COLCFV-292

A Guide
to Financial
Statement
Disclosures

Recent Titles from QUORUM BOOKS

Boards of Directors: Their Changing Roles, Structure, and Information Needs
Charles N. Waldo

A Compendium of State Statutes and International Treaties in Trust and Estate Law
M. Henner

Utilizing Consultants Successfully: A Guide for Management in Business, Government, the Arts and Professions
Herman R. Holtz

International Broadcasting by Satellite: Issues of Regulation, Barriers to Communication
Jon T. Powell

Corporate and Commercial Free Speech: First Amendment Protection of Expression in Business
Edwin P. Rome and William H. Roberts

The Impact of Office Automation on Clerical Employment, 1985–2000: Forecasting Techniques and Plausible Futures in Banking and Insurance
J. David Roessner, Robert M. Mason, Alan L. Porter, Frederick A. Rossini, A. Perry Schwartz, and Keith R. Nelms

The Learning Curve: A Management Accounting Tool
Ahmed Belkaoui

Willing Workers: The Work Ethics in Japan, England, and the United States
Tamotsu Sengoku, translated by Koichi Ezaki and Yuko Ezaki

University-Industry Research Partnerships: The Major Legal Issues in Research and Development Agreements
Bernard D. Reams, Jr.

Managing the Corporate Image: The Key to Public Trust
James G. Gray, Jr.

Interstate Banking: Strategies for a New Era: Conference Proceedings
Federal Reserve Bank of Atlanta, sponsor

Marketing with Seminars and Newsletters
Herman Holtz

Corporate PACs and Federal Campaign Financing Laws: Use or Abuse of Power?
Ann B. Matasar

A GUIDE
TO FINANCIAL
STATEMENT
DISCLOSURES

Paul Munter AND
Thomas A. Ratcliffe

Q **QUORUM BOOKS**
NEW YORK·WESTPORT, CONNECTICUT·LONDON

657.3
M97g

Library of Congress Cataloging-in-Publication Data

Munter, Paul, 1952–
  A guide to financial statement
disclosures.

  Bibliography: p.
  Includes index.
  1. Disclosure in accounting. 2. Financial
statements. I. Ratcliffe, Thomas A. (Thomas Arthur)
II. Title.
HF5658.M86 1986   657'.3   85-9603
ISBN 0-89930-032-4 (lib. bdg. : alk. paper)

Copyright © 1986 by Paul Munter and Thomas A. Ratcliffe

All rights reserved. No portion of this book may be
reproduced, by any process or technique, without the
express written consent of the publisher.

Library of Congress Catalog Card Number: 85-9603
ISBN: 0-89930-032-4

First published in 1986 by Quorum Books

Greenwood Press, Inc.
88 Post Road West, Westport, Connecticut 06881

Printed in the United States of America

The paper used in this book complies with the
Permanent Paper Standard issued by the National
Information Standards Organization (Z39.48-1984).

10 9 8 7 6 5 4 3 2 1

Contents

UNIVERSITY LIBRARIES
CARNEGIE-MELLON UNIVERSITY
PITTSBURGH, PENNSYLVANIA 15213

    Bibliography   267

    Index   271

List of Exhibits

List of Abbreviations

AICPA	American Institute of Certified Public Accountants
APB	Accounting Principles Board
APBO	Accounting Principles Board Opinion
APBS	Accounting Principles Board Statement
ARB	Accounting Research Bulletin
ARD	Accounting Research Division
ARS	Accounting Research Study
ASR	Accounting Series Release
CAP	Committee on Accounting Procedure
CPI	Consumer Price Index for all urban consumers
EAC	Earnings available to common stockholders
EPS	Earnings per share
ERISA	Employee Retirement Income Security Act of 1974
FASB	Financial Accounting Standards Board
FASBIN	Financial Accounting Standards Board Interpretation
FIFO	First in, first out
GAAP	Generally accepted accounting principles
GAAS	Generally accepted auditing standards
G & G	Geological and geophysical
ITC	Investment tax credit
LCM	Lower of cost or market
LIFO	Last in, first out
NRV	Net realizable value
R & D	Research and development
SEC	Securities and Exchange Commission
SFAC	Statement of Financial Accounting Concepts
SFAS	Statement of Financial Accounting Standards

A Guide
to Financial
Statement
Disclosures

1
The Nature of Generally Accepted Accounting Principles

To provide financial statement users with a common basis for evaluating the financial statements of business enterprises, the accounting profession has, over time, developed a set of accounting principles used to prepare financial statements. In order to narrow the alternatives that exist in practice, the American Institute of Certified Public Accountants (AICPA) (formerly the American Institute of Accountants) has designated bodies with the authority for issuing promulgated generally accepted accounting principles (GAAP). From the period 1939 to the present, three distinct bodies have been so designated: the Committee on Accounting Procedures (CAP) (1939–1959), the Accounting Principles Board (APB) (1959–1973), and the Financial Accounting Standards Board (FASB) (1973 to the present). The documents issued by these bodies have significantly reduced the divergence existing in practice; however, much difference still exists. The purpose of this chapter is to trace the development of promulgated GAAP and discuss their applicability and authority.

DEVELOPMENT OF PROMULGATED GAAP

The CAP was the first body designated by the AICPA to establish preferable accounting principles. The CAP was a committee of the AICPA and it issued a total of 51 Accounting Research Bulletins (ARBs), the first 42 of which were codified into ARB No. 43, "Restatement and Revision of Accounting Research Bulletins."

The work of the CAP was extremely important to the development of GAAP. Among the important developments in reporting the results of

3

operations of the business enterprise has been the trend to adhere more closely to the all-inclusive concept of income determination. However, the CAP faced two severe problems in developing a comprehensive set of GAAP.

The first problem was that it promulgated accounting principles on a piece-meal basis rather than developing a conceptual framework within which accounting principles could be promulgated. As a consequence, the CAP was subjected to a significant amount of criticism for its "brushfire" approach to accounting rule-making.

Additionally, as ARB No. 43 pointed out, "The authority of opinions reached by the [CAP] rests upon their general acceptability." Consequently, although practitioners were called upon to justify departures from the principles adopted by the CAP, in reality, business enterprises were free to depart from such principles without such justification. Therefore, GAAP truly meant general acceptance at that time.

Owing to the confluence of these two problems, the demise of the CAP was inevitable. As a consequence, the AICPA established the APB as its senior technical body with the sole authority to promulgate GAAP. In conjunction with the creation of the APB, the AICPA also established the Accounting Research Division (ARD). The purpose of the ARD was twofold. First, the ARD would research topics that the APB had on its technical agenda for the purpose of providing background information and theoretical discussions of the alternative methods currently available in practice. Additionally, however, the ARD was supposed to aid the APB in establishing the basic postulates and broad operating principles of accounting. As will be discussed later, these attempts proved largely unsuccessful.

Rather than developing a cohesive set of accounting postulates and principles, the APB also developed accounting principles on a piece-meal basis. This resulted in 31 APB Opinions (APBOs) being issued in the period from 1959 to 1973. Perhaps the effect of a lack of cohesion can be illustrated best with regard to the APB's deleberations on accounting for leases.

APBO No. 5, "Reporting of Leases in Financial Statements of Lessees," provided a set of criteria that the lessee should apply in determining whether the lease was a capital or an operating lease. APBO No. 7, "Accounting for Leases in Financial Statements of Lessors," provided a different set of criteria for the lessor to apply in determining whether the lease was a capital or an operating lease. As a consequence, there was a significant lack of symmetry in accounting for leases by lessees and lessors.

The APB also was plagued with the same problem that beset the CAP. Initially, the authority of APBOs rested solely with their general acceptance. However, in October 1964, the AICPA took an initial step to increase the authority of APBOs. The AICPA resolved that

1. GAAP are those principles that have authoritative support.
2. APBOs constitute "substantial authoritative support."
3. "Substantial authoritative support" can exist for accounting principles that differ from APBOs.
4. No distinction should be made between ARBs on matters of accounting principles and APBOs.
5. If an accounting principle that differs materially in its effect from one accepted in an APBO (or ARB) is applied in financial statements, the reporting member must decide whether the principle has substantial authoritative support and is applicable in the circumstances. If he concludes that it does have substantial authoritative support, he will give an unqualified opinion and see that the fact of the departure is disclosed in a note to the financial statements.

As a result of this resolution, the authority of the existing ARBs and APBOs was increased substantially. However, two factors caused continued departures from ARBs and APBOs. First, the AICPA stated that substantial authoritative support could be derived from sources other than ARBs and APBOs. Consequently, there was no burden of proof placed upon the business enterprise that chose to depart from a promulgated GAAP—only a call for disclosure of the departure.

Even more importantly, the AICPA had no enforcement mechanism at this time. Thus, even if substandard reporting did result from departing from promulgated GAAP, the AICPA did not have the ability to take any punitive action against the reporting member.

The APB, in an effort to improve the disclosure of accounting principles adopted by business enterprises, promulgated APBO No. 22, "Disclosure of Accounting Policies," in 1972. APBO No. 22 required that business enterprises include, as an integral part of financial statements, a description of all significant accounting policies. The disclosure should include, but was not limited to, accounting practices and methods adopted from a set of existing acceptable alternatives, those that are peculiar to the industry in which the business enterprise operates, and any unusual or innovative applications of GAAP. Although APBO No. 22 required additional disclosures, the determination of whether the principles adopted had substantial authoritative support still was made by the business enterprise and its auditor.

Owing to the increasing dissatisfaction with the APB and the concern over the AICPA exercising sole authority to promulgate GAAP, the APB was replaced with the FASB in 1973. The FASB was established as a semiautonomous body separate from the direct control of the AICPA. The FASB is now designated as the body with the authority to promulgate GAAP. Unlike the CAP and APB, the FASB issues two types of documents that constitute promulgated GAAP. These are Statements of Financial Accounting Standards (SFASs) and FASB Interpretations (FASBINs). Additionally, the FASB issues Technical Bulletins (TBs) to address specific implementation questions on a timely basis.

CURRENT AUTHORITY AND APPLICABILITY OF PROMULGATED GAAP

Actions taken by the AICPA and the Securities and Exchange Commission (SEC) in 1973 greatly increased the authority and enforceability of promulgated GAAP. The AICPA adopted its Code of Professional Ethics effective for March 1, 1973. The code applies directly to all persons who are members of the AICPA. It also applies indirectly to all persons in the public accounting profession since state licensing boards typically look to the AICPA for guidance on ethical matters.

Rule 202 of the AICPA's Code of Professional Ethics states that a member shall not permit his name to be associated with financial statements in such a manner as to imply that he is acting as an independent public accountant unless he has complied with generally accepted auditing standards (GAAS) promulgated by the AICPA. Among the ten GAAS is the first standard of reporting, which asserts that the auditor's report shall state whether the financial statements are presented in accordance with GAAP. Therefore, if an accountant is associated with financial statements, he must state whether the statements conform to GAAP.

Rule 203 of the AICPA's Code of Professional Ethics further states that a member shall not express an opinion that financial statements are presented in conformity with GAAP if they contain a material departure from promulgated GAAP, unless it can be demonstrated that owing to unusual circumstances, the financial statements would otherwise be misleading. In such cases, the report must describe the departure, the effects of the departure, and the reason for the departure.

An auditor is precluded from expressing an unqualified opinion on the financial statements if the statements are not prepared in accordance with promulgated GAAP. Therefore, the confluence of Rules 202 and 203 and GAAS requires that the financial statements be prepared in accordance with promulgated GAAP if the independent accountant is to comply with the AICPA's Code of Professional Ethics when he is associated with the financial statements.

The adoption of the Code of Professional Ethics made two significant changes in the authority of promulgated GAAP. First, the burden of proof was shifted to the departing enterprise. Now, it is up to the business enterprise to show that the departure from promulgated GAAP is necessary to prevent the financial statements from being misleading. The second major change was that with the adoption of the code, the AICPA had an enforcement mechanism. Members are ethically bound to comply with the code. Furthermore, most states have ethical standards that are at least as stringent as the AICPA's. As a consequence, violation of the ethical standards of the AICPA can potentially result in a revocation of the accountant's license to practice.

Even more significant than the actions taken by the AICPA—from the standpoint of the enforceability of promulgated GAAP—was the issuance of Accounting Series Release (ASR) No. 150 by the SEC on December 20, 1973. The SEC is legally empowered, through various acts of Congress, to prescribe the methods that should be followed in the preparation of financial statements for SEC registrants. The SEC can legally impose any accounting method it wishes upon registrants [e.g., reserve recognition accounting (RRA)]. In ASR No. 150, the SEC stated that principles, standards, and practices promulgated by the FASB in its SFASs and FASBINs will be considered to have substantial authoritative support. Furthermore, principles, standards, and practices that are contrary to such promulgations will not be considered to have substantial authoritative support by the SEC. However, it is important to note that the SEC reserved its right to exercise its statutory authority to set accounting standards—a right that it occasionally exercises. Nevertheless, the issuance of ASR No. 150 significantly enhanced the authority of promulgated GAAP.

APPLICABILITY OF GAAP

In general, promulgated GAAP apply primarily to business enterprises organized for a profit. Therefore, promulgated GAAP do not apply specifically to not-for-profit enterprises. There are, however, exceptions to these general rules.

Certain promulgated GAAP are deemed to be appropriate for not-for-profit enterprises and should therefore be applied in such instances. For example, Statement of Position 78-1 extends the accounting for marketable equity securities promulgated in SFAS No. 12 to hospitals.

In addition, certain promulgated GAAP are deemed not to be necessary for fairly presenting financial position, results of operations, and changes in financial position. For example, nonpublic enterprises are exempted from earnings per share (EPS) and segment disclosures by SFAS No. 21.

Further, in 1962, the AICPA recognized that different accounting principles may be necessary for business enterprises that are regulated for rate-making purposes than for those that are not so regulated. In SFAS No. 72, the FASB provided the conditions under which the different accounting treatment by a regulated enterprise is acceptable. The difference results primarily from deferring and amortizing to subsequent periods costs that would normally be expensed immediately [e.g., research and development (R & D) costs]. However, such differing treatment is acceptable for external reporting only when it is clear that the cost will be recoverable out of future revenues.

DEVELOPING A CONCEPTUAL FRAMEWORK OF FINANCIAL REPORTING

As was noted, the failure to develop a conceptual framework of financial reporting was largely responsible for the demise of both the CAP and the APB. When the FASB began operations in 1973, it placed the conceptual framework project on its technical agenda. To date, five Statements of Financial Accounting Concepts (SFACs) have been issued.

The CAP never made a concerted effort to develop a conceptual framework of accounting; however, the APB—with the aid of the ARD—was supposed to develop a set of postulates and broad operating principles of accounting. The ARD at its inception commissioned two studies to address these matters. The results of these studies were published in Accounting Research Study (ARS) Nos. 1, "The Basic Postulates of Accounting," and 3, "A Tentative Set of Broad Accounting Principles for Business Enterprises." The APB in Statement (APBS) No. 1, "Statement by the Accounting Principles Board," rejected the conclusions of ARS Nos. 1 and 3, saying "that while these studies are a valuable contribution to accounting thinking, they are too radically different from present generally accepted accounting principles for acceptance at this time."

The APB then channeled its efforts into the piece-meal standard-setting process that the CAP had used. However, both the APB and ARD later undertook a comprehensive study of what constituted GAAP. The results of these studies were published in APBS No. 4, "Basic Concepts and Accounting Principles Underlying Financial Statements of Business Enterprises," and ARS No. 7, "Inventory of Generally Accepted Accounting Principles for Business Enterprises." Both studies were self-professed attempts to define and describe GAAP as they currently existed. Therefore, neither study met the needs of the profession for assessing new problems that arose in practice.

As a result of the failure of its predecessors, the FASB was largely applauded when it placed the conceptual framework project on its initial technical agenda. While the progress of the FASB has been slow, the business community remains generally supportive of its efforts to develop a conceptual framework of accounting.

SFAC No. 1, "Objectives of Financial Reporting by Business Enterprises," was significant in that it identified investors, creditors, and potential investors as primary users of financial statements. As a consequence, the need of the users of financial statements is information that will allow for prediction of the timing, amount, and uncertainty of future cash flows accruing to them. Therefore, the objectives of financial reporting are to provide users with information that will enable them to predict cash flows. In doing so, the users must be able to assess the earning power of the enterprise, since this will determine the cash flows accruing to the enterprise, and cash flows must accrue to the enterprise before they can accrue to investors and creditors.

As a first step in operationalizing the concepts espoused in SFAC No. 1, the FASB has begun requiring current cost information to be disclosed by certain large, publicly held enterprises. This requirement, as promulgated in SFAS No. 33, requires information on income from continuing operations on a current cost basis, purchasing power gain or loss, and increase or decrease in specific prices of inventories and property, plant, and equipment both before and after general inflation. Theoretically, this information should provide financial statement users with better information with which to determine the earning power of the reporting enterprise. The promulgation of SFAS No. 33 represents a significant step in implementing portions of the conceptual framework of accounting.

The FASB has also issued SFAC No. 2, "Qualitative Characteristics: Criteria for Selecting and Evaluating Financial Accounting and Reporting Policies." Among the significant projects that the FASB is discussing relative to the conceptual framework are an analysis of funds flow and liquidity.

In SFAC No. 3, "Elements of Financial Statements," the FASB provided authoritative definitions of the financial statement elements such as assets, liabilities, revenues, and expenses. Finally, in SFAC No. 5, the FASB provided general guidelines as to when economic events should be recognized and how they should be displayed in the financial statements. (SFAC No. 4 discusses the applicability of the other SFACs to not-for-profit organizations.)

While progress often has been criticized for being too slow, it is important to note that the FASB has devoted a significant amount of its energies to the development of a conceptual framework of financial reporting. The ultimate goal is for the project to provide the accounting profession with guidance when problems arise in practice that have not been specifically addressed by promulgated GAAP.

CONCLUSION

The purpose of this chapter has been to trace the development and authority of promulgated GAAP. Further, a discussion of the FASB's conceptual framework project should provide a basis for assessing future developments in financial accounting and reporting.

2
Basic Financial Statements

COMPLETE SET OF FINANCIAL STATEMENTS

When a reporting entity is preparing a complete set of financial statements that purport to present financial position, changes in financial position, and results of operations in accordance with GAAP, several statements are required. A complete set of financial statements should include the following financial information:

1. Balance sheet
2. Income statement
3. Statement of retained earnings (may be combined with the income statement)
4. Statement of changes in financial position (PRE 12-31-89)
5. Statement of stockholders' equity
6. Summary of significant accounting policies
7. Disclosure of segments of business activities (public companies)
8. Notes to the financial statements.

Additionally, because investors are typically interested in the trend, for the reporting entity, comparative financial statements are usually reported. Further, in certain instances, supplementary information is required to be disclosed. Required supplementary information that must be provided by certain entities includes: (1) the effect of inflation on the reporting entity and (2) a summary of mineral right extractive activities. Exhibit 2.1 illustrates a complete set of financial statements presented in comparative form. The reader should note that all of the required information is included.

Exhibit 2.1
Basic Financial Statements: Monsanto Company

Statement of Consolidated Income			Monsanto Company and Subsidiaries
(Dollars in millions, except per share)			
	1984	1983	1982
Net Sales	$6,691	$6,299	$6,325
Cost of goods sold	4,846	4,738	4,826
Gross Profit	1,845	1,561	1,499
Marketing and administrative expenses	722	681	691
Technological expenses	446	359	329
	1,168	1,040	1,020
Operating Income	677	521	479
Interest expense	(100)	(96)	(82)
Interest income	92	73	63
Other income — net	38	72	41
	30	49	22
Income Before Income Taxes and Extraordinary Items	707	570	501
Income taxes	268	201	172
Income Before Extraordinary Items	439	369	329
Extraordinary Items:			
Tax benefits from utilization of ex-U.S. loss carryforwards		33	
Gain from exchange of debt for common shares			23
Net Income	$ 439	$ 402	$ 352
Earnings per Share:			
Before extraordinary items	$ 5.42	$ 4.48	$ 4.10
Extraordinary items		0.41	0.29
After extraordinary items	$ 5.42	$ 4.89	$ 4.39

The above statement should be read in conjunction with pages 49 through 53 of this report.

Key Financial Statistics			
	1984	1983	1982
Net Sales as a Percent of Total Assets	105%	98%	104%
Net Income as a Percent of Net Sales	7%	6%	6%
Percent Return on Average Shareowners' Equity			
After extraordinary items	12%	11%	10%
Percent Return on Average Capital Employed*			
After extraordinary items	10%	10%	9%

*Capital employed is the sum of short-term debt, long-term debt and shareowners' equity. The beginning of the year and the end of the year capital employed are averaged and divided into net income after adding back the aftertax effect of interest costs.

BALANCE SHEET

The purpose of the balance sheet (or statement of financial position) is to report the financial position of the reporting entity at a point in time. Thus, the balance sheet contains a listing of what an entity owns at the reporting date (assets), what it owes at that date (liabilities), and the interests of its stockholders (stockholders' equity). The individual disclosures included in the balance sheet are discussed in several chapters (e.g., working capital, long-term investments, long-term bonds).

Exhibit 2.1 (continued)

Statement of Consolidated Financial Position	Monsanto Company and Subsidiaries	
(Dollars in millions, except per share)		At December 31
Assets	**1984**	1983
Current Assets:		
Cash, time deposits and certificates of deposit	$ 149	$ 164
Short-term securities, at cost which approximates market	310	493
Trade receivables, net of allowances of $49 in 1984 and $44 in 1983	1,078	1,115
Miscellaneous receivables and prepaid expenses	221	205
Inventories	839	778
	2,597	2,755
Investments and Other Assets:		
Investments in affiliates	119	113
Other assets	283	275
	402	388
Property, Plant and Equipment, at Cost:		
Land	81	74
Buildings	732	667
Machinery and equipment	5,094	4,938
Mineral rights and oil and gas properties	765	716
Construction-in-progress	247	244
	6,919	6,639
Less accumulated depreciation	3,545	3,355
	3,374	3,284
Total Assets	**$6,373**	$6,427
Liabilities and Shareowners' Equity		
Current Liabilities:		
Accounts payable	$ 497	$ 500
Wages and commissions	110	108
Income and other taxes	69	104
Miscellaneous accruals	249	255
Short-term debt	277	253
	1,202	1,220
Long-Term Debt	824	937
Deferred Credits and Other Liabilities:		
Deferred income taxes	661	558
Other liabilities	52	45
	713	603
Shareowners' Equity:		
Common stock — authorized, 200,000,000 shares, par value $2; issued, 82,197,097 shares in 1984 and 40,977,448 shares in 1983	164	82
Additional contributed capital	855	936
Accumulated currency adjustment	(319)	(200)
Reinvested earnings	3,110	2,853
	3,810	3,671
Less treasury stock, at cost (3,916,071 shares in 1984 and 56,152 shares in 1983)	176	4
	3,634	3,667
Total Liabilities and Shareowners' Equity	**$6,373**	$6,427

The above statement should be read in conjunction with pages 49 through 53 of this report.

(continued)

Exhibit 2.1 (continued)

Statement of Changes in Consolidated Financial Position	Monsanto Company and Subsidiaries		
(Dollars in millions)			
Sources (Uses) of Funds	1984	1983	1982
Operations:			
Income before extraordinary items	$ 439	$ 369	$ 329
Charges not using (credits not providing) funds:			
Depreciation, depletion and obsolescence	491	517	439
Deferred income taxes	103	71	85
Other	(25)	(9)	27
Funds provided from operations, before changes in working capital and extraordinary items	1,008	948	880
Investment and Other Transactions:			
Extraordinary tax benefits from utilization of ex-U.S. loss carryforwards		33	
Working capital changes:			
Trade receivables	37	(39)	(3)
Inventories	(61)	46	49
Other current assets	(16)	(65)	38
Accounts payable and accrued liabilities	(42)	147	(69)
Short-term debt	24	122	(44)
Total working capital changes	(58)	211	(29)
Foreign currency adjustments on working capital	(58)	(47)	(60)
Property, plant and equipment additions	(614)	(560)	(673)
Proceeds from property disposals	39	39	31
Acquisitions and investments	(94)	(208)	(11)
Other	60	49	34
	(725)	(483)	(708)
Financial Transactions:			
Long-term financing	12	49	38
Long-term debt reduction	(127)	(87)	(149)
Extraordinary gain from exchange of debt for common shares			23
Issuance of common stock	—	—	75
Treasury stock purchases	(184)	(14)	(13)
Dividends	(182)	(170)	(158)
	(481)	(222)	(184)
Increase (Decrease) in Funds	$ (198)	$ 243	$ (12)
Increase (Decrease) in Elements of Funds:			
Cash, time deposits and certificates of deposit	$ (15)	$ 21	$ (66)
Short-term securities	(183)	222	54
Increase (Decrease) in Funds	$ (198)	$ 243	$ (12)

The above statement should be read in conjunction with pages 49 through 53 of this report.

OVERVIEW OF RESULTS OF OPERATIONS

Inasmuch as financial statement users assign significant informational value to income statement data, authoritative rule-making bodies in the accounting profession have promulgated several pronouncements for the purpose of enhancing the comparability and understandability of enterprise results of operations. The trend in these pronouncements has been to move away from the current operating performance theory of

Exhibit 2.1 (continued)

Statement of Consolidated Shareowners' Equity		Monsanto Company and Subsidiaries	
(Dollars in millions, except per share)	**1984**	1983	1982
Common Stock:			
Balance, January 1	$ 82	$ 82	$ 80
New shares issued (138,117, 11,289 and 988,075 shares in 1984-1982, respectively)	—	—	2
Par value of stock issued in two-for-one stock split	82		
Balance, December 31	$ 164	$ 82	$ 82
Additional Contributed Capital:			
Balance, January 1	$ 936	$ 931	$ 853
New shares issued	—	—	73
Par value of stock issued in two-for-one stock split	(82)		
Other	1	5	5
Balance, December 31	$ 855	$ 936	$ 931
Accumulated Currency Adjustment:			
Balance, January 1	$ (200)	$ (122)	$
Initial translation adjustment for SFAS No. 52			(16)
Translation adjustments	(121)	(84)	(111)
Income taxes	2	6	9
Transferred to net income			(4)
Balance, December 31	$ (319)	$ (200)	$ (122)
Reinvested Earnings:			
Balance, January 1	$2,853	$2,621	$2,423
Deferred tax adjustment for SFAS No. 52			4
Net income	439	402	352
Preferred dividends ($2.06 per share in 1984, $2.75 per share in 1983 and 1982)	—	—	—
Common dividends ($2.25, $2.075 and $1.975 per share for 1984-1982, respectively)	(182)	(170)	(158)
Balance, December 31	$3,110	$2,853	$2,621
Common Stock in Treasury:			
Balance, January 1	$ (4)	$ (22)	$ (26)
Shares purchased (4,053,300, 159,570 and 171,940 shares in 1984-1982, respectively)	(184)	(14)	(13)
Conversion of convertible securities and issuances under employee stock plans (349,837, 471,966 and 313,192 shares in 1984-1982, respectively)	12	32	17
Balance, December 31	$ (176)	$ (4)	$ (22)

The above statement should be read in conjunction with pages 49 through 53 of this report.

Key Financial Statistics–Common Stock Data		**1984**	1983	1982
Stock Price	High	$53⅞	$58⅛	$44½
	Low	40⅝	37⅛	28¼
Per Common Share:	Dividends	2.25	2.075	1.975
	Shareowners' Equity	46.43	44.83	42.99

(*continued*)

Exhibit 2.1 (continued)

Notes to Financial Statements
Monsanto Company and Subsidiaries

Where applicable, per share amounts and the number of common shares have been restated to reflect the June 1984 two-for-one common stock split.

Significant Accounting Policies

The Company's significant accounting policies are italicized in the following Notes to Financial Statements.

Basis of Consolidation

The consolidated financial statements include the Company and its majority-owned subsidiaries. Intercompany transactions have been eliminated in consolidation. Companies in which Monsanto has an ownership interest between 20 and 50 percent are included in "Investments in affiliates" in the Statement of Consolidated Financial Position and Monsanto's share of these companies' income or loss is included in "Other income — net" in the Statement of Consolidated Income.

Principal Acquisitions and Divestitures

In May 1984, Monsanto acquired Continental Pharma, S.A., which has pharmaceutical manufacturing and research facilities in Belgium. Its products are marketed principally in Europe and Asia.

In July 1983, Monsanto purchased for $178 million the interest of The General Electric Company p.l.c. (GEC) in Fisher Controls International, Inc. (FCII). This increased the Company's ownership in FCII to 100 percent from the previous 66½ percent. The excess purchase price above FCII's net assets attributable to GEC's interest was $81 million, which is being amortized on a straight-line basis over 20 years.

In June 1983, Monsanto sold the European acrylic fibers business to Montefibre, a subsidiary of Montedison (Italy). The pretax loss provision of $20 million ($18 million, or $0.23 per share, net of tax) was established in 1982 and was included in cost of goods sold as obsolescence expense. This business was part of the Fibers and Intermediates operating unit and had 1982 sales of approximately $139 million.

In June 1983, Monsanto acquired at net book value Montefibre's 50 percent interest in Polyamide Intermediates Limited (PIL), a nylon intermediates joint venture in the United Kingdom. This resulted in Monsanto

having sole ownership in PIL, whose operations are reported as part of the Fibers and Intermediates operating unit.

Had Monsanto owned 100 percent of Continental Pharma, FCII and PIL since January 1, 1983, Monsanto's net income would not have changed significantly.

Depreciation

	1984	1983	1982
Depreciation, depletion and obsolescence:			
Depreciation and depletion	**$449**	$456	$396
Obsolescence (including gains and losses from divestitures)	**42**	61	43
Total depreciation, depletion and obsolescence	**$491**	$517	$439

The cost of plant and equipment is depreciated using the straight-line method over weighted average periods of 23 years for buildings and 12 years for machinery and equipment.

Supplemental Data

	1984	1983	1982
Raw material and energy costs	**$2,522**	$2,345	$2,435
Employee compensation and benefits	**1,689**	1,687	1,736
Income and other taxes	**482**	368	394
Rent expense	**80**	83	78
Technological expenses:			
Research and development	**370**	290	264
Engineering, commercial development and patent	**76**	69	65
Total technological expenses	**446**	359	329
Interest expense:			
Total interest costs incurred	**117**	126	128
Less capitalized interest	**17**	30	46
Net interest expense	**100**	96	82
Equity in affiliates' income (loss)	**18**	15	(11)
Foreign currency gains (losses) — including equity in affiliates' currency gains and losses	**2**	5	(15)

reporting earnings to the all-inclusive approach to income statement presentation. This trend is readily apparent through an analysis of APBO No. 30, "Reporting the Results of Operations," and SFAS No. 16, "Prior Period Adjustments." In APBO No. 30, the APB concluded that essentially all items of profit or loss should be included in the determination of income, with the various components of income segregated and clearly disclosed by nature and source. In SFAS No. 16, the FASB severely restricted the number of items, events, and transactions that could be precluded from the income statement by specifying the two

Exhibit 2.1 (continued)

Currency Translation

    In accordance with Statement of Financial Accounting Standards No. 52, most of Monsanto's ex-U.S. operations' financial statements are translated into U.S. dollars using current exchange rates. Unrealized currency adjustments in the Statement of Consolidated Financial Position are accumulated in shareowners' equity. The financial statements of ex-U.S. operations that operate in hyperinflationary economies, including Brazil, Mexico and Argentina, are translated at either current or historical exchange rates, as appropriate, and currency adjustments are included in net income.

    Major currency exposures are the British pound sterling and Belgian franc. Other important currencies include the German mark, French franc, Canadian dollar, Australian dollar, Japanese yen and Mexican peso. Currency restrictions are not expected to have a significant effect on Monsanto's cash flow, liquidity or capital resources.

    Foreign currency translation gains on long-term debt in hyperinflationary countries in 1983 and 1982 have been reclassified from "Cost of goods sold" to "Other income — net" to be consistent with the classification for 1984.

Inventory Valuation

    Inventories are stated at cost or market, whichever is less. Actual cost is used for raw materials and supplies, and standard cost, which approximates actual cost, is used for finished goods and goods in process. Standard cost includes direct labor, raw material and manufacturing overhead based on practical capacity. The cost of substantially all U.S. inventories is determined by the last-in, first-out (LIFO) method, generally reflecting the effects of inflation on cost of goods sold sooner than other inventory cost methods. The cost of other inventories (approximately 25 percent of all inventories) is generally determined by the first-in, first-out (FIFO) method.

    Inventories at December 31, 1984 and 1983 would have been $432 million and $453 million, respectively, higher than reported if the FIFO basis of inventory valuation (which approximates current cost) had been used for all inventories. Monsanto's LIFO inventory policies make it impractical to identify inventories by classification (i.e., finished goods, goods in process, raw materials and supplies). The liquidation of lower cost inventory "tiers" under the LIFO method increased 1982 earnings approximately $83 million before taxes.

Oil and Gas Activities

    Oil and gas exploration and production activities are accounted for using the successful efforts method.

Income Taxes

    The components of income before income taxes were:

		1984	1983	1982
	U.S.	$442	$419	$425
	Ex-U.S.	265	151	76
Total		**$707**	**$570**	**$501**

The components of income tax expense were:

		1984	1983	1982
Current:	Federal	$ 72	$103	$ 53
	State	21	6	8
	Ex-U.S.	56	45	39
		149	154	100
Deferred:	Federal	72	11	72
	State	3	4	4
	Ex-U.S.	44	(1)	(4)
		119	14	72
Tax effect of loss carryforward			33	
Total		**$268**	**$201**	**$172**

    The sources of timing differences in the recognition of revenue and expense for tax and financial statement purposes and the tax effect of each were:

	1984	1983	1982
Depreciation, depletion and obsolescence	$ 92	$ 19	$ 49
Intangible drilling and development costs	11	(3)	19
Interest capitalization	—	8	18
Other	16	(10)	(14)
Total	**$119**	**$ 14**	**$ 72**

    Factors causing the effective tax rate to differ from the statutory rate were:

	1984	1983	1982
Federal statutory rate	46%	46%	46%
Investment and R&D tax credits	(5)	(6)	(11)
Lower ex-U.S. tax rates	(3)	(1)	—
Benefits attributable to DISC earnings	(2)	(3)	(3)
Other	2	(1)	2
Effective income tax rate	**38%**	**35%**	**34%**

    Investment tax credits are recorded as a reduction of income tax expense in the year they reduce the federal income tax liability. Investment tax credits for 1984-1982 were $30 million, $26 million and $53 million, respectively.

    Income taxes have not been provided on $472 million of undistributed earnings of

(continued)

Exhibit 2.1 (continued)

---

subsidiaries either because any taxes on dividends would be offset substantially by foreign tax credits or because Monsanto intends to indefinitely reinvest those earnings.

Earnings per Share

Earnings per share were computed using the weighted average number of common and common equivalent shares outstanding each year, adjusted for the two-for-one stock split (80,909,755, 82,215,156 and 79,950,996 in 1984-1982, respectively). Common share equivalents (335,979, 563,622 and 319,716 in 1984-1982, respectively) consist primarily of common stock issuable upon exercise of outstanding stock options. Earnings per share assuming full dilution were not different significantly from the primary amounts.

Pension Plans

Most Monsanto employees are covered by noncontributory pension plans. Upon retirement, many Monsanto employees are also provided other benefits, principally medical and life insurance. *Pension costs are funded as accrued and include current service and amortization of unfunded prior service costs generally over periods of 10 to 30 years. Other postretirement benefits are not currently funded and are expensed as incurred.*

Pension expense for all plans was $116 million, $131 million and $136 million in 1984-1982, respectively. The 1984 decrease in pension expense reflects higher investment returns and reduced numbers of employees. Pension expense was 7 percent of total compensation in 1984 and 8 percent in 1983 and 1982.

The 1984-1982 expense recorded for other postretirement benefits was $18 million, $13 million and $8 million, respectively.

Estimated benefit and asset information at year-end for Monsanto's pension plans is presented below. Net assets of the pension trusts were measured at market value and accumulated benefits were estimated from actuarial valuations, principally using the entry age normal actuarial cost method.

		1984	1983
Actuarial present value of accumulated plan benefits:			
	Vested	**$1,554**	$1,463
	Nonvested	**184**	178
Total		**$1,738**	$1,641
Net assets available for benefits		**$2,074**	$1,958

U.S. salaried and hourly employees are covered by two principal plans. The funding and company cost assumptions for these plans

include an investment return of 7.5 percent used in determining the actuarial present values. The actuarial assumptions also include an overall average salary increase of 6.5 percent for the salaried employees plan. The actuarial present value of additional projected benefits from future salary increases for the U.S. salaried employees plan at December 31, 1984 was approximately $280 million. Accumulated plan benefits included in the above table for these major U.S. plans were approximately $1,617 million at December 31, 1984.

Short-Term Debt and Credit Arrangements

		1984	1983
Notes payable:	Banks	**$ 43**	$ 52
	Others		75
Bank overdrafts		**111**	102
Current portion of long-term debt		**123**	24
Total		**$277**	$253

Monsanto has available $300 million in U.S. and Eurocurrency Revolving Credit Agreements. The U.S. agreement ($200 million) is effective through 1989, with interest rates generally at or below prevailing prime interest rates. The $100 million Eurocurrency agreements are subject to reductions beginning in 1986 and terminating in 1987. Interest rates under these agreements are at a margin above the London or Luxembourg interbank offered rates. No borrowings were made under the above credit facilities through February 22, 1985.

In addition, certain ex-U.S. subsidiaries have aggregate short-term loan facilities of $266 million, under which loans totaling $43 million were outstanding at December 31, 1984. Interest on these loans is related to various ex-U.S. bank rates.

Long-Term Debt

Long-term debt (exclusive of current maturities):

	1984	1983
Industrial development bond obligations, weighted average interest rate of 7½%, due 1986 to 2021	**$252**	$247
8% notes due 1985		100
4¾% promissory notes due 1993	**39**	44
9⅛% sinking fund debentures due 1997	**67**	67
8½% sinking fund debentures due 2000	**127**	127
3¾% income debentures due 2002	**77**	77
4¼% income debentures due 2008	**50**	50
8¾% sinking fund debentures due 2008	**169**	169
Capitalized lease obligations	**5**	7
Other	**38**	49
Total	**$824**	$937

---

types of events that should be accounted for as direct adjustments to retained earnings.

THE MODEL INCOME STATEMENT

The authoritative literature in accounting requires that income statement components be segregated into (1) income from continuing opera-

Exhibit 2.1 (continued)

Maturities and sinking fund requirements on long-term debt are $123 million, $23 million, $22 million, $18 million and $16 million for 1985-1989, respectively.

Covenants of certain loan agreements restrict maximum borrowings and dividend payments. It is not anticipated that additional future borrowings will be affected by these restrictions, and none of the Company's reinvested earnings were restricted as to dividend payments at December 31, 1984.

Commitments and Contingencies

Commitments in connection with uncompleted additions to property and investments in affiliates were approximately $178 million at December 31, 1984. Monsanto was contingently liable as guarantor of bank loans and for discounted customers' receivables totaling approximately $60 million at December 31, 1984.

Monsanto is a party to a number of lawsuits, which it is vigorously defending, arising in the normal course of business. Certain of these actions seek damages in very large amounts. While the results of litigation cannot be predicted with certainty, management believes, based upon the advice of Company counsel, that the final outcome of such litigation will not have a material adverse effect on Monsanto's consolidated financial position.

Capital Stock

At December 31, 1984, there were 39,070 common shares reserved for conversion of convertible securities and 6,015,830 common shares reserved for employee stock options.

The Company called for the redemption of all of the outstanding $2.75 Cumulative Convertible Preferred Stock at $73 per share effective October 15, 1984. Prior to the redemption date, preferred stock shareowners had the option of converting each share of preferred stock held into 2.24 shares of common stock.

Stock Option Plans

At December 31, 1984, there were 2,756,830 shares under options outstanding for the Company's 1974 and 1984 Management Incentive Plans at prices ranging from $24.25 to $57.59. Options for 1,525,360 shares were exercisable at December 31, 1984. During 1984, 1,800,699 options were granted and 106,568 options, granted at prices ranging from $24.97 to $44.03 per share, were exercised.

Stock appreciation rights (SARs) are authorized to be granted under both the 1974 and 1984 Plans, including retroactive grants for unexercised options. At December 31, 1984, SARs related to options for 805,138 shares were outstanding; of these, 390,526 were exercisable. During 1984, SARs related to options for 565,941 shares were granted and 12,836 were exercised.

Segment Information

Certain operating unit segment data for 1984-1982 appear on page 36 and are integral parts of the accompanying financial statements. The principal product lines included in each operating unit are shown in this segment data. The principal unusual charge included in the Operating Unit and World Area Segment Data is discussed in the "Principal Acquisitions and Divestitures" note to the financial statements. The liquidation of lower cost inventory "tiers" under the LIFO method increased 1982 operating income by $20 million, $27 million and $35 million for Fibers and Intermediates, Industrial Chemicals and Polymer Products, respectively.

Total sales between operating units (made on a market price basis) were $304 million, $297 million and $311 million in 1984-1982, respectively. These sales were significant for Industrial Chemicals ($142 million, $140 million and $151 million in 1984-1982, respectively) and Fibers and Intermediates ($116 million, $101 million and $91 million in 1984-1982, respectively). Inter-area sales, which are sales from one Monsanto location to another Monsanto location in a different world area, also were made on a market price basis.

Certain corporate expenses, primarily those related to the overall management of the Company, were not allocated to the operating units or world areas. Interest expense, interest income and other income — net, as shown in the Statement of Consolidated Income, are the only reconciling items between operating income and income before income taxes. Nonoperating assets principally include investments, and a portion of cash, time deposits and certificates of deposit, and short-term securities.

(continued)

tions, (2) discontinued operations, (3) extraordinary items, and (4) cumulative effects of changing accounting principles. Exhibit 2.2 presents a model income statement that should provide operational guidance in formulating disclosures applicable to nonroutine gains and losses. The authoritative source references in the exhibit refer to paragraph numbers in promulgated GAAP and should be useful in referring back to applicable documents for authoritative support.

Exhibit 2.1 (continued)

Net sales by entities in each world area were:

	Unaffiliated Customers			Inter-Area (Between Monsanto Entities)		
	1984	1983	1982	**1984**	1983	1982
United States	**$4,914**	$4,596	$4,483	**$ 534**	$ 526	$ 467
Europe-Africa	**945**	924	1,079	**207**	188	108
Canada	**278**	259	227	**9**	6	3
Latin America	**203**	192	221	**6**	4	2
Asia-Pacific	**351**	328	315	**33**	25	21
Eliminations				**(789)**	(749)	(601)
Total consolidated	**$6,691**	$6,299	$6,325	**$ —**	$ —	$ —

Operating income and total assets by entities in each world area were:

	Operating Income (Loss)			Total Assets		
	1984	1983	1982	**1984**	1983	1982
United States	**$ 477**	$ 434	$ 458	**$5,088**	$5,110	$4,711
Europe-Africa	**192**	137	39	**772**	696	790
Canada	**25**	24	5	**105**	92	81
Latin America	**4**	(4)	3	**178**	180	166
Asia-Pacific	**31**	15	11	**257**	203	172
Eliminations	**2**	(35)	8	**(253)**	(362)	(268)
Corporate expenses	**(54)**	(50)	(45)			
Nonoperating assets				**226**	508	425
Total consolidated	**$ 677**	$ 521	$ 479	**$6,373**	$6,427	$6,077

Following is a reconciliation of ex-U.S. operating income and total assets to the Company's equity in the net income and net assets of consolidated ex-U.S. subsidiaries:

	1984	1983	1982
Operating income	**$ 252**	$ 172	$ 58
Interest expense	**(53)**	(65)	(70)
Interest income	**36**	28	17
Other income — net	**29**	36	61
Income taxes (including extraordinary tax benefits of loss carryforwards)	**(108)**	(45)	(35)
Net income of consolidated ex-U.S. subsidiaries	**$ 156**	$ 126	$ 31
Total operating assets	**$1,312**	$1,171	$1,209
Total liabilities	**519**	470	440
Net assets of consolidated ex-U.S. subsidiaries	**$ 793**	$ 701	$ 769

MEASURING AND DISCLOSING DISCONTINUED OPERATIONS

Discontinued operations represent operations of a business segment that have been sold, spun-off, or otherwise disposed of, or, although still operating, that are the subject of a formal plan of disposal. A business segment in this sense refers to a separate major line of business or class of customer. As such, a segment may constitute a subsidiary, division, department, or any other unit where assets and results of operations are physically and operationally segregable for financial reporting purposes. It should be noted that if an enterprise disposes of what is considered a major segment but continues to operate in the same line of business, the disposal of this portion of the business does not constitute discontinuing a business segment.

Exhibit 2.1 (continued)

Financial Summary				Monsanto Company and Subsidiaries	
(Dollars in millions, except per share)	**1984**	1983[2]	1982[3,4]	1981	1980
Operating Results					
Net Sales	**$6,691**	$6,299	$6,325	$6,948	$6,574
Operating Income	**677**	521	479	702	210
Net Income	**$ 439**	$ 402	$ 352	$ 445	$ 149
As a Percent of Net Sales	**7%**	6%	6%	6%	2%
As a Percent of Average Shareowners' Equity	**12%**	11%	10%	15%	5%
As a Percent of Average Capital Employed	**10%**	10%	9%	11%	5%
Earnings per Share[1]	**$ 5.42**	$ 4.89	$ 4.39	$ 5.75	$ 2.05
Year-end Financial Position					
Total Assets	**$6,373**	$6,427	$6,077	$6,069	$5,796
Working Capital	**1,395**	1,535	1,503	1,486	1,226
Property, Plant & Equipment:					
Gross	**$6,919**	$6,639	$6,530	$6,218	$6,074
Net	**3,374**	3,284	3,313	3,184	3,109
Long-Term Debt	**$ 824**	$ 937	$1,003	$1,110	$1,371
Shareowners' Equity	**3,634**	3,667	3,490	3,330	2,808
Current Ratio	**2.2**	2.3	2.6	2.4	2.1
Percent of Long-Term Debt to Total Capitalization	**18%**	20%	22%	25%	33%
Other Data					
Property, Plant & Equipment Additions	**$ 614**	$ 560	$ 673	$ 668	$ 781
Depreciation, Depletion and Obsolescence	**491**	517	439	263	547
Interest Expense	**100**	96	82	101	112
Research and Development Expense	**370**	290	264	233	208
Income Taxes	**268**	201	172	248	57
Stock Price:[1] High	**$ 53⅞**	$ 58⅛	$ 44½	$ 43¾	$ 35⅛
Low	**40⅝**	37⅛	28¼	29¾	21⅛
Price/Earnings Ratio on Year-end Stock Price	**8**	11	9	6	17
Per Common Share:[1]					
Dividends	**$ 2.25**	$2.075	$1.975	$1.875	$1.775
Shareowners' Equity	**46.43**	44.83	42.99	42.18	38.82
Common Shareowners	**71,343**	69,787	75,943	79,029	82,441
Common Shares Outstanding (in millions)[1]	**78**	82	81	79	72
Employees	**50,754**	48,835	52,199	57,391	61,836

[1]Per share amounts and shares outstanding have been restated to reflect the June 1984 two-for-one common stock split.
[2]Net income for 1983 includes extraordinary tax benefits of $33 million, or $0.41 per share, from the utilization of ex-U.S. loss carryforwards.
[3]Net income for 1982 includes an extraordinary gain of $23 million, or $0.29 per share, from an exchange of debt for common shares.
[4]In 1982, the requirements of Statement of Financial Accounting Standards No. 52, "Foreign Currency Translation," were adopted.

(continued)

Exhibit 2.1 (continued)

Operating Unit Segment Data

	Net Sales			Operating Income (Loss)			Research and Development		
	1984	1983	1982	1984	1983	1982	1984	1983	1982
Agricultural Products	$1,256	$1,167	$1,165	$438	$400	$441	$107	$ 78	$ 65
Biological Sciences	168	152	146	(95)	(54)	(35)	66	41	33
Fibers and Intermediates	1,194	1,170	1,257	79	55	(21)	45	41	39
Industrial Chemicals	937	856	810	90	88	101	35	22	18
Polymer Products	1,877	1,830	1,786	152	70	13	41	40	44
Electronic Materials and Fabricated Products	519	355	357	5	(66)	(64)	25	24	23
Fisher Controls	537	528	588	35	37	52	19	10	14
Oil and Gas	203	241	216	27	41	37			
Corporate items and eliminations				(54)	(50)	(45)	32*	34*	28*
Total consolidated	**$6,691**	$6,299	$6,325	**$677**	$521	$479	**$370**	$290	$264

*Corporate R&D expenses are allocated on a weighted average basis of investment to operating units in determining operating income (loss).

	Total Assets			Capital Expenditures			Depreciation and Obsolescence		
	1984	1983	1982	1984	1983	1982	1984	1983	1982
Agricultural Products	$1,215	$1,214	$1,049	$ 67	$104	$ 89	$ 76	$ 70	$ 57
Biological Sciences	339	225	141	75	84	42	29	21	18
Fibers and Intermediates	992	1,071	1,150	83	79	90	97	115	135
Industrial Chemicals	892	810	777	90	61	162	74	75	56
Polymer Products	1,179	1,163	1,135	85	64	72	88	96	74
Electronic Materials and Fabricated Products	437	406	433	74	37	57	41	37	30
Fisher Controls	515	487	418	25	27	27	15	16	13
Oil and Gas	578	543	549	107	101	130	69	85	55
Nonoperating assets	226	508	425	8	3	4	2	2	1
Total consolidated	**$6,373**	$6,427	$6,077	**$614**	$560	$673	**$491**	$517	$439

The above data should be read in conjunction with the "Segment Information" note to the financial statements on page 52.

For 1984, the Company has realigned its financial reporting of Operating Unit Segments to better reflect the future direction of the Company's operations. Nutrition chemicals, health care and the corporate biological research effort have been combined to form a new segment, Biological Sciences. Corporate biological research and health care were previously included in corporate staff expense and allocated to Operating Unit Segments. Biological research directly related to Agricultural Products is included as an expense of that segment. The Oil and Gas operations are also presented as a separate segment.

Agricultural Products

Net Sales	1984	1983	1982
Herbicides and other agricultural chemicals	$1,256	$1,167	$1,165

Sales and operating income in 1984 increased 8 and 10 percent, respectively. Sales volume of *Roundup* herbicide increased 6 percent,

a slightly less than expected rate due to abnormal weather conditions in parts of the United States and Europe. Sales volume of *Lasso* herbicide also increased 6 percent year to year. The higher operating income from sales more than offset the increased research and new product development expenditures.

In November 1984, the United States Environmental Protection Agency (EPA) announced that it will conduct a Special Review to determine whether *Lasso* herbicide may cause an unreasonable adverse effect on humans or the environment. Pending the results of the review, Monsanto and the EPA agreed to modifications in the use of *Lasso*, which do not significantly affect the majority of uses for *Lasso*. Monsanto's tests conclude that *Lasso* poses no unreasonable adverse effects to humans or the environment, and the Company believes that the EPA review will reach a similar conclusion. The Company expects no significant effect on operating results from this review.

The operating results and any gain or loss associated with the discontinuance of a business segment should be separately disclosed in the statement of income immediately after income from continuing operations. Any gains or losses on disposal should not be considered extraordinary, but rather should be separately disclosed, net of tax, in the

Exhibit 2.1 (continued)

Sales in 1983 increased slightly from 1982, while operating income declined as a result of the 1983 PIK program.

Biological Sciences

Net Sales	1984	1983	1982
Human health care and nutrition products	$168	$152	$146

Sales in 1984 increased, reflecting the acquisition of Continental Pharma in May 1984. Sales volume of *Alimet*, an animal feed supplement, continued to grow, but selling prices remained depressed, largely because of the effects of the strong U.S. dollar and competition from ex-U.S. manufacturers. Operating losses, which have increased over the three-year period, are a result of significant biological research expenditures in both human health care and animal nutrition, along with facility start-up costs and expanded marketing efforts. Sales increased slightly in 1983 versus 1982.

Fibers and Intermediates

Net Sales	1984	1983	1982
Man-made fibers	$880	$824	$880
Textile intermediates	314	346	377

Sales in 1984 increased 2 percent, net of the 1983 nitrogen products divestiture. Operating income increased 44 percent over the prior year, reflecting the continued strong demand and improved pricing for nylon carpet fibers and chemical intermediates. Demand slowed and prices slipped, however, in the last quarter of 1984. Sales volume of branded nylon carpet fibers was particularly strong in 1984. Higher plant facility utilization also contributed to the higher earnings levels. Partially offsetting these improvements were higher costs of natural gas and the loss of income from the nitrogen products business. Sales in 1983 were lower than 1982 due to divested businesses and lower selling prices, offset somewhat by higher sales volume. Operating income in 1983 increased over 1982 due to higher sales volume, lower costs and the elimination of 1982 divested business losses. The operating loss in 1982 included $35 million in obsolescence charges relating to divestitures, partially offset by a $20 million benefit from non-replacement of lower cost LIFO inventories.

Industrial Chemicals

Net Sales	1984	1983	1982
Detergent and fine chemicals	$628	$587	$552
Specialty chemicals	309	269	258

Sales in 1984 increased 9 percent due to higher volumes for most products. Operating income was about the same in 1984 as compared with 1983. Improved efficiencies from higher plant facility utilization and reduced raw materials costs were offset by increased other manufacturing costs and research and development expenditures. Sales in 1983 were 6 percent higher than 1982, the principal increase being in detergent materials. Operating income declined in 1983 due to nonrecurring gains recognized in 1982, including a $27 million favorable impact of non-replacement of lower cost LIFO inventories.

Polymer Products

Net Sales	1984	1983	1982
Plastics	$874	$809	$775
Resin products	693	742	742
Rubber chemicals and instruments	310	279	269

A stronger worldwide economy pushed 1984 sales volume higher, especially sales to the automotive and housing industries. This increase more than offset the lost sales from divested and shutdown businesses. Operating income more than doubled in 1984, principally from sales volume gains in higher margin products and from improved plant facility utilization and elimination of 1983 divested business losses.

Sales in 1983 increased slightly over the preceding year due to higher volume offset by lower selling prices and business divestments. Operating income improved in 1983 from better manufacturing performance, offset in part by net charges of $24 million relating to various divestments and shutdowns of facilities. Operating income in 1982 included a $35 million favorable impact from non-replacement of lower cost LIFO inventories.

Electronic Materials and Fabricated Products

Net Sales	1984	1983	1982
Electronic-grade silicon wafers and engineered products	$519	$355	$357

Sales in 1984 increased 46 percent, largely due to higher volume and prices of silicon wafers and fabricated products, coupled with increased construction project activity in Monsanto Enviro-Chem Systems, Inc. The year 1984 was a turning point for electronic materials, with silicon wafer sales increasing 84 percent. These factors, together with higher electronic materials plant facility utilization and lower raw materials costs, resulted in a $71 million profit improvement over 1983.

(continued)

Exhibit 2.1 (continued)

Sales in 1983 were level with the prior year, with volume gains in electronic materials and fabricated products offset by decreased construction project activity in Enviro-Chem. Operating losses in 1983 were essentially the same as the prior year.

Fisher Controls

Net Sales	1984	1983	1982
Valves, regulators and electronic process controls	**$537**	$528	$588

Sales and operating income in 1984 were virtually the same as 1983. Improved operations in North and Latin America were offset by a one time acquisition-related technological expense and by continuing weak European performance, due to the adverse impact of the strong U.S. dollar and the depressed capital goods market.

In 1983, sales were lower than the previous year as price increases did not offset lower volume. Operating income in 1983 was 29 percent lower than the preceding year, reflecting the depressed worldwide capital goods market.

Oil and Gas

Net Sales	1984	1983	1982
Oil and gas	**$203**	$241	$216

Reduced oil and gas volumes resulted in lower 1984 sales and operating income. Also affecting the year to year operating income comparison are lower exploration and production expenses in 1984. Sales and operating income were higher in 1983 as compared to 1982 due primarily to higher oil and gas volumes.

Exploration efforts in 1984 were concentrated principally in the United States and United Kingdom North Sea, and current production was carried out primarily in the United States and Canada. Total spending for exploration amounted to $71 million, $55 million and $46 million for 1984, 1983 and 1982, respectively.

Net Quantities of Developed and Undeveloped Proved Reserves

	1984	1983	1982
Oil[1]			
Beginning of year	**42**	38	34
Extensions and discoveries	**9**	7	5
Production	**(4)**	(4)	(4)
Other changes — net	**(1)**	1	3
End of year	**46**	42	38
Natural Gas[2]			
Beginning of year	**587**	607	599
Extensions and discoveries	**19**	28	46
Production	**(34)**	(44)	(38)
Other changes — net	**6**	(4)	
End of year	**578**	587	607
Combined — Oil Equivalent[3]			
End of year	**142**	140	139

[1]Stated in millions of barrels.
[2]Stated in billions of cubic feet.
[3]Stated in millions of barrels (approximately six thousand cubic feet of gas equals one barrel of oil).

Estimated future net cash flows data related to proved reserves follow. Future selling prices and costs were determined by using the actual 1984 year-end levels, with a 10 percent interest rate used for discounting.

Standardized Measure of Discounted Future Net Cash Flows

	1984	1983	1982
Future cash inflows	**$3,068**	$3,222	$3,491
Future production and development costs	**730**	761	736
Future income tax expenses	**992**	1,047	1,190
Future net cash flows	**1,346**	1,414	1,565
Annual discount for estimated timing of cash flows	**888**	926	1,113
Standardized measure of discounted future net cash flows	**$ 458**	$ 488	$ 452

World Area Segment Data						
	Net Sales			Operating Income (Loss)		
	1984	1983	1982	1984	1983	1982
United States	**$4,498**	$4,243	$4,086	**$518**	$453	$441
Europe-Africa	**968**	943	1,092	**93**	44	33
Canada	**292**	274	244	**61**	51	29
Latin America	**360**	305	353	**22**	11	(9)
Asia-Pacific	**573**	534	550	**55**	27	19
Unallocated corporate items				**(54)**	(50)	(45)
Affiliates' equity (income) loss included in individual world areas				**(18)**	(15)	11
Total consolidated	**$6,691**	$6,299	$6,325	**$677**	$521	$479

Exhibit 2.1 (continued)

As required by generally accepted accounting principles, world area segment data (page 52) in the Notes to Financial Statements are prepared on an "entity basis." This means sales and income of the legal entity are assigned to the area where the entity is located (e.g., a sale from the U.S. to Brazil is reported as a U.S. sale). However, Monsanto normally views its results on an "area basis" wherein sales and income are assigned to the customer location (e.g., a sale from U.S. to Brazil is reported as a Brazilian sale). The table on the preceding page summarizes Monsanto's "area basis" results.

United States

Approximately two-thirds of Monsanto's worldwide sales are to customers in the United States. Sales for 1984 were up 6 percent, net of divestitures. The stronger economic environment benefited most product lines, especially housing and automotive-related businesses. In addition, silicon wafer sales to the semiconductor industry increased substantially. Agricultural products sales benefited from the United States government's discontinuation of the 1983 PIK program which resulted in volume growth in *Lasso* and related products.

Operating income in 1984 increased 14 percent. Sales volume improved along with better plant facility utilization. However, the strong U.S. dollar resulted in greater import competition from ex-U.S. competitors, which in turn adversely affected selected products selling prices and profits. In addition, the Company incurred higher technological expense in support of the numerous growth programs.

For 1983, sales increased 4 percent from 1982 due to the stronger economy partially offset by the 1983 PIK program. Operating income in 1983 increased 3 percent due to lower raw material costs and better plant facility utilization.

Europe-Africa

Sales in 1984 increased 3 percent over the preceding year as the European economic environment improved. Operating income more than doubled, benefiting from strong acrylonitrile and nylon intermediate profits. This increase in sales and operating income was accomplished despite the adverse effects of the strong U.S. dollar on the competitiveness of United States exports as well as the adverse translation effect on ex-U.S. currency denominated sales and income. Sales of *Roundup* herbicide increased in spite of abnormal weather conditions.

Sales in 1983 decreased 14 percent as compared to 1982, reflecting the divestiture of the acrylic fibers business, reduced agricultural products sales due to drought and adverse economic conditions. Operating income for 1983 improved over 1982, however, due principally to

the elimination of losses of the discontinued acrylic fibers business.

Canada

Sales in 1984 increased 7 percent, while operating income improved $10 million. Monsanto benefited from good detergent products and crop chemicals sales. In addition, sales to the automotive industry grew. Sales and operating income increased in 1983, as compared to 1982.

Latin America

Sales in 1984 increased 18 percent and operating income doubled to $22 million. Results in Brazil improved, where agricultural products sales continued to grow. In addition, Monsanto's Mexican equity affiliate experienced higher profitability. Sales in 1983 decreased from the prior year, as Brazil suffered from recession-induced conditions. Operating income in 1983 improved as higher earnings of a Mexican equity affiliate more than offset lower Brazilian results.

Asia-Pacific

This world area showed strong year to year sales and operating income gains, led by agricultural products sales volume growth throughout the area, higher United States exports of other products and improved operating income in Australia. These accomplishments were achieved despite the adverse effects of the strong U.S. dollar on the competitiveness of United States exports as well as the adverse translation effect on ex-U.S. currency denominated sales and income.

Sales declined slightly in 1983 principally due to depressed United States exports resulting from the strong U.S. dollar. Operating income in 1983 was up 42 percent over 1982, due to improved results in Australia and increased earnings from a Japanese equity affiliate.

A reconciliation of 1984 area basis sales and operating income to ex-U.S. entity basis sales and operating income (reflected in the Notes to Financial Statements) follows:

	Net Sales	Operating Income
Ex-U.S. entities	$2,032	$252
U.S. exports	950	25[1]
Ex-U.S. affiliates' equity income		18
Less: Inter-area eliminations	(789)	
Ex-U.S. entities' operating income on sales to U.S.		(64)
Ex-U.S. area basis	2,193	231
U.S. area basis	4,498	518
Affiliates' equity income included in ex-U.S. areas		(18)
Unallocated corporate expenses		(54)
Total consolidated	**$6,691**	**$677**

[1]Net of allocated costs.

(continued)

Exhibit 2.1 (continued)

Quarterly Data

		First Quarter	Second Quarter	Third Quarter	Fourth Quarter	Total Year
Net Sales	1984	$1,732	$1,801	$1,599	$1,559	$6,691
	1983	1,483	1,612	1,553	1,651	6,299
Gross Profit	1984	526	534	410	375	1,845
	1983	370	417	378	396	1,561
Income Before Extraordinary Items	1984	175	145	78	41	439
	1983	99	105	99	66	369
Net Income	1984	175	145	78	41	439
	1983	101	114	115	72	402
Earnings per Share						
Before Extraordinary Items	1984	2.13	1.77	0.97	0.55	5.42
	1983	1.21	1.27	1.21	0.79	4.48
After Extraordinary Items	1984	2.13	1.77	0.97	0.55	5.42
	1983	1.24	1.38	1.40	0.87	4.89

Agricultural products sales are traditionally concentrated in the first half of the year and are generally more profitable than sales of other segments. Sales and profit improvement in the first half of 1984 resulted from the favorable agricultural products environment and continued improvement in worldwide economic conditions.

However, the United States economy moderated somewhat during the last half of 1984 and the strengthening of the U.S. dollar increased import and price competition.

There were no major nonrecurring or unusual items in 1984. The 1983 items increasing (decreasing) earnings per share were as follows:

1983	First Quarter	Second Quarter	Third Quarter	Fourth Quarter	Total Year
Extraordinary tax benefits from loss carryforwards	$ 0.03	$ 0.11	$ 0.19	$ 0.08	$ 0.41
Change in accounting estimate of annual effective tax rate	(0.06)	(0.09)	0.15		
Net losses from facilities shut down or sold		(0.07)	(0.02)	(0.14)	(0.23)
Total	$(0.03)	$(0.05)	$ 0.32	$(0.06)	$ 0.18

Inflation-Adjusted Data

Year Ended December 31, 1984	Historical Cost	Current Cost
Net sales	$6,691	$6,691
Cost of goods sold, excluding depreciation	4,397	4,400
Depreciation expense	449	587
All other expenses — net	1,138	1,138
Income taxes	268	268
Net income	$ 439	$ 298

Current cost amounts shown above attempt to measure the effect of inflation on cost of goods sold and depreciation. Other historical amounts, including income taxes, are not adjusted for inflation to arrive at current cost net income. All current cost amounts are stated in average 1984 dollars using the U.S. Consumer Price Index (the "translate-restate" method).

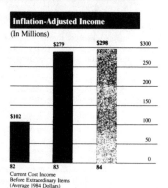

Inflation-Adjusted Income (In Millions)

Current Cost Income Before Extraordinary Items (Average 1984 Dollars)

discontinued operations section of the income statement (Refer back to Exhibit 2.2 and notice the two-tier disclosure.)

In attempting to measure the amounts to be included in discontinued operations, two definitions must be understood. The measurement date of a disposal is the date on which management having the authority to

Exhibit 2.1 (continued)

The 1984 increase in current cost of inventories and property, plant and equipment was $204 million. At December 31, 1984, the current cost of inventory and property, plant and equipment (net of accumulated depreciation) was $1,271 million and $4,051 million stated in year-end 1984 dollars.

The current cost of inventories was estimated using the FIFO (first-in, first-out)

inventory method. Cost of goods sold on a current cost basis was approximated using the LIFO method, or similar techniques. The current cost of property, plant and equipment was estimated generally by using construction and equipment indexes. Current cost accumulated depreciation and related expenses were estimated using the same overall method and lives as used on a historical cost basis.

Selected Financial Data

	1984	1983	1982	1981	1980
Historical cost, as reported[1]:					
Net sales	**$6,691**	$6,299	$6,325	$6,948	$6,574
Income — Before extraordinary items	**439**	369	329	445	149
— Per share	**5.42**	4.48	4.10	5.75	2.05
Total assets	**6,373**	6,427	6,077	6,069	5,796
Long-term debt	**824**	937	1,003	1,110	1,371
Dividends per common share	**2.25**	2.075	1.975	1.875	1.775
Current cost (average 1984 dollars):					
Net sales	**$6,691**	$6,567	$6,807	$7,935	$8,288
Income (loss) — Before extraordinary items	**298**	279	102	263	(11)
— Per share	**3.68**	3.39	1.28	3.39	(0.15)
Purchasing power gain on monetary items	**32**	30	36	112	170
Increase in specific prices of inventory and property over (under) increase caused by general inflation	**1**	(234)	(235)	(13)	(324)
Aggregate foreign currency adjustment, net of taxes	**(143)**	(103)	(177)		
Net assets	**4,677**	4,853	5,038	5,573	5,124
Other data (average 1984 dollars):					
Dividends per common share	**$ 2.26**	$ 2.17	$ 2.13	$ 2.16	$ 2.26
Year-end common stock price	**43.39**	53.94	40.57	38.75	41.32
Average consumer price index	**311.1**	298.4	289.1	272.4	246.8

[1]In 1982, the requirements of Statement of Financial Accounting Standards No. 52, "Foreign Currency Translation," were adopted.

Comparisons of investment levels (including capital expenditures, and research and other growth-oriented investments) are distorted by inflation. Inflation-adjusted data may be useful in evaluating whether total investment levels, in "real dollars," have increased. In addition, such data may be useful in evaluating, on a broad financial basis, whether current profitability levels

are providing sufficient funds for growth-oriented investments. As discussed below, a comparison of Monsanto's inflation-adjusted funds provided from operations and funds used for investment expenditures indicates that the Company has generated sufficient cash to fund a significant portion of those growth-related investments.

Total Investment

	1984	1983	1982	1981	1980
Capital expenditures	**$ 614**	$ 560	$ 673	$ 668	$ 781
Investments	**94**	208	11	2	64
R&D expenditures	**370**	290	264	233	208
Total (historical cost)	**$1,078**	$1,058	$ 948	$ 903	$1,053
Total (average 1984 dollars)	**$1,078**	$1,103	$1,020	$1,031	$1,327

Total Investment Remains High, But Components Have Changed

Monsanto's "total investment" level — capital expenditures, investments (acquisitions,

venture capital, etc.), and research and development expenditures — remains high, but the underlying components of investment have changed. In recent years, expenditures for research

(continued)

Exhibit 2.1 (continued)

and development and investments have increased while traditional capital expenditures have moderated. This trend is consistent with the strategy shift from certain commodity and capital intensive businesses to selected high technology, specialty products with a higher value added component.

    This "total investment" includes expenditures to: (1) maintain the existing earnings

base, and (2) increase future income levels. Monsanto considers its current cost depreciation and estimated "maintenance" research and development costs for existing businesses to approximate the amount of investment needed to maintain existing earnings levels. The remaining investment may be considered as new growth investment.

Investment Analysis

	1984	1983	1982	1981	1980
Investment to maintain existing earnings base	$ 694	$ 673	$ 693	$ 713	$ 691
New growth investment	384	430	327	318	636
Total (average 1984 dollars)	$1,078	$1,103	$1,020	$1,031	$1,327

Discretionary Cash Flow Is Sufficient to Fund Significant Portion of Growth-Related Investments

    In recent years, Monsanto has generated sufficient discretionary cash flow to fund all or a significant portion of the growth-oriented investments. "Discretionary cash flow" is defined as cash flow from operations (after working capital changes), before research and development expenditures, less dividends, debt repayments and investment to maintain the existing earnings base.

Discretionary Cash Flow
(Average 1984 Dollars — In Millions)

Discretionary Cash Flow

	1984	1983	1982	1981	1980
Historical cost	$309	$489	$245	$171	$206
Average 1984 dollars	$309	$510	$264	$195	$260
Discretionary cash flow as a percent of new growth investment (average 1984 dollars)	80%	119%	81%	61%	41%

    Monsanto's cost reduction and asset management programs, coupled with the pruning of unprofitable businesses, have been significant cash flow contributors. Proceeds from the sale of assets have also contributed funds for growth. In addition, Monsanto's strong financial position provides substantial unused debt and equity capacity for funding future investment requirements.

Company Has Demonstrated Ability to Fund Future Growth

    Management believes that Monsanto has demonstrated its ability to generate sufficient earnings and cash flow to provide for real future growth beyond that required to maintain its existing earnings base, including inflation-adjusted replacement capital requirements.

approve disposals commits to a formal plan to sell or abandon a business segment. At a minimum, this plan should include an identification of the major assets to be disposed, the expected method of disposal, the period estimated to complete the disposal, an active program to find a buyer if disposal is to be through sale, the estimated results of operations of the segment from the measurement date to the disposal date, and the estimated proceeds or salvage to be realized on disposal. The disposal date is the date on which the sale is closed or the operations cease, whichever is appropriate in the particular circumstances.

Exhibit 2.1 (continued)

Management Report

Monsanto Company management is responsible for the fair presentation and consistency of all financial data included in this Annual Report. Where necessary, the data reflect management estimates.

Management is also responsible for maintaining a system of internal accounting control to provide reasonable assurance that assets are safeguarded against material loss from unauthorized use or disposition and that authorized transactions are properly recorded to permit the preparation of accurate financial data. Cost-benefit judgments are an important consideration in this regard. The effectiveness of internal controls is maintained by: (1) personnel selection and training; (2) division of responsibilities; (3) establishment and communication of policies; and (4) ongoing internal review programs and audits.

As ratified by shareowner vote at the 1984 Annual Meeting, Deloitte Haskins & Sells was appointed to examine, and express an opinion as to the fair presentation of, the consolidated financial statements. This opinion appears below.

Monsanto's Audit Committee, consisting of five non-employee directors, meets with Controllership, Internal Audit and Deloitte Haskins & Sells personnel to review internal controls, financial reporting and accounting practices. Deloitte Haskins & Sells and internal auditors meet with the Committee, with and without management present, to discuss their examinations, the adequacy of internal controls and the quality of financial reporting.

Richard J. Mahoney
President
and
Chief Executive Officer

Francis A. Stroble
Senior Vice President
and
Chief Financial Officer

February 22, 1985

Independent Auditors' Opinion

To the Shareowners of Monsanto Company:

We have examined the statement of consolidated financial position of Monsanto Company and Subsidiaries as of December 31, 1984 and 1983 and the related statements of consolidated income, shareowners' equity and changes in financial position for each of the three years in the period ended December 31, 1984. Our examinations were made in accordance with generally accepted auditing standards and, accordingly, included such tests of the accounting records and such other auditing procedures as we considered necessary in the circumstances.

In our opinion, such consolidated financial statements present fairly the financial position of Monsanto Company and Subsidiaries at December 31, 1984 and 1983, and the results of their operations and changes in their financial position for each of the three years in the period ended December 31, 1984, in conformity with generally accepted accounting principles applied on a consistent basis.

Deloitte Haskins & Sells

Saint Louis, Missouri
February 22, 1985

Following the accounting tradition of recognizing losses as soon as possible and postponing the recognition of gains as long as possible, promulgated GAAP require that if a loss is anticipated on disposal of a business segment, the loss should be recognized at the measurement date whereas anticipated gains should be recognized as realized, which typically is the disposal date. The determination of whether a gain or loss is expected on disposal should encompass two factors: (1) an estimate of operating results from the measurement date to the disposal

Exhibit 2.2
Model Income Statement Format

Authoritative Source

Unusual or infrequently occurring items: APBO No. 30, p. 26.	Gain from sale of securities	XXX
	Income from continuing operations before income taxes	XXX
	Provision for income taxes	XXX
	Income from continuing operations	XXX
Discontinued operations: APBO No. 30, p. 8.	Discontinued operations:	
	Income (loss) from operations of discontinued Division X (less applicable income taxes of $X)	XXX
	Loss on disposal of Division X (less applicable income taxes of $X)	XXX XXX
	Income before extraordinary item and cumulative effect of accounting change	XXX
Extraordinary items: APBO No. 30, p. 10/ APBO No. 11, p. 60/ SFAS No. 4, p. 8/ SFAS No. 15, p. 21.	Loss from destruction of physical facility due to natural disaster (less applicable income taxes of $X)	XXX XXX
Accounting changes: APBO No. 20, p. 20.	Cumulative effect of change in accounting method of depreciation (less applicable income taxes of $X)	XXX XXX
	Net income	XXX
EPS: APBO No. 15, p. 16/ APBO No. 30, pp. 9 & 12	Earnings per common share:	
	Income from continuing operations	$X.XX
	Discontinued operations	X.XX
	Income before extraordinary items	$X.XX
	Extraordinary items	X.XX
	Cumulative effect of change in principle	X.XX
	Net income	$X.XX
	Items of profit and loss excluded from income statement: Correction of errors	

Exhibit 2.2 (continued)

Prior period adjustments: APBO No. 9, p. 25/ SFAS No. 16, p. 11.	Adjustments that result from realization of income tax benefits of pre-acquisition operating loss carryforward of purchased subsidiaries

Source: William W. Holder, M. Herschel Mann, and Thomas A. Ratcliffe, "Reporting the Results of Operations," *CPA Journal* (April 1978):80.

date and (2) an estimate of net realizable value of the net assets being disposed of compared with the carrying amount of the net assets. If the confluence of these two factors results in an estimated loss, this loss should be recognized at the measurement date through disclosure in the second tier of discontinued operations. Costs and expenses that are incurred as a direct result of discontinuing operations, e.g., severance pay and additional pension cost, should be included in the determination of this estimated gain or loss. Other costs and expenses that would have been recognized regardless of the decision to dispose, e.g., normal accruals, should be excluded from this estimation.

The first line in the discontinued operations disclosure should represent operating results of the discontinued segment from the beginning of the reporting period to the measurement date. Although when these earnings were generated or losses incurred they represented continuing operations, these results will not recur in subsequent time periods, and accordingly this amount should be disclosed, net of tax, in discontinued operations.

In addition to the disclosures required in the body of the income statement pertaining to discontinued operations, the notes to the financial statements covering the period encompassing the measurement date should include the following:

1. The identity of the business segment that has been or will be disposed of
2. The expected disposal date, if known
3. The expected manner of disposal
4. A description of any remaining assets and liabilities of the segment at the financial statement date
5. The operating income or loss and any proceeds from segment disposal during the period from the measurement date to the financial statement date.

These disclosures also should be made in reporting periods subsequent to the measurement date, including the period of disposal, and the information in (5) should be compared with prior estimates.

DETERMINING AND DISCLOSING EXTRAORDINARY ITEMS

Current promulgated GAAP severely restrict the number of items, events, or transactions that now may be classified as extraordinary items and thus disclosed "below the line" (as shown in Exhibit 2.2). There should exist a presumption that an activity is ordinary unless either of the following is met:

1. The item, event, or transaction must be both unusual in nature and infrequently occurring, considering the environment in which an enterprise operates. Unusual in nature means the activity should be highly abnormal and clearly unrelated, or only incidentally related, to typical business activity, and infrequency of occurrence means the activity should be of a type not reasonably expected to recur in the foreseeable future.
2. Promulgated GAAP require that the accounting effects of the item, event, or transaction be classified as extraordinary. Examples of this type of activity would include recognizing the tax effects of operating loss carryforwards in other than the loss year (see APBO No. 11), gains and losses on the extinguishment of debt (see SFAS Nos. 4, 15, and 64), and asset dispositions by a pooled enterprise (see APBO No. 16).

Pragmatically, the most common disclosures of extraordinary items currently are those required by promulgated GAAP coupled with gains and losses resulting from natural disasters such as hurricanes and tornadoes. In applying materiality thresholds for determining whether to classify an item, event, or transaction as extraordinary, effects on income before extraordinary items and the trend of annual earnings before extraordinary items should be considered. The items, events, or transactions should be considered individually in applying the materiality thresholds unless there exists a series of related transactions arising from a single specific and identifiable event or plan of action; in the latter case, the related transactions should be aggregated in applying materiality thresholds.

Disclosure of Unusual or Infrequently Occurring Items

Some questions have been raised concerning the disclosure of transactions that meet the criterion of being either unusual in nature or infrequently occurring but not both. Promulgated GAAP require that these types of transactions of a material amount be disclosed as a separate line item in income from continuing operations. These items may not be disclosed net of tax so that no misleading inference may be drawn concerning whether they are extraordinary. Examples of transactions that may meet this either/or test would be material writedowns of receivables or foreign exchange gains or losses.

EARNINGS PER SHARE DISCLOSURES

At a minimum, EPS disclosures should be made for income from continuing operations, discontinued operations, income before extraordinary items, income after extraordinary items, cumulative effect of accounting changes, and net income. The unique problems associated with EPS disclosures are discussed in Chapter 13.

PRIOR PERIOD ADJUSTMENTS—STATEMENT OF RETAINED EARNINGS

As opposed to presenting a set of definitive criteria to be used in determining what items of profit or loss should be excluded from income determination, promulgated GAAP now specifically identify the items, events, or transactions that constitute prior period adjustments. The two specific accounting events that should be accounted for as prior period adjustments in annual financial reports are (1) corrections of errors in prior period financial statements and (2) adjustments that result from the realization of income tax benefits of pre-acquisition operating loss carryforwards of purchased subsidiaries. The accounting effects of these two events should be treated as adjustments to the beginning balance of retained earnings for the current reporting period. To the extent that previously issued financial statements that contained errors are reissued, they should be changed to reflect correct accounting treatments. Other changes typically reflected in the retained earnings statement are net income for the year, dividends, and retroactive accounting changes.

REPORTING CHANGES IN FINANCIAL POSITION

Prior to 1971, presentation of a funds statement was encouraged but not required (see APBO No. 3, "The Statement of Source and Application of Funds") for financial statements to be in comformity with GAAP. While a significant number of companies were presenting a funds statement, others were not. This diversity in reporting practices was evident even within the same industry. In addition, the form and content of funds statements varied widely. In an attempt to provide consistency related to reporting changes in financial position, the APB issued APBO No. 19, "Reporting Changes in Financial Position."

Applicability of the Provisions of APBO No. 19

The provisions of APBO No. 19 apply to all profit-oriented businesses presenting both an income statement and a balance sheet in conformity with GAAP. The provisions apply whether or not the balance sheet is classified. If a classified balance sheet is provided, the statement of changes in financial position may be presented on a cash, near cash, or working capital basis. Companies that do not provide a classified balance sheet should present the statement either on a cash or near cash basis.

Overview of APBO No. 19

The APB, in requiring the presentation of a statement of changes in financial position, adopted the concept of "all financial resources." Under this concept, all the significant aspects of a company's financial and investing activities, regardless of their effect on cash or working capital, should be disclosed. Examples of items not affecting cash or working capital that are disclosed in the statement would include the acquisition or disposal of long-term assets in exchange for debt or equity securities.

The format used in the statement of changes in financial position should be the one making the most informative presentation in the applicable circumstances. However, APBO No. 19 provides basic guidelines that should be followed. In addition, it also recommends that the title of the statement should be "Statement of Changes in Financial Position."

Concept of Funds

APBO No. 19 does not state a specific concept of "funds" that should be used. Instead, the statement should use the funds concept that presents the most useful portrayal of the financing and investing activities of the company. Some of the types of funds that may be emphasized are (1) cash, (2) cash and temporary investments (marketable securities), (3) net quick assets, and, (4) working capital.

The concept of funds used should be described accurately. In addition, it should be relevant in relation to the company and the particular financial statements. For example, the working capital concept should not be used for a company not presenting a classified balance sheet.

Funds Provided or Used in Operations

The statement of changes in financial position should prominently disclose working capital or cash provided from or used in operations for the period. The APB recommends that the effects of extraordinary items be separately stated. Likewise, the effects of discontinued operations and accounting changes logically should be disclosed separately.

Two methods of disclosing the amount of funds provided from operations are acceptable. The first method, which is used most commonly, begins with income or loss from continuing operations. From this amount, items that did not use (or provide) working capital or cash are added back (or deducted). Examples of those items not requiring the use of funds include depreciation, amortization, and noncurrent deferred taxes. The items added back or deducted are not sources or uses of working capital but are adjustments to income to reconcile to sources provided by operations. A common format of this method can be illustrated by the following:

Income from continuing operations		$15,000
Add (deduct) items not requiring outlay of working capital in the current period		
Depreciation	$2,000	
Amortization	1,000	
Deferred income taxes (credit)	(500)	2,500
Working capital generated by continuing operations		$17,500
Working capital generated by discontinued operations		(1,500)
Working capital generated by extraordinary items		2,000
Working capital generated by accounting change		1,000
Working capital generated by operations		$19,000

The second method begins with total revenues that provide working capital or cash. From this amount, operating expenses affecting working capital or cash are subtracted. Either of the two methods will result in the same amount of funds provided by operations.

In addition to working capital or cash provided from operations, all other significant financing or investing activities affecting the type of funds used should be clearly disclosed. Examples of these items include

1. Funds used to purchase long-term assets
2. Proceeds from sales of long-term assets not in the normal course of business
3. Issuance, assumption, redemption, and repayment of long-term debt
4. Issuance, redemption, or purchase of capital stock
5. Certain distributions to shareholders.

Financing or Investing Transactions Not Affecting Funds

APBO No. 19, under the "all financial resources" concept, requires the disclosure of all investing and financing transactions including those that do not involve the receipt of disbursement of working capital or cash funds. Examples of these transactions include

1. Conversion of long term debt or preferred stock to long-term debt or preferred stock to common stock
2. Acquisition of long-term assets through the use of long-term debt or equity
3. Exchange of long-term assets directly for other long-term assets (however, normal trade-in should be reported on a net basis).

These transactions should be disclosed clearly in the statement. The practical result is the disclosure of a source of funds offset by a corresponding use of funds. An exception to the disclosure requirements is made for "book entries" such as stock dividends or stock splits.

Changes in the Elements of Working Capital

Regardless of whether the working capital concept of funds is used, net changes of each element of working capital should be disclosed for the current period. If funds are defined as working capital, the changes in the elements should be disclosed in a tabulation accompanying the statement. One method of disclosing this information is illustrated, as follows:

	1981	1982	Increase or (Decrease)
Current Assets			
Cash	$10,000	$ 8,000	$(2,000)
Accounts receivable	15,000	19,000	4,000
Prepaid insurance	2,000	1,000	(1,000)
Inventory	30,000	36,000	6,000
Total current assets	$57,000	$64,000	$ 7,000
Current Liabilities			
Accounts payable	$ 7,000	$ 9,000	$ 2,000
Accrued liabilities	4,000	7,000	3,000
Notes payable (current)	12,000	10,000	(2,000)
Total current liabilities	$23,000	$26,000	$ 3,000
Increase in working capital	$34,000	$38,000	$ 4,000

If cash is used as the concept of funds, the changes of elements of working capital will be properly disclosed in the body of the statement. No separate statement is needed since the changes in the current accounts appear in the statement.

Other Considerations

The statement of changes in financial position should be included for each period an income statement is presented. However, the detail of net changes in each element of working capital is required only for the current year.

Isolated statistics of working capital or cash provided from operations, especially per share information, should not be presented in annual reports to shareholders. However, if per share amounts are included, the minimum disclosure should include amounts for inflow from operations, inflow from other sources, and total outflow. In addition, each per share amount should be clearly identified with the proper amounts in the statement.

STOCKHOLDERS' EQUITY

Because not all stockholders' equity transactions are reflected in the combined statement of income and retained earnings, entities are also required to include a schedule or statement that depicts the other changes in stockholders' equity accounts. Accordingly, this statement would demonstrate transactions such as issuance of stock, treasury stock, stock dividends, and issuance of rights (see Chapter 12).

SUMMARY OF SIGNIFICANT ACCOUNTING POLICIES

Because entities may use different accounting principles to report similar transactions, APBO No. 22, "Accounting Policies," requires entities to disclose the significant accounting principles used. This is typically the first note to the financial statements (see Exhibit 2.1). Included in this disclosure usually is information regarding the basis of consolidation, inventory methods, depreciation methods, and methods of accounting for investment tax credits.

SEGMENT DISCLOSURES

Public entities are required by SFAS No. 14 to disclose information by segments of the business. Additional disclosures are also specified by this statement. Chapter 14 delineates these reporting requirements.

NOTES TO FINANCIAL STATEMENTS

As a final requirement, entities must report all material or important information in their financial statements. To avoid a cluttering effect, the notes to the financial statements are used to expand on the summarized data included (see Exhibit 2.1).

SUPPLEMENTARY DISCLOSURES

The FASB requires certain entities to make supplementary (unaudited) disclosures. These requirements are elaborated in Chapter 15.

SUMMARY

This chapter provides an overview of information included in a complete set of financial statements to give the reader a frame of reference. The subsequent chapters amplify on these illustrations by specific items in the financial statements and provide detail of how that information is derived.

3
Working Capital Disclosures

THE NATURE OF CURRENT ASSETS AND CURRENT LIABILITIES

Accounting for and classifying assets and liabilities involve three primary determinations: existence, evaluation, and classification.

Classification in accounting implies the grouping of like items to provide meaningful summaries of financial data. The criteria chosen to effect such groupings can greatly influence a financial statement user's ability to understand the financial position and operations of a company, to make meaningful comparisons over time and among other companies, and to predict future profitability and cash flow. In addition to facilitating comprehension, comparison, and projection of financial information, the specific objective of designating certain assets and liabilities as current is to provide a measure of liquidity. Along with the income statement and the statement of changes in financial position, the current/noncurrent classification of assets and liabilities is essential to the evaluation of

1. The present and expected solvency of a company
2. The availability of funds for distribution
3. The degree of choice available to management in the commitment of funds to specific forms of investment.

Chapter 3A of ARB No. 43 is the primary source of GAAP applicable to the classification of assets and liabilities. The stated objective of the CAP in Chapter 3A is to develop criteria necessary to define current assets and current liabilities in relation to the operating cycle of a business. Thus, an important purpose of balance sheet classification is to set forth a comparison of the resources and obligations necessary to finance daily operations and to measure financial flexibility and viability during the time that cash is invested in the process of earning revenues. ARB No. 43 specifies working capital, the excess of current assets over current liabilities, as an important indicator of short-term solvency. That is, working capital identifies the relatively liquid portion of total enterprise capital that constitutes a margin or buffer for meeting obligations within the ordinary operating cycle of a business.

OVERVIEW OF CURRENT ASSETS

Chapter 3A of ARB No. 43 defines current assets as cash and other assets or resources that are reasonably expected to be realized in cash or sold or consumed during the normal operating cycle of the business or within one year, whichever is greater. Examples of current assets include the following:

1. Cash and cash equivalents available for current operations
2. Inventories of merchandise, supplies, and manufacturing processes
3. Receivables due within the current operating cycle (or one year if longer)
4. Marketable securities intended as secondary cash resources available for current operations
5. Prepaid expenses and deferred charges that benefit or relate to the current period.

The operating cycle concept provides an operational means of separating short-term from long-term commitments. Chapter 3A of ARB No. 43 describes the operating cycle as the length of time required for capital to "circulate" within the current asset group, i.e., from cash, to inventory, to sale, to receivables, to cash. The objective of accounting for current assets is to identify those resources that are directly involved in this process or that are liquidated or consumed during the term of one cycle (or one year, whichever is longer). Accordingly, the following items are specifically excluded from the current asset classification:

1. Cash and equivalents restricted from use for current operations, designated for the acquisition or construction of noncurrent assets, or segregated for the payment of debts properly classified as long-term
2. Receivables not due within the current operating cycle (or one year if longer)
3. Investments of a permanent nature, i.e., intended for purposes of control, affiliation, or continuing business advantage
4. Cash surrender value of life insurance policies
5. Depreciable assets

6. Land and other natural resources

7. Prepayments and deferrals that are chargeable to the operations of years subsequent to the current period.

OVERVIEW OF CURRENT LIABILITIES

The CAP defines a current liability as an obligation that is expected to be liquidated by either a current asset or the creation of another current liability. In addition to emphasizing the solvency aspect of the current classification, ARB No. 43 expresses an operational perspective by stating that the current liability classification is intended to include obligations for items that have entered into the operating cycle. Examples of current liabilities include the following:

1. Obligations related to the operating cycle, such as trade payables, unearned revenues, and accruals for payroll expenses, commissions, rents, royalties, and taxes

2. Short-term debts and current maturities of long-term liabilities (amounts due within one year)

3. Estimates of known obligations, such as vested vacation benefits

4. Certain loss contingencies.

The objective of accounting for current liabilities is to identify those obligations that will require the use of unrestricted cash, the liquidation of a current asset, or the creation of another short-term debt. Consequently, the current liability classification does not include obligations that will be refinanced on a long-term basis or debts to be paid with noncurrent assets (e.g., reclassification after nine years on a ten-year bond issue and its related sinking fund would seriously distort the current ratio for the tenth year).

ACCOUNTING FOR RECEIVABLES

Although the term "receivables" could include any claim of one entity for money, goods, or services from another entity, the receivables encountered most often are trade accounts receivable, notes receivable, and receivables from related parties (e.g., officers, employees, shareholders, or affiliates). Receivables should be stated at the estimated amount of cash to be realized. Any decline in the maximum collectible amount is recognized as an expense (e.g., bad debt expense) or as a reduction in revenues (e.g., sales allowances for defective goods). Receivables due within the current operating cycle, or one year if longer, are classified as current assets. The treatment of related party receivables is not unusual except that these amounts must be reported separately in the financial statements and not included under a general heading such as "notes receivable" or "accounts receivable." The balance of this section will explain the accepted methods of (1) accounting for potentially uncollectible trade receivables and (2) valuation of trade receivables when a "right of return" exists.

COLLECTIBILITY OF RECEIVABLES

The uncertainty that generally exists regarding the collectibility of receivables constitutes a contingency within the meaning of paragraph 1 of SFAS No. 5, entitled "Accounting for Contingencies." Consequently, estimated bad debt expense must be accrued if it is material and probable and can be reasonably estimated. The degree to which receivables have been "impaired" may be estimated based on experience, an analysis of individual accounts, or reference to appropriate industry averages.

Except in unusual cases, the very process of selling on account implies that bad debt expenses are probable. Assuming that a reasonable estimate (or range) of those losses is generally possible, SFAS No. 5 would seem to preclude the use of the direct write-off method. That is, the method of recognizing bad debt expense only when individual accounts become uncollectible cannot be sued in lieu of recognizing probable losses not yet attributable to specific accounts. The direct write-off method is therefore inappropriate unless bad debts are immaterial, are not "likely" to occur, or cannot reasonably be estimated. In all other cases, bad debts should be estimated at least annually, charged to expense, and credited to an allowable for doubtful accounts to provide a proper matching of expenses with revenue. When specific accounts are subsequently determined to be uncollectible, they should be written off (or down) by charging the allowance and crediting accounts receivable.

If a reasonable estimate of probable bad debt losses cannot be made, the conditions for accrual [paragraph 8 (b) of SFAS No. 5] are not met and the disclosures required by paragraph 10 of SFAS No. 5 must be made. In this case, if there is significant uncertainty as to collection, the installment method, the cost recovery method, or some other method of revenue recognition may be most apprppriate (see paragraph 12 of APBO No. 10).

REVENUE RECOGNITION WHEN RIGHT OF RETURN EXISTS

SFAS No. 48, entitled "Revenue Recognition When Right of Return Exists," sets forth criteria for recognizing revenue—and consequently for valuing receivables—when buyers have a right to return a product, whether by contract or by existing practice. The product may be returned for a refund, credit, or exchange either by the ultimate customer or by an entity engaged in reselling the product to others. Transactions to which SFAS No. 48 apply typically include sales when customer satisfaction is guaranteed or when a retailer has a right to return unsold items. SFAS No. 48 does not apply to service industries, transactions involving real estate or leases, or a buyer's prerogative to return defective merchandise.

Prior to issuance of the AICPA's Statement of Position 75-1, from which SFAS No. 48 was extracted, accounting practices varied considerably among three basic approaches:

1. No recognition of a sale until unconditional acceptance of the product
2. Recognition of a sale reduced by an allowance for estimated returns
3. Recognition of a sale with no allowance for returns.

To encourage more uniformity, the AICPA established criteria that had to be met before revenue could be recognized. The FASB adopted the AICPA position that sales revenue, when the right of product return exists, should not be recognized in the year of sale unless all of the following conditions are met:

1. The seller's price to the buyer is substantially fixed or determinable at the date of sale.
2. The buyer has paid the seller, or the buyer is obligated to pay the seller and the obligation is not contingent on resale of the product.
3. The buyer's obligation to the seller would not be changed in the event of theft or physical destruction or damage of the product.
4. The buyer acquiring the product for resale has economic substance apart from that provided by the seller.
5. The seller does not have significant obligations for future performance to directly bring about resale of the product by the buyer.
6. The amount of future returns can be reasonable estimated.

Thus, sales cannot be recognized until the right of return has expired or until the required conditions are met, whichever occurs first.

When all of the above criteria are satisfied, product sales should be recognized immediately. However, SFAS No. 48 requires that both sales revenue and cost of sales be reduced to reflect estimated returns and that any "costs or losses" expected to result from those returns be accrued in accordance with SFAS No. 5. The FASB provides no guidance regarding the implementation of these requirements. However, a theoretically correct approach would be to establish an allowance to reduce the carrying value of accounts receivable by the gross margin applicable to probable returns. If, for example, only one sale was recognized and the entire shipment was considered a probable return, the net receivable would represent the cost of the returned goods.

INVENTORY PRICING

The term "inventory" refers to those items of tangible personal property that (1) are held for sale in the ordinary course of business, (2) are in the process of production for such sale, or (3) are to be currently consumed in the production of goods or services to be available for sale. The phrase "in the ordinary course of business" limits the inventory classification to merchandise and manufactured goods that a company is in the business of selling. Materials and supplies used to produce manufactured goods are includable as inventory only to the extent of current consumption, i.e., materials and supplies for use within one operating cycle (or one year if longer). Excluded from inventory are significant quantities of materials to be used on the production of noninventory items; plant and equipment whether before, during, or after "regular" use in operations; and securities or other items held for resale but incidental to the operations of the company. Inventories are, by definition, current assets.

As set forth in Chapter 4 of ARB No. 43, the major objective of accounting for inventories is determination of income through the matching of costs with related revenues. This requires that the cost of goods available for sale be allocated between items sold and items left in inventory at the end of each accounting period. The first step in this process is to determine the physical quantities of goods on hand. ARB No. 43 permits either a periodic count or a prudent reliance on perpetual records for this purpose. That is, physical counts should be made at least annually or by an on-going rotation system in order to maintain the integrity of the perpetual record. All goods to which a business has legal title should be included in inventory regardless of physical location, e.g., whether in transit, out on consignment, or in the warehouse.

The second step in the matching process is to assign accounting values to goods sold and to ending inventory. The balance of this section will discuss issues pertinent to the task of pricing inventory, including the concept of cost, departures from cost, and assumptions as to the flow of costs.

DEFINITION OF COST

In general, GAAP require that assets be stated at cost. As applied to inventories, ARB No. 43 defines cost as the sum of applicable expenditures and charges directly or indirectly incurred in bringing an article to its existing condition and location. Thus, the cost of merchandise will include the purchase price as well as any taxes, freight, storage, and other material amounts incurred in getting the product ready for sale. The cost of manufacturing inventories will include similar costs for acquisition of direct materials, but also will include charges for direct labor as well as allocations of overhead expenses such as utilities and maintenance of plant and equipment.

Application of the cost principle to manufactured items becomes a matter of judgment when deciding whether particular items of overhead are period or product costs. ARB No. 43 establishes a criterion on normalcy for making such determination. That is, under some circumstances, items such as idle facility expense, excessive spoilage, double freight, and rehandling costs may be so abnormal as to require treatment as current period charges rather than as a portion of the inventory cost. ARB No. 43 further provides that general, administrative, and selling expenses are period costs, except for that portion of general and administrative expense that may be clearly related to production.

ARB No. 43 permits the pricing of inventories by standard costs as long as the standards are current and the result reasonably approximates some other accepted cost flow assumption [e.g., first in, first out (FIFO) or average cost].

DEPARTURE FROM COST

When the utility of inventory items falls below recorded cost, whether owing to physical deterioration, obsolescence, changes in price levels, or other causes, ARB No. 43 requires that the loss be recognized in the period of the decline. ARB No. 43 specifies that this requirement can be satisfied by pricing inventories at the lower of cost or market (LCM).

For the purposes of applying the LCM rule, the term "market" means replacement cost, by purchase or by reproduction, but with an upper and lower limit. The upper limit (ceiling) is net realizable value (NRV). That is, market cannot exceed the expected sales price less additional costs of completion and disposal. The lower limit (floor) is NRV less a normal profit margin. The lower limit will exceed replacement cost when a decline in replacement cost is not accompanied by a similar decline in projected selling price, e.g., in the case of existing sales contracts at fixed prices. The purpose of the lower limit is to avoid recognizing a loss in the current period that will result in an abnormal profit in a subsequent period.

The cost-to-market comparison may be applied to individual items, to major categories, or to the inventory as a whole. ARB No. 43 requires that the method chosen be that that most clearly reflects periodic income. If, for example, an inventory of materials can be segregated into operational categories that relate to separate products, determination of LCM for each category may be most appropriate. On the other hand, a retailer of furniture and appliances should apply the LCM rule separately to each item of inventory.

REQUIRED DISCLOSURES

In addition to the reporting requirements, GAAP require that financial statements disclose the following:

1. Method of determining inventory costs
2. Whether inventories are stated at cost or LCM
3. Significant losses resulting from LCM adjustments
4. Existence of firm purchase commitments and any material losses resulting therefrom
5. Existence of any restrictions or claims on inventories imposed by loans or other agreements.

ACCOUNTING FOR CONTINGENCIES

SFAS No. 5 defines a contingency as an existing condition, situation, or set of circumstances involving uncertainty as to possible gain or loss to an enterprise that will ultimately be resolved when one or more future events occur. SFAS No. 5 further explains that not all uncertainties constitute contingencies, i.e., that estimates of the amount of known obligations or costs do not involve uncertainty as to the existence of loss but only as to the exact amount of losses or expenses. Therefore, obligations such as vested vacation benefits, which are known to exist but are estimated as to amount, would not qualify as contingencies within the meaning of SFAS No. 5. Examples of loss contingencies include

1. Collectibility of receivables
2. Obligations related to product warranties and product defects
3. Risk of loss or damage by fire or other hazards
4. Threat of expropriation of assets
5. Pending or threatened litigation, claims, and assessments
6. Guarantees of the indebtedness of others
7. Agreements to repurchase receivables (or related property) that have been sold.

SFAS No. 5 requires accrual of a loss contingency when events confirm that the loss is "likely" to occur and when the amount of the loss can be "reasonably estimated." Probability (likelihood) of a loss may be perceived any time prior to issuance of the financial statements, but accrual is not appropriate unless the item, event, or transaction that precipitated the loss occurred on or before the balance sheet date. (However, disclosure of loss contingencies arising after the date of financial statements is required if the statements would otherwise be misleading.) FASBIN No. 14 explains that when the reasonable estimate of a loss is a range (and the test of probability is met), the minimum amount in the range should be accrued unless some amount within the range is a "better estimate" than any other. Although a single amount from the range is recognized as a charge against income, the full extent of the range must be disclosed.

If one but not both of the two criteria for accrual is met, disclosure of a loss contingency is required if there exists at least a "reasonable possibility" that a loss may have occurred. Reasonable possibility is defined as less than likely (probable) but more than remote. Disclosure must include an explanation of the nature of the contingency as well as an estimate of the possible loss or a range of loss. If an estimate cannot be obtained, a statement to that effect must be made. An exception to the disclosure requirement is granted in the case of unasserted claims or assessments. If there has been no manifestation by a potential claimant of an awareness of a possible claim or assessment, disclosure is not required unless it is considered probable that a claim will be asserted and there is a reasonable possibility that the outcome will be unfavorable.

Without regard to the disclosure criteria just discussed, SFAS No. 5 requires disclosure of certain loss contingencies even though the possibility of loss is remote (slight). These include

1. Guarantees of the indebtedness of others
2. Obligations of commercial banks under standby letters of credit
3. Guarantees to repurchase receivables (or related property) that have been sold or assigned.

FASBIN No. 34 explains that guarantees of the indebtedness of others include indirect guarantees, i.e., agreements that require the guarantor to advance funds to the debtor company upon the occurrence of specified events (such as reduction of the debtor's working capital below a required minimum level).

General or unspecified business risks do not meet the conditions for accrual set forth previously, and no disclosure about such risks is required.

SFAS No. 5 explicitly reaffirms the principle that a liability cannot be created by an appropriation of retained earnings. Consequently, costs or losses must not be charged to such an appropriation as a substitute for the requirements of SFAS No. 5 nor can any portion of retained earnings be transferred to income. However, there is no requirement that precludes retained earnings appropriations for loss contingencies to supplement the loss accrual.

The provisions of ARB No. 50 continue in effect with regard to gain contingencies. Therefore, possible gains are not recognized in the in-

Exhibit 3.1

Comparative Balance Sheets: Atlantic Richfield Company

Assets	1979	1978
Current Assets:		
Cash	$ 162,535,000	$ 21,870,000
Time deposits and certificates of deposit	154,908,000	76,015,000
Marketable securities, at cost, approximating market value	95,657,000	239,767,000
Accounts and notes receivable, less allowance for doubtful accounts of		
$20,074,000 and $17,989,000, respectively	1,880,319,000	1,053,352,000
Inventories	1,222,692,000	1,222,629,000
Prepaid expenses and other current assets	188,228,000	74,696,000
	3,704,339,000	2,688,329,000
Investments and Long-Term Receivables:		
Affiliated companies accounted for on the equity method	285,018,000	344,911,000
Other investments and long-term receivables, at cost	261,089,000	312,012,000
	546,107,000	656,923,000
Fixed Assets:		
Property, plant and equipment, including capitalized leases	14,162,602,000	12,880,730,000
Less accumulated depreciation, depletion and amortization	4,676,361,000	4,359,761,000
	9,486,241,000	8,520,969,000
Deferred Charges	96,700,000	123,031,000
	$13,833,387,000	$11,989,252,000

come statement until they are realized. Gain contingencies may be disclosed, but no implication as to the possibility of realization may be made.

CLASSIFICATION OF SHORT-TERM OBLIGATIONS EXPECTED TO BE REFINANCED

SFAS No. 6 is not relevant unless a classified balance sheet is prepared, since the issue in question is one of classification. In addition, this statement does not apply to liabilities directly associated with the operating cycle of a business, e.g., trade payables and accruals for wages or other operating expenses.

Exhibit 3.1 (continued)

Liabilities and Shareholders' Equity	1979	1978
Current Liabilities:		
Accounts payable	$ 1,334,625,000	$ 785,905,000
Notes payable	124,050,000	197,851,000
Taxes payable, including excise taxes collected from customers	454,405,000	288,600,000
Long-term debt due within one year	69,967,000	71,917,000
Advances and production payments due within one year	23,839,000	14,225,000
Capital lease obligations due within one year	23,802,000	36,107,000
Accrued interest	72,165,000	93,343,000
Other	207,221,000	173,782,000
	2,310,074,000	1,661,730,000
Long-Term Debt	2,570,104,000	2,626,777,000
Advances and Production Payments	483,720,000	513,412,000
Capital Lease Obligations	563,583,000	669,131,000
Deferred Income Taxes	1,404,959,000	926,309,000
Other Deferred Credits	381,443,000	361,402,000
Shareholders' Equity:		
Cumulative preferred stock 3.75% series B, par $100 (aggregate value in voluntary liquidation $35,728,000); shares authorized and issued 352,000	35,200,000	35,200,000
$3 Cumulative convertible preference stock, par $1 (aggregate value in liquidation $44,158,000); shares authorized 746,530; shares issued 551,975	552,000	666,000
$2.80 Cumulative convertible preference stock, par $1 (aggregate value in liquidation $312,487,000); shares authorized 9,954,081; shares issued 4,464,105	4,464,000	6,783,000
Common stock, par $5; shares authorized 150,000,000; shares issued 115,771,583	578,858,000	558,266,000
Capital in excess of par value of stock	924,792,000	882,340,000
Net income retained for use in the business	4,575,638,000	3,747,236,000
	6,119,504,000	5,230,491,000
	$13,833,387,000	$11,989,252,000

(continued)

SFAS No. 6 establishes conditions that must be met in order to exclude short-term obligations from current liabilities. The first condition is that management must intend to refinance an obligation on a long-term basis. The second condition is that this intent must be demonstrated in one of two ways: (1) by actual issuance (between the balance sheet date and the date the statements are released) of equity securities or long-term debt for purposes of the refinancing or (2) by securing a financing agreement before the balance sheet is issued, which clearly permits the company to refinance short-term obligations on a long-term basis. In order to adequately demonstrate that management has both the

Exhibit 3.1 (continued)

4. Inventories

Inventories are recorded when purchased, produced or manufactured and are stated at the lower of cost or market. The cost of inventories is determined using the last-in, first-out method except for materials and supplies which are valued at or below cost. Total inventories at Dec. 31 comprised the following categories (thousands of dollars):

	1979	1978
Crude oil and petroleum products	$ 400,951	$ 438,866
Chemical products	153,176	129,133
Metal manufacturing	370,134	394,597
Non-petroleum mineral resources	57,651	53,877
Materials and supplies	240,780	206,156
Total	$1,222,692	$1,222,629

5. Short-Term Debt

At Dec. 31, 1979, the Company had bank credit arrangements totaling $655 million, including a $200 million revolving credit agreement available jointly to Atlantic Richfield and its wholly owned subsidiaries when guaranteed by Atlantic Richfield. The Company also had open lines of credit of over $450 million for Atlantic Richfield and/or ARCO Credit Corporation. At Dec. 31, 1979, there were no borrowings under any of these bank credit arrangements.

The notes payable, including commercial paper, outstanding at Dec. 31, 1979 and 1978, had an average interest rate of 13.26 percent and 10.11 percent respectively. During 1979 and 1978, the maximum amount outstanding at any month-end was $215 million and $447 million, respectively, while the average amount outstanding was $173 million and $376 million, respectively. The weighted average interest rate was 10.72 percent and 7.70 percent for 1979 and 1978, respectively.

6. Compensating Balances

The Company is expected to maintain compensating balances for various banking arrangements. At Dec. 31, 1979 and 1978, compensating balances approximated $37 million and $64 million, respectively. Compliance with compensating balance requirements is determined on an average basis, so that effectively on any given date none of the Company's cash is restricted by these requirements. During 1979 and 1978, the Company was in compliance with the compensating balance requirements.

9. Advance Payments and Production Payments

At Dec. 31, 1979, the Company had outstanding $117 million under agreements for advance payments covering the future delivery of natural gas and other retained production payments.

At Dec. 31, 1979, $391 million was outstanding on a hydrocarbon production payment on certain leasehold, mineral and other interests. The production payment will be discharged solely from production from the interest conveyed, over the period between now and Sept. 30, 1987.

14. Other Commitments and Contingencies

At Dec. 31, 1979, the Company had entered into projects and commitments relating to the construction of facilities and other items amounting to approximately $2.3 billion, including approximately $1.0

Exhibit 3.1 (continued)

billion for domestic oil and gas development of which $540 million is for the development of the North Slope of Alaska; $970 million for manufacturing facilities, of which $450 million relates to Anaconda; $100 million for development of coal resources; and $80 million for transportation facilities. The uncertainties inherent in such projects may result in curtailment, postponement or cost escalation of certain of these projects.

In addition to commitments of the Company, there were other contingent liabilities with respect to guarantees, throughput agreements, and other matters arising in the ordinary course of business which, in the aggregate, amounted to approximately $330 million. No material loss is anticipated with respect to these contingencies.

Since mid-July 1973, the Company and certain other petroleum companies have been named as defendants in a number of civil antitrust actions brought against them by Federal or state agencies, or by private individuals as class actions, which allege violations of Federal and state monopoly and restraint of trade statutes. The various types of relief sought in such actions include the divestiture of certain segments of the Company's operations and other significant relief. In addition, the Company and/or its subsidiaries are defendants in various other large civil actions. The Company is unable to predict the outcome of these actions at this time, but believes they can be successfully defended; however, certain adverse decisions in such actions could have a significant effect on the scope and nature of the Company's operations. Final judicial determination of these actions is expected to take a number of years.

In addition, the Company is a defendant in numerous other suits involving smaller amounts in which it is not covered by insurance. Although the legal responsibility and financial impact in respect to such litigation cannot presently be ascertained, the Company does not anticipate that these suits will result in the payment by the Company of monetary damages which in the aggregate would be material in relation to the net assets of the Company and its subsidiaries.

The petroleum industry in the United States continues to be subject to government regulations under the Department of Energy (DOE), including crude oil and refined product allocation and price control. Although these regulations are extremely complex and subject to continuous change, the Company believes it has complied substantially with the regulations as issued. However, differing interpretations by regulatory authorities could result in remedial actions and/or civil penalties which might have a material impact on the Company's future operations.

The environment for the domestic and international petroleum industry, including the Company, is now highly uncertain. In 1980, over 70 percent of the Company's capital program is directed toward domestic energy related projects. The breadth and duration of U.S. government controls, particularly DOE regulations, possible actions by certain foreign governments, extent and form of regulation of natural gas, proposed industry dismemberment, and anticipated increased taxation at the Federal, state and local level, may have an adverse effect on the Company but are, by their nature, unpredictable.

intent and the ability to refinance short-term obligations, a financing arrangement must have all of the following characteristics:

1. The agreement must not expire or be cancelable within one year of the balance sheet date (or the operating cycle if longer).
2. No violations of the agreement are in existence that have not been waived by the lender.
3. The terms of the financing agreement are readily determinable, e.g., duration, interest rate, and available proceeds.
4. The lendor or investor is financially capable of honoring the agreement.

Once management's intent and ability to refinance a short-term obligation have been demonstrated, the amount to be reclassified must be determined. If qualifying equity securities or long-term liabilities have been issued during the subsequent period, the amount of short-term debt to be classified as noncurrent may not exceed the proceeds from those securities or long-term obligations; i.e., any excess must remain as a current liability. The same comparison is made in the case of a qualifying financing agreement. That is, the maximum amount of short-term debt to be reclassified may not exceed the funds available from the financing agreement. If funds provided by the agreement can fluctuate, the amount of reclassification is limited to the minimum funds expected to be received from the agreement between the maturity date of the short-term obligation and the end of the fiscal year (or the end of the operating cycle, whichever is greater).

Short-term obligations that qualify for reclassification may be reported as long-term debt, or they may be placed in a separate category between current and then long-term liabilities. This hybrid category should be titled "short-term obligations expected to be refinanced."

FASBIN No. 8 addresses the question of classification when a short-term obligation is repaid after the balance sheet date, and before the statements are released, long-term debt or equity securities are issued to replenish current assets. The interpretation concludes that any obligation requiring the use of current assets during the ensuing fiscal year must be classified as a current liability as of the balance sheet date. Thus, the funds obtained through long-term financing must be received before repayment of the short-term obligation in order to exclude that amount from current liabilities.

SFAS No. 6 requires the following footnote disclosures:

1. A general description of the financing agreement
2. The terms of any new obligations incurred or expected to be incurred
3. Equity securities issued or expected to be issued.

ACCOUNTING FOR COMPENSATED ABSENCES

SFAS No. 43 establishes standards of accounting for employee compensated absences such as vacation, illness, and holidays. It does not apply to severance or termination pay, post-retirement benefits, deferred compensation, stock or stock options issued to employees, or other long-term fringe benefits such as group insurance and long-term disability pay.

SFAS No. 43 requires accrual of a liability for compensated absences if all of the following conditions are met:

1. The obligation for future compensation relates to employee services already performed.
2. The obligation relates to rights that vest or accumulate.
3. Payment of the compensation is probable.
4. The amount can be reasonably estimated.

If the first three conditions are satisfied, but a reasonable estimate cannot be made, that fact must be disclosed.

An exception to the accrual requirement is granted in the case of liabilities for nonvesting accumulating rights to receive sick pay benefits. The FASB concluded that the amounts involved would not justify the cost of estimating payments contingent upon future illness. However, if sick pay benefits vest or if they are normally paid without an illness-related absence, the exception will not apply, and the criteria set forth above will govern.

Exhibit 3.1 provides a disclosure illustrative of working capital. Notice that the balance sheet separates out current assets and liabilities from other items. Also observe that some disclosure is made parenthetically (such as the allowance for uncollectibles on the receivables) and other disclosures are included in the notes.

4
Property, Plant, and Equipment Disclosures

OVERVIEW OF DEPRECIABLE ASSETS

Depreciable assets comprise the long-lived tangible fixed assets that are used in business operations and are not intended for sale. Various terms such as "plant assets," "plant and equipment," and "property, plant, and equipment" are used synonymously with the term "tangible fixed assets." Depreciable assets include all tangible fixed assets with the exception of land, which, because of its unlimited life, is not depreciable.

Depreciable assets typically are reflected in the balance sheet at historical cost less accumulated depreciation. Land is reflected in the balance sheet at cost. Generally depreciable assets should not be reflected in the balance sheet at appraisal, market, or current values that are above historical cost. Appraisal values for depreciable assets may be reflected in the balance sheet when an enterprise has undergone a quasi-reorganization for the assets have been purchased with equity securities by the nonpublic enterprise. However, a permanent decline in the value of depreciable assets below historical cost should be reflected in the balance sheet by writing down assets to their net realizable value and recognizing the loss immediately. Otherwise appraisal values should not be used to reflect the cost of depreciable assets. The purpose of this section is to illustrate accounting and reporting practices applicable to depreciable assets.

DETERMINING THE COST OF DEPRECIABLE ASSETS

Depreciable assets are recorded at their historical cost, which is generally the fair value of the consideration given or the fair value of the consideration received, whichever is more clearly evident. Determination and consideration of historical cost will depend on the circumstances surrounding the asset's acquisition. In addition, certain repairs may be capitalized as part of an asset's depreciable value. This section will discuss the determination of the historical cost of an asset at the date of its acquisition and at a date subsequent to the asset's acquisition.

Date of Acquisition—Interest Cost

When an asset is acquired in exchange for a monetary asset, the cost of the asset will include all the expenditures necessary to bring it to the condition and location of its intended use. The expenditures capitalized as the cost of the asset would include

1. Invoice price less cash or other discounts
2. Freight-in cost
3. Installation cost
4. State and federal excise taxes
5. For buildings, the cost of excavating for the foundation of a new building and all repair costs incurred because of neglect by the building's previous owner
6. Interest cost incurred during the asset's construction, if any.

Per SFAS No. 34, entitled "Capitalization of Interest Cost," interest should be capitalized for

1. Assets that are constructed or produced for an enterprise's own use
2. Assets that are intended for sale or lease produced as discrete projects (e.g., airplanes, buildings, oil rigs).

Conversely, capitalization of interest cost is prohibited for

1. Inventories that are manufactured routinely or repetitively produced in large quantities
2. Assets that are already being used in the earning activities of an enterprise or are ready for use by an enterprise
3. Assets that are not being used in the earning activities of an enterprise or are not being prepared for such use.

The amount of interest capitalized is determined by applying an appropriate interest rate to the average accumulated expenditures for the asset during the period. However, the amount of interest cost capitalized in an accounting period should not exceed the amount of interest actually incurred during that period. The interest rate(s) is applied to capitalized expenditures (net of progress payments) requiring payments of cash, transferring of assets, and incurring of a liability on which interest is recognized.

The capitalization period should begin when the following conditions are present:

1. Expenditures for the asset have been made.
2. Activities necessary to prepare the asset for its intended use are in progress. The term "activities" is construed broadly to encompass more than physical construction. Activities include all the steps required to prepare the asset for its intended use, e.g., development of design plans or acquiring permits from a governmental body during the pre-construction stage and steps taken after construction has begun such as modifications of designs due to technical problems and litigation.
3. Interest cost is being incurred.

The interest capitalization period should end when the asset is substantially complete and ready for its intended use. Determining when an asset is substantially complete for accounting purposes may present problems at times. Hence, for accounting purposes, the asset is deemed to be substantially complete when it is ready for its intended use or is placed into service.

Costs Incurred Subsequent to the Date of Acquisition

All post-acquisition costs incurred in relation to land are capitalized. Normally post-acquisition costs related to land include the cost of additions and improvements to land. Although land is not a depreciable asset, additions and improvements to land are. Examples of additions and improvements include building fences, sidewalks, and parking lots. The costs capitalized would include all the expenditures necessary to bring the asset to the condition and location of its intended use, including interest costs incurred during the construction of these improvements.

Post-acquisition costs also will be incurred in relation to depreciable assets. However, not all post-acquisition costs related to depreciable assets should be capitalized. Normally, post-acquisition costs would include

1. Ordinary repair and maintenance costs on depreciable assets
2. Additions and improvements to depreciable assets
3. Replacements and overhauls on depreciable assets.

[Note: (2) and (3) are commonly referred to as "extraordinary repairs."]

DEPRECIATION

Depreciation is defined in *Accounting Terminology Bulletin* No. 1, entitled "Review and Resume," as being a system of accounting which aims to distribute the cost or other basic value of tangible capital assets, less salvage value (if any), over the estimated useful life of the unit (which may be a group of assets) in a systematic and rational manner. It is a process of allocation, not of valuation. Depreciation for the year is the portion of the total charge under such a system that is allocated to the year.

When the depreciation figure is derived by a "systematic and rational" method, it is recorded as a debit to an expense account and a credit to a contraaccount entitled "accumulated depreciation."

Methods of Depreciation

A number of systematic and rational methods for computing depreciation have been developed. The methods provide varying patterns of expense recognition over the life of a tangible asset.

Straight-line Depreciation

The straight-line method computer depreciation depends strictly upon the passage of time. Under this method, an equal amount of expense is charged to each period of the service life of the asset. Depreciation is computed by dividing the original cost of the asset, less any salvage value, by the number of accounting periods in the estimated useful life of the asset.

The straight-line method is theoretically justified when the asset to be depreciated will be of approximately equal benefit during each year of its service life.

Units of Production Method

The units of production method computes depreciation based upon the activity of the asset being depreciated. Under this method, a per unit charge is multiplied by the actual units of output for the period. This per unit charge is computed by dividing the original cost of the asset, less any salvage value, by the estimated number of units to be produced during the asset's life. If the number of units produced cannot be estimated, this method may be employed by substituting service hours for units or production.

The units of production method is theoretically justified when usage is the main factor causing the expiration of the asset.

Accelerated Depreciation Methods

The CAP of the AICPA addressed accelerated depreciation methods in ARB No. 44 (revised) issued in July 1958. The committee concluded that the declining balance method is one of those that meets the requirements of being systematic and rational. In those cases where the expected productivity of revenue earning power of the asset is relatively greater during the earlier years of its life, or where maintenance charges tend to increase during the later years, the declining balance method may well provide the most satisfactory allocation of cost. The conclusions of this bulletin also apply to other methods, including the sum-of-the-years'-digits method, which produces substantially similar results. ARB No. 44 was issued in response to the provisions of the Internal Revenue Code of 1954, which allowed reducing charge depreciation. The regulations issued by the Internal Revenue Service limit the amount of depreciation to be expensed by any company for any reason. They limit each period to not more than double the amount that may be recognized under the straight-line method. This regulation created the double-declining balance method of depreciation.

Declining Balance Method

Under the declining balance method of depreciation, the rate to be used is computed by applying a percentage to straight-line depreciation. Residual value is ignored in computing this rate. However, the undepreciated balance of the asset may not be reduced below the residual value amount. Therefore, each year the undepreciated balance of the asset is multiplied by the rate to be used, and to the extent that this amount does not reduce the book value of the asset below the residual value, this amount is charged to expense for the period.

Sum-of-the-Years'-Digits Method

The sum-of-the-years'-digits method is another accelerated depreciation method widely used. Under this method, a fraction is determined each period, and this fraction is multiplied by the cost of the asset, less the residual value, to determine the depreciation expense for the period. The denominator to the fraction is the sum of the years' digits for the life of the asset, and remains constant. The numerator is the years' digits in reverse order, reducing by one each year.

Group and Composite Depreciation

Composite depreciation applies an average depreciation rate to a group of assets. When the average rate is applied to homogeneous assets having similar characteristics and service lives, the method is referred to as group depreciation. When the average rate is applied to heterogeneous assets having dissimilar characteristics and service lives, the procedure is referred to as composite depreciation. The only difference in the mechanics of the two methods is the calculation of the average rate.

Under the group method, all assets in the group are recorded in one asset account. Depreciation is then computed by multiplying an average depreciation rate by the balance in the group asset account. The average rate is computed by subtracting the estimated residual value from the cost of the assets and by dividing this difference by the estimated service lives of the assets. When a unit of the group is retired, the group asset account is credited for the original cost of the unit. The accumulated depreciation account is debited for the original cost of the unit less any residual recovery. No gains or losses are recognized on retirement of single assets in the group.

Balance Sheet Presentation

APBO No. 12, entitled "Omnibus Opinion—1967," requires that the balance sheet, or the notes thereto, report the following: (1) balances of major classes of depreciable assets by nature or function; (2) accumulated depreciation, either by major classes or depreciable assets or in total; and (3) a general description of the methods used in computing depreciation for the major classes or operational assets.

Depreciation Disclosures

APBO No. 12 requires the following disclosures to be made in the financial statements or in notes thereto:

1. Depreciation expense for the period
2. Balances for major classes of depreciable assets, by nature or function, at the balance sheet date
3. Accumulated depreciation, either by major classes of depreciable assets as in total, at the balance sheet date
4. A general description of the method or methods used in computing depreciation with respect to major classes of depreciable assets.

OVERVIEW OF NATURAL RESOURCES

For financial accounting and reporting purposes, natural resources are defined as regenerative or nonregenerative resources that are either presently in or on the earth's surface and are subject to exploitation. Exploitation would include activities such as prospecting, exploration, mining, development, or other form of extractive activity. These resources are commonly referred to as "wasting" assets. "Wasting" assets include but are not limited to the following:

1. Timber resources
2. Crude oil and natural gas
3. Metals such as copper, gold, iron, lead, nickel, platinum, silver, tin, titanium, tungsten, uranium, and zinc
4. Coal
5. Salt
6. Sulfur

7. Gravel, sand, and stone

8. Shale and clay.

Items (2) through (7) are considered to be nonregenerative mineral resources that are not susceptible to attempts by man to replace them to their original state.

Determining the Cost of Natural Resources

Determining the cost of timber resources presents for the most part little difficulty. Expenditures that are capitalized include

1. Direct acquisition costs

2. Indirect acquisition costs incurred, such as broker fees and legal fees in connection with leasing or purchasing property, recording fees, and other related costs associated with acquiring properties

3. Carrying charges, which are substantial costs incurred for fire protection, insect and disease control, and other maintenance costs applicable to unharvested standing timber.

Determining the cost of nonregenerative mineral resources is contingent upon the method of accounting adopted to account for the resources. One of the most significant and controversial issues in accounting and reporting in the extractive industries concerns the identification of the kinds of costs that should be capitalized and the kinds that should be charged to expense as incurred. Hence, two methods of accounting for these resources are widely accepted in the extractive industries: full costing and successful efforts costing.

Under the full costing accounting concept, all costs incurred in prospecting for mineral reserves and in acquiring, exploring, and developing mineral reserves related to these costs are capitalized and amortized based upon production. Operating costs such as lifting costs and general administrative overhead costs applicable to current production are charged to expense as incurred.

Under the successful efforts accounting concept, only those costs resulting directly in identifiable future benefits through the discovery, acquisition, or development of specific discrete mineral reserves are capitalized. Conversely, costs that provide no identifiable future benefits are generally charged to expense as incurred or are written off as a loss when the costs are determined to be nonproductive. Under this concept, the types of costs usually charged to expense include those relating to (1) geological and geophysical (G & G) studies, (2) carrying of undeveloped properties, (3) nonproductive exploration, and (4) general and administrative activities.

The preceding discussion provides only a general overview of the differences between full costing and successful efforts accounting.

Exhibit 4.1

Fixed Asset Disclosures: Vulcan Materials Company

	1979	1978
Assets		
Current assets		
Cash, including certificates of deposit: 1979, $4,158,823; 1978, $2,009,019 (Note 1)	$ 12,210,708	$ 10,161,924
Marketable securities at cost (approximates market)	18,750,635	23,753,961
Notes and accounts receivable:		
Customers (less allowance for doubtful accounts:		
1979, $3,489,140; 1978, $3,373,075)	103,526,505	86,849,003
Other	3,452,886	4,500,073
Inventories (Note 2)	71,273,901	62,659,935
Prepaid expenses	2,087,112	1,850,893
Total current assets	211,301,747	189,775,789
Investments and long-term receivables	3,662,553	3,718,703
Property, plant and equipment—net (Note 3)	322,567,342	286,170,053
Deferred charges and other assets	5,364,352	5,835,846
Total	$542,895,994	$485,500,391

	1979	1978
Liabilities and Shareholders' Equity		
Current liabilities		
Current maturities:		
Long-term debt	$ 2,475,953	$ 2,564,037
Capitalized lease obligations	768,594	599,690
Notes payable (Note 4)	1,534,479	1,791,342
Accounts payable and accruals	65,492,099	58,730,050
Income taxes	15,641,879	12,889,912
Total current liabilities	85,913,004	76,575,031
Long-term debt (Note 5)	86,990,030	91,731,947
Long-term capitalized lease obligations (Note 6)	9,502,581	10,269,831
Deferred credits		
Income taxes	50,479,000	43,845,200
Management incentive and other compensation	4,632,706	3,899,556
Total deferred credits	55,111,706	47,744,756
Shareholders' equity		
Common stock, $1 par value (Note 9)	11,643,399	11,643,399
Capital in excess of par value	9,307,191	9,381,290
Retained earnings (Note 10)	288,268,464	242,858,700
Total	309,219,054	263,883,389
Less cost of stock in treasury	3,840,381	4,704,563
Total shareholders' equity	305,378,673	259,178,826
Total	$542,895,994	$485,500,391

Exhibit 4.1 (continued)

3. Property, Plant and Equipment
Balances of major classes of assets and allowances for depreciation, depletion and amortization at December 31 are as follows:

	1979	1978
At cost:		
Land and land improvements	$ 39,056,433	$ 35,833,348
Buildings	27,486,198	25,733,953
Machinery and equipment	467,770,344	420,087,402
Leaseholds and leasehold improvements	9,061,159	8,435,632
Oil and gas properties-proved	23,408,105	11,501,020
Construction in progress	11,144,042	10,869,765
Total	577,926,281	512,461,120
Less allowances for depreciation, depletion and amortization	258,229,201	230,574,591
Total	319,697,080	281,886,529
Oil and gas properties-unproved, net	2,870,262	4,283,524
Property, plant and equipment-net	$322,567,342	$286,170,053

Balances referable to capitalized leases which are included in property, plant and equipment at December 31 are as follows:

	1979	1978
Land and land improvements	$ 336,716	$ 336,716
Buildings	122,882	122,882
Machinery and equipment	16,523,639	16,562,103
Leasehold improvements	67,750	67,750
Total	17,050,987	17,089,451
Less allowance for amortization	8,803,238	7,920,170
Property, plant and equipment-net	$ 8,247,749	$ 9,169,281

Amortization of capitalized leases amounted to $915,053 in 1979 and $2,033,261 in 1978. The 1978 amount includes $624,000 of accelerated amortization of ammonia facilities at Wichita, Kansas, referable to the discontinuance of operations.

(continued)

Exhibit 4.1 (continued)

5. Long-term Debt

Long-term debt, exclusive of current maturities, at December 31 is summarized as follows:

	1979	1978
10¼% sinking fund debentures	$57,000,000	$60,000,000
8⅞% notes payable to insurance company	16,400,000	17,850,000
6⅝% pollution control revenue bonds	6,800,000	6,800,000
6¾% notes payable to insurance companies	4,797,500	5,320,000
Other notes (rates ranging from 4½% to 9%)	1,992,530	1,761,947
Total	$86,990,030	$91,731,947

The 10¼% debentures are due in 2000 and are subject to annual sinking fund requirements of $3,000,000 in the years 1981-1999. During 1979 the company acquired $3,000,000 principal amount of its 10¼% debentures and has the option to use these debentures to satisfy future sinking fund requirements. The 8⅞% notes are payable in annual installments of $1,450,000 in the years 1980 through 1990 with the balance of $1,900,000 maturing in 1991; the 6⅝% pollution control revenue bonds issued on behalf of the company in November 1978 are payable in installments of $1,000,000 in the years 1998 and 1999 and installments of $1,200,000 in the years 2000-2003; and the 6¾% notes are payable in annual installments of $522,500 in the years 1980 through 1988 with the balance of $617,500 maturing in 1989.

The aggregate principal payments for the five years subsequent to December 31, 1979, are 1980—$2,475,953; 1981—$5,412,916; 1982—$5,357,689; 1983—$5,342,661; and 1984—$5,342,661.

Exhibit 4.2
Natural Resource Disclosures: E. I. Du Pont de Nemours and Company

Oil and Gas Producing Activities

The disclosures on pages 64 through 66 are presented in accordance with the provisions of Statement of Financial Accounting Standards No. 69. Unless otherwise noted, these data reflect the oil and gas producing activities of Conoco subsequent to its acquisition by Du Pont on August 1, 1981.

Estimated Proved Reserves of Oil and Gas

The reserve quantities below exclude royalty interests of others. Royalty interests in foreign reserves that are dependent upon rates of production or prices were calculated using projected rates of production and prices that existed at the time the quantities were estimated. Oil reserves comprise crude oil, condensate and natural gas liquids expected to be removed for the company's account from its natural gas deliveries.

	Total Worldwide		United States		Europe		Other Foreign[1]
	Oil	Gas	Oil	Gas	Oil	Gas	Oil
	(Oil in million barrels and gas in billion cubic feet)						
Proved Developed and Undeveloped Reserves							
Acquisition of Conoco on August 1, 1981	1,444	3,537	379	2,621	385	916	680
Revisions of previous estimates	17	(1)	15	8	1	(9)	1
Extensions, discoveries and other additions ..	27	89	14	82	12	7	1
Production	(54)	(136)	(21)	(109)	(9)	(27)	(24)
December 31, 1981	1,434	3,489	387	2,602	389	887	658
Revisions of previous estimates	87	11	57	96	28	(85)	2
Extensions, discoveries and other additions ..	18	187	17	135	—	52	1
Production	(131)	(333)	(50)	(262)	(24)	(71)	(57)
Sales of in-place reserves[2]	(61)	(268)	(61)	(268)	=	=	=
December 31, 1982[2]	1,347	3,086	350	2,303	393	783	604
Proved Developed Reserves							
August 1, 1981	1,052	2,744	364	2,272	35	472	653
December 31, 1981	1,085	2,886	380	2,418	72	468	633
December 31, 1982[2]	1,014	2,616	344	2,199	89	417	581

Capitalized Costs Relating to Oil and Gas Producing Activities

	Total	Proved Properties	Unproved Properties
At December 31, 1981:			
Gross cost	$4,143	$3,369	$774
Accumulated depreciation, depletion, amortization and valuation allowances	177	148	29
Net cost	$3,966	$3,221	$745
At December 31, 1982[2]:			
Gross cost	$4,873	$3,990	$883
Accumulated depreciation, depletion, amortization and valuation allowances	640	534	106
Net cost	$4,233	$3,456	$777

[1] Dubai, Libya and Indonesia.

[2] December 31, 1982 reserve quantities and capitalized costs exclude amounts applicable to properties sold to Petro-Lewis Corporation and others (see page 16); for this purpose, these transactions are reflected as sales of in-place reserves in 1982.

(*continued*)

Exhibit 4.2 (continued)

Costs Incurred in Oil and Gas Producing Activities[1]

	Total Worldwide	United States	Europe	Other Foreign[2]
Five months ended December 31, 1981:				
Acquisition of proved properties	$ 18	$ 18	$ —	$ —
Acquisition of unproved properties	101	100	—	1
Exploration	206	138	25	43
Development	304	188	77	39
Year ended December 31, 1982:				
Acquisition of proved properties	6	6	—	—
Acquisition of unproved properties	140	129	—	11
Exploration	458	288	78	92
Development	797	389	338	70

Results of Operations for Oil and Gas Producing Activities[3]

	Total Worldwide	United States	Europe	Other Foreign[2]
Five months ended December 31, 1981:				
Revenues:				
Sales to unaffiliated customers	$ 667	$ 479	$ 98	$ 90
Transfers to other company operations	1,027	367	220	440
Total	1,694	846	318	530
Expenses:				
Exploration	173	130	13	30
Production	497	367	80	50
Depreciation, depletion, amortization and valuation provisions	196	110	41	45
Income taxes	703	138	144	421
Total	1,569	745	278	546
Results of operations	$ 125	$ 101	$ 40	$ (16)
Year ended December 31, 1982:				
Revenues:				
Sales to unaffiliated customers	$1,952	$1,150	$504	$ 298
Transfers to other company operations	2,555	866	318	1,371
Total	4,507	2,016	822	1,669
Expenses:				
Exploration	388	264	56	68
Production	1,100	787	206	107
Depreciation, depletion, amortization and valuation provisions	543	319	122	102
Income taxes	2,014	359	347	1,308
Total	4,045	1,729	731	1,585
Results of operations	$ 462	$ 287	$ 91	$ 84

[1] These data comprise all costs incurred in the activities shown, whether capitalized or charged to expense at the time they were incurred.

[2] Dubai, Libya and Indonesia, except for acquisition of unproved properties and exploration costs which cover all areas outside the United States and Europe.

[3] Revenues are based on market prices determined at the point of delivery from the producing unit. All royalty payments are reflected as reductions in revenues in this tabulation. Results of oil and gas producing activities are included in the Petroleum Exploration and Production segment information in Note 21 on page 60, along with results of tar sands, oil shale and certain other activities; in that tabulation, foreign royalty payments are reflected as costs.

Exhibit 4.2 (continued)

Standardized Measure of Discounted Future Net Cash Flows and Changes Therein Relating to Proved Oil and Gas Reserves

The information below has been prepared in accordance with Statement of Financial Accounting Standards No. 69, which requires the standardized measure of discounted future net cash flows to be based on sales prices, costs and statutory income tax rates in effect at the time the projections are made, and a 10 percent per year discount rate.

The projections should not be viewed as realistic estimates of future cash flows nor should the "standardized measure" be interpreted as representing current value to the company. Material revisions to estimates of proved reserves may occur in the future; development and production of the reserves may not occur in the periods assumed; and actual prices realized and actual costs in-

curred are expected to vary significantly from those used. The company's investment and operating decisions are not based on the information presented below, but on a wide range of reserve estimates that includes probable as well as proved reserves and on different price and cost assumptions than reflected in this information.

The December 31, 1980 Conoco data shown below predate Du Pont's August 1, 1981 acquisition of Conoco, but are included to provide a basis for explaining changes in the standardized measure for the full-year 1981. The December 31, 1980 data exclude Conoco's 52.9% interest in Hudson's Bay Oil and Gas Company Limited, which was disposed of during the second quarter of 1981.

	Total Worldwide	United States	Europe	Other Foreign[1]
December 31, 1980				
Standardized measure of discounted				
future net cash flows	$ 5,379	$ 3,148	$ 1,811	$ 420
December 31, 1981				
Future cash flows				
Revenues	$54,843	$17,550	$15,387	$21,906
Production costs	(11,518)	(7,325)	(3,137)	(1,056)
Development costs	(1,933)	(341)	(1,096)	(496)
Income tax expense	(32,688)	(4,533)	(8,307)	(19,848)
Future net cash flows	8,704	5,351	2,847	506
Discount to present value at a 10% annual rate	(3,849)	(2,241)	(1,379)	(229)
Standardized measure of discounted				
future net cash flows	$ 4,855	$ 3,110	$ 1,468	$ 277
December 31, 1982[2]				
Future cash flows				
Revenues	$48,355	$15,556	$14,050	$18,749
Production costs	(9,830)	(6,542)	(2,443)	(845)
Development costs	(1,845)	(374)	(993)	(478)
Income tax expense	(28,147)	(3,935)	(7,806)	(16,406)
Future net cash flows	8,533	4,705	2,808	1,020
Discount to present value at a 10% annual rate	(3,966)	(2,202)	(1,275)	(489)
Standardized measure of discounted				
future net cash flows	$ 4,567	$ 2,503	$ 1,533	$ 531

[1]Dubai, Libya and Indonesia.

[2]Excludes future cash flows related to reserve quantities sold to Petro-Lewis Corporation and others (see page 16).

The aggregate standardized measure of discounted future net cash flows decreased $288 during 1982. This change reflects pretax decreases of $3,407 due to sales and transfers of oil and gas produced and $1,323 due to net changes in sales and transfer prices and in production costs. Partially offsetting these factors were a $2,180 accretion of the beginning pretax amount of the standardized measure and a net $2,018 decrease in the discounted amount of income taxes. Other, less significant, variances include those attributable to the exclusion from December 31, 1982 balances of amounts applicable to properties sold to Petro-Lewis Corporation and others (see page 16),

additions and revisions to reserve estimates, and changes in development costs.

The aggregate standardized measure decreased $524 during 1981. The principal source of this change was a pretax decrease of $3,457 due to sales and transfers of oil and gas produced. Largely offsetting this factor were a $2,337 accretion of the beginning pretax amount of the standardized measure and a net $1,044 decrease in the discounted amount of income taxes. Other, less significant, variances include those attributable to additions and revisions to reserve estimates and changes in development costs.

(continued)

Exhibit 4.2 (continued)

Undeveloped Petroleum Acreage
(thousands of acres at December 31)

	Gross 1982	Gross 1981	Net 1982	Net 1981
Worldwide	**103,609**	**118,432**	**35,688**	**40,043**
United States operations	**9,062**	**8,130**	**6,180**	**5,640**
Onshore	8,127	7,174	5,835	5,305
Texas	1,790	1,358	1,207	781
Montana	1,284	1,146	588	627
North Dakota	1,097	918	227	309
California	850	613	721	527
Other	3,106	3,139	3,092	3,061
Offshore and Alaska	935	956	345	335
Gulf of Mexico	711	625	211	144
Atlantic	97	193	55	104
Pacific	57	62	35	38
Alaska	70	76	44	49
International operations	**94,547**	**110,302**	**29,508**	**34,403**
Europe	**4,512**	**4,629**	**2,190**	**2,451**
United Kingdom	2,614	2,614	1,612	1,619
Norway	892	784	144	126
Italy	805	875	378	565
The Netherlands	106	106	32	32
Spain	95	250	24	109
Africa	**64,758**	**76,998**	**15,701**	**19,580**
Chad	32,236	32,236	8,059	8,059
Central African Republic	18,200	18,200	4,550	4,550
Libya	12,600	12,600	2,058	2,058
Egypt	1,722	13,962	1,034	4,913
Middle East	**956**	**956**	**287**	**287**
Dubai	956	956	287	287
Asia Pacific	**22,798**	**26,196**	**9,807**	**10,562**
Indonesia	22,798	26,196	9,807	10,562
Latin America	**1,523**	**1,523**	**1,523**	**1,523**
Brazil	1,523	1,523	1,523	1,523

Sources of Refined Products*
(barrels per calendar day)

	1982	1981
Worldwide	**626,608**	**623,128**
United States	**399,925**	**418,703**
Crude oil and condensate processed	282,871	290,987
Other feedstocks processed	14,869	10,539
Natural gas liquids recovered	20,310	18,678
Purchases	75,381	87,494
Inventory decrease	6,494	11,005
International	**226,683**	**204,425**
Crude oil and condensate processed	103,889	97,318
Other feedstocks processed	51,788	43,674
Purchases	63,661	65,293
Inventory decrease (increase)	7,345	(1,926)

*These sources supply products for outside sales and for internal uses, including refinery fuel, petrochemical feedstocks and other uses.

Refinery Capacities and Operations
Rated Crude Oil and Condensate
Distillation Capacity at Year End
(barrels per calendar day)

	1982	1981
Worldwide	**546,000**	**596,500**
United States[1]	**381,000**	**431,500**
Lake Charles, Louisiana[2]	156,500	156,500
Ponca City, Oklahoma	134,000	134,000
Billings, Montana[3]	48,500	52,500
Denver, Colorado[4]	32,500	32,500
Santa Maria, California	9,500	9,500
Paramount, California[5]	—	46,500
United Kingdom	**130,000**	**130,000**
Federal Republic of Germany[6]	**35,000**	**35,000**

Crude Oil and Condensate Processed
at Refineries by Sulfur Content
(barrels per calendar day)

	1982	1981
Worldwide	**386,760**	**388,305**
United States	**282,871**	**290,987**
Low sulfur[7]	238,241	242,434
High sulfur	44,630	48,553
United Kingdom (low sulfur)[7]	**84,594**	**77,278**
Federal Republic of Germany[6]	**19,295**	**20,040**
Low sulfur[7]	11,423	11,910
High sulfur	7,872	8,130

Product Yields by Volume
(percent of total yield)

	1982	1981
United States:		
Motor gasoline	49.9	48.9
Middle distillate	29.3	27.0
Residual fuel oil and asphalt	9.0	9.6
Other	11.8	14.5
United Kingdom:		
Motor gasoline	27.5	28.4
Middle distillate	41.2	41.8
Residual fuel oil	2.1	.5
Other	29.2	29.3
Federal Republic of Germany[6]**:**		
Motor gasoline	40.4	46.6
Middle distillate	22.1	23.0
Residual fuel oil	22.3	22.1
Other	15.2	8.3

[1] A 23,500-barrel-per-day refinery in Wrenshall, Minn., operational for the first part of 1981, was shut down in May of that year.

[2] A 32,500-barrel-per-day interest in the refinery, formerly held by Monsanto, was acquired in August 1981 as part of the merger with Conoco.

[3] Decrease in rated capacity resulted from reduced availability of light Canadian condensate.

[4] The Denver refinery, which was extensively damaged by an explosion and fire in 1978, resumed operations in April 1981.

[5] The Paramount refinery was closed in July 1982 and sold in December 1982.

[6] Represents Conoco's 25 percent interest in a refinery at Karlsruhe.

[7] Low-sulfur crude oil and condensate contain no more than 0.5 percent sulfur by weight.

Exhibit 4.2 (continued)

Well Completions	Development		Exploration	
	1982	1981	1982	1981
United States:				
Gross wells	969.0	1,134.0	87.0	99.0
Net wells	263.0	358.8	52.1	50.1
Oil	152.4	192.2	5.5	3.9
Gas	86.0	129.9	3.2	6.6
Dry	24.6	36.7	43.4	39.6
International:				
Gross wells	62.0	87.0	40.0	36.0
Net wells	12.3	17.2	10.4	11.0
Oil	11.0	16.5	2.8	1.8
Gas	1.0	—	.3	1.8
Dry	.3	.7	7.3	7.4

Petroleum and Coal Five-Year Review
(Dollars in millions)

	1982	1981	1980	1979	1978
CAPITAL EXPENDITURES[1]					
Petroleum exploration:					
United States operations:					
Acquisition of leases	$ 128.9	$ 166.2	$ 117.6	$ 135.0	$ 44.1
Wells and equipment	137.9	150.6	65.4	51.8	33.7
International operations:					
Acquisition of leases	40.2	45.9	67.9	13.0	8.7
Wells and equipment	68.6	47.3	36.8	15.8	10.4
Subtotal	**375.6**	**410.0**	**287.7**	**215.6**	**96.9**
Petroleum production:					
United States operations	396.4	500.7	380.1	242.6	226.3
International operations	408.5	326.6	305.4	275.5	228.9
Subtotal	**804.9**	**827.3**	**685.5**	**518.1**	**455.2**
Petroleum refining and natural gas processing:					
United States refining	198.4	148.0	80.9	70.2	39.9
International refining	18.0	39.1	23.4	29.0	23.9
Natural gas processing[2]	33.6	52.3	19.1	24.1	19.9
Subtotal	**250.0**	**239.4**	**123.4**	**123.3**	**83.7**
Petroleum marketing:					
United States operations	24.3	18.8	14.9	12.4	8.5
International operations	25.9	26.8	25.4	16.4	20.6
Subtotal	**50.2**	**45.6**	**40.3**	**28.8**	**29.1**
Petroleum transportation:					
United States operations	48.7	85.0	65.0	23.9	17.2
International operations	1.2	24.0	4.4	2.9	6.8
Subtotal	**49.9**	**109.0**	**69.4**	**26.8**	**24.0**
Total Petroleum	**1,530.6**	**1,631.3**	**1,206.3**	**912.6**	**688.9**
Coal:					
Coal and surface lands[3]	60.3	87.9	26.2	17.3	16.2
Plant and equipment	273.3	188.1	173.1	164.9	136.8
Total Coal	**333.6**	**276.0**	**199.3**	**182.2**	**153.0**
Total Petroleum and Coal	**$1,864.2**	**$1,907.3**	**$1,405.6**	**$1,094.8**	**$841.9**
United States	$ 1,271.5	$ 1,392.3	$ 931.9	$ 734.7	$ 540.4

(continued)

Exhibit 4.2 (continued)

Petroleum and Coal Five-Year Review Continued
(Dollars in millions)

	1982	1981	1980	1979	1978
CASH EXPLORATION EXPENSES					
United States petroleum operations	$ 148.4	$ 115.1	$ 69.2	$ 44.0	$ 33.3
International petroleum operations	70.7	73.9	44.7	28.0	22.8
Petroleum	219.1	189.0	113.9	72.0	56.1
Coal	9.2	11.8	11.4	12.5	10.2
Total	**$ 228.3**	**$ 200.8**	**$ 125.3**	**$ 84.5**	**$ 66.3**
UNDEVELOPED PETROLEUM ACREAGE (at December 31)[4]					
Net acreage—Worldwide (thousands of acres)	**35,688**	**40,043**	**51,749**	**43,979**	**50,909**
United States operations	6,180	5,640	4,173	3,517	3,290
International operations	29,508	34,403	47,576	40,462	47,619
PROVED PETROLEUM RESERVES (at December 31)[1]					
Petroleum liquids—Worldwide (million barrels)	**1,539**	**1,637**	**1,723**	**1,793**	**1,719**
United States	350[5]	387	403	398	413
Europe	452	446	452	461	409
Africa, Middle East and Asia Pacific	737	804	868	934	897
Natural gas—Worldwide (billion cubic feet)	**3,197**	**3,617**	**3,743**	**4,102**	**4,146**
United States	2,303[5]	2,602	2,660	2,681	2,704
Europe	894	1,015	1,083	1,181	1,158
Africa and Middle East	—	—	—	240	284
PETROLEUM PRODUCTION[1]					
Petroleum liquids production—Worldwide					
(thousands of barrels daily)	**401**	**375**	**389**	**408**	**398**
United States operations	**136**	**139**	**148**	**159**	**165**
Crude oil and condensate	125	126	134	143	151
Onshore	99	105	114	122	128
Texas	51	55	60	64	67
Wyoming	15	17	18	20	20
California	9	10	10	11	11
Other	24	23	26	27	30
Offshore	26	21	20	21	23
Louisiana	25	20	19	20	22
California	1	1	1	1	1
Natural gas liquids	11	13	14	16	14
International operations	**265**	**236**	**241**	**249**	**233**
United Kingdom	53	41	17	16	3
Norway	21	15	6	1	—
Other International (Dubai, Libya and Indonesia)	191	180	218	232	230

[1] See Definition of Terms on page 72.

[2] Includes transportation and storage facilities for natural gas and gas liquids.

[3] Includes $20.5 for the 1982 acquisition of a 49 percent interest in Gollin Wallsend Coal Company Limited.

[4] Does not reflect tar sands and oil shale properties, which at December 31, 1982 contained an estimated 1.4 billion tons of tar, a portion of which is potentially recoverable, and 1.3 billion barrels of shale oil. These resources are not currently under production or development and would not be commercially recoverable under present costs and market prices.

[5] Excludes reserves sold to Petro-Lewis Corporation and others (see page 16).

Exhibit 4.2 (continued)

Petroleum and Coal Five-Year Review Continued

	1982	1981	1980	1979	1978
Natural gas deliveries—Worldwide (million cubic feet daily) ...	**931**	**899**	**1,007**	**1,050**	**1,127**
United States operations	**718**	**737**	**778**	**834**	**869**
Onshore	466	511	539	573	567
Texas	164	172	187	206	204
New Mexico	140	171	183	180	178
Oklahoma	78	86	74	90	94
Other	84	82	95	97	91
Offshore	252	226	239	261	302
International operations (United Kingdom)	**213**	**162**	**229**	**216**	**258**
PETROLEUM REFINING (thousands of barrels daily)					
Refinery inputs processed—Worldwide	**453**	**443**	**448**	**525**	**481**
United States operations	**297**	**302**	**293**	**346**	**354**
By own refineries	297	301	293	346	354
Crude oil and condensate	282	290	284	337	344
Other feedstocks	15	11	9	9	10
By others for Conoco	—	1	—	—	—
International operations (Western Europe)	**156**	**141**	**155**	**179**	**127**
By United Kingdom refinery	121	109	115	127	100
Crude oil and condensate	85	77	86	112	84
Other feedstocks	36	32	29	15	16
By nonconsolidated affiliate for Conoco	35	32	37	39	14
Crude oil and condensate	19	20	29	33	14
Other feedstocks	16	12	8	6	—
By others for Conoco	—	—	3	13	13
PETROLEUM MARKETING					
Sales of refined products—Worldwide					
(thousands of barrels daily)	**532**	**526**	**543**	**617**	**638**
United States operations	**321**	**332**	**338**	**394**	**426**
Motor gasoline	163	158	166	188	204
LPG and natural gasoline	25	26	22	23	23
Commercial jet fuel	22	22	19	19	24
Middle distillate	68	59	73	94	92
Residual fuel oil and asphalt	28	49	42	54	66
Other products	15	18	16	16	17
International operations	**211**	**194**	**205**	**223**	**212**
Western Europe	203	187	193	213	204
Motor gasoline	72	69	72	72	65
Middle distillate	89	87	85	88	98
Residual fuel oil	19	11	15	29	20
Other products	23	20	21	24	21
Far East	8	7	12	10	8
Retail marketing outlets—Worldwide[1][2]	**7,542**	**7,741**	**7,628**	**7,362**	**8,462**
United States operations	5,489	5,708	5,605	5,275	6,425
International operations (Western Europe)	2,053	2,033	2,023	2,087	2,037
PETROLEUM TRANSPORTATION					
Pipeline shipments (thousands of barrels daily):					
Pipeline shipments	629	576	648	685	688
Equity in pipeline shipments of nonconsolidated affiliates	328	319	319	349	349

[1]At December 31.

[2]Outlets owned by Conoco and others that sell the company's refined products.

(continued)

Exhibit 4.2 (continued)

Petroleum and Coal Five-Year Review Continued

	1982	1981	1980	1979	1978
COAL ACTIVITIES (millions of tons)[1]					
Recoverable coal resources at January 1[2]	**12,250**	**14,324**	**14,511**	**14,093**	**14,166**
Purchased resources	231	357	485	289	284
Resources sold in place	(2)	(985)[3]	(127)	(200)	(153)
Production	(45)	(39)	(45)	(47)	(38)
Revisions and other changes	(197)	(1,407)	(500)	376	(166)
Recoverable coal resources at December 31[2]	**12,237**	**12,250**	**14,324**	**14,511**	**14,093**
Steam coal	**10,937**	**10,758**	**12,772**	**12,702**	**12,201**
Eastern and midwestern United States	5,079	5,004	5,478	5,318	5,127
Western United States[4]	5,825	5,669	7,205	7,160	6,851
Canada	33	85	89	224	223
Metallurgical coal	**1,300**	**1,492**	**1,552**	**1,809**	**1,892**
Eastern United States	993	1,128	1,138	1,384	1,484
Canada	307	364	414	425	408
Coal production[5]	**45**	**39**	**45**	**47**	**38**
Steam coal	39	35	39	42	35
Metallurgical coal	6	4	6	5	3
Average realized mine price (per ton)[6]	**$33.30**	**$29.52**	**$27.65**	**$25.94**	**$23.80**

[1]Coal activities data do not include Consol's 49 percent interest, acquired during 1982, in Gollin Wallsend Coal Company Limited, an Australian company, nor do the tables include resource or production data for other affiliates. Such amounts are immaterial in the aggregate.

[2]Not all of these resources are commercially recoverable under present prices and costs. See Definition of Terms on page 72. The breakdown of recoverable coal resources is as follows:

	1982	1981	1980
Demonstrated Reserves	7,253	7,410	7,661
Other Identified Resources	4,984	4,840	6,663
Total	12,237	12,250	14,324

The 12.2 billion tons at year-end 1982 consist of 11 billion tons owned or leased, and 1.2 billion tons for which the company has preferential leasing rights granted by the Federal government. These rights include 0.5 billion tons that are located on an Indian reservation and are currently being contested by the tribal lessors. It is possible that these Indian reservation leasing rights will either be honored or that the rights will be converted to other leases. The leased resources include 1 billion tons leased from the Federal government subject to certain "due diligence" production requirements commencing in 1985. The resources are located in nearly every major coal-producing region in North America.

[3]Includes approximately 650 million tons related to properties that were exchanged for oil shale properties.

[4]West of the Mississippi River.

[5]In addition to its own production, Consol supervises production for certain of its affiliates and other companies. Supervised production totaled 5.9 million tons during 1982, compared with 3.9 million tons during 1981.

[6]The average realized mine price per ton of coal reflects sales of both steam and metallurgical coal sold at a wide range of prices, including substantial sales made under long-term contracts.

Exhibit 4.2 (continued)

After-Tax Operating Income

Sales and other income less all directly allocable expenses, net of taxes, but before deduction of certain corporate expenses (net of taxes). Corporate expenses consist of items such as interest and debt expense; salaries, employee benefit costs and other costs related to general corporate activities; corporate advertising and contributions programs; and certain exchange gains and losses.

Total Debt to Total Capitalization Ratio

Total short and long-term borrowings and capital lease obligations divided by the sum of these amounts, stockholders' equity and minority interests in consolidated subsidiaries.

Capital Expenditures

Expenditures for property, plant and equipment and investment in affiliates. The total includes the costs of wells determined to be unsuccessful and additions to capital leases.

Petroleum Liquids Production and Natural Gas Deliveries

The company's interest in production or deliveries, plus related royalty volumes outside the United States.[1] Petroleum liquids production comprises crude oil, condensate and natural gas liquids (NGL) removed for the company's account from its natural gas deliveries. Natural gas deliveries represent deliveries from leases and, in the United States, are before removal of NGL.

Proved Petroleum Liquids and Natural Gas Reserves

The company's interest in reserves, plus related royalty volumes outside the United States.[1] Petroleum liquids reserves comprise crude oil, condensate and natural gas liquids (NGL) expected to be removed for the company's account from its natural gas deliveries. Natural gas reserves in the United States have not been reduced for the expected removal of such NGL due to its immaterial effect.

Proved reserves are the volumes in known reservoirs which, based upon geological and engineering data, can be expected with reasonable certainty to be commercially recoverable under present prices, costs, regulatory practices and technology.

Proved developed reserves are recoverable through wells as currently completed or by recompleting existing wells where the cost of recompletion would be small relative to the cost of a new well. Proved undeveloped reserves are recoverable only by drilling additional wells or incurring relatively major recompletion costs.

Recoverable Coal Resources

Identified resources[2] whose existence and recoverability are evidenced by geological, geophysical and engineering data. They are limited to quantities that can be extracted from known deposits, after deducting anticipated losses from mining, preparation or processing, using current technology and mining practices.

Identified resources are classified as (1) demonstrated reserves[2], which are or would be *commercially mineable* under present prices and operating costs (however, the resultant operating margins would not necessarily be sufficient in all cases to recover economically mine development and construction costs if incurred today), and (2) other identified resources, which are only *potentially commercially mineable*.

[1] Except for volume data appearing on page 64, which exclude all royalty volumes, as required by Statement of Financial Accounting Standards No. 69.

[2] Usage of these terms is consistent with that of the Geological Survey Circular 831, "Principles of a Resource/Reserve Classification for Minerals."

Depletion

Depletion is the accounting allocation of the cost of a natural resource against revenue as it is exploited. Cost depletion is required for financial accounting purposes. Under the cost method, allocation is accomplished by dividing the cost of the asset, less any residual value, by the estimated number of units that can be withdrawn. This unit rate is then multiplied by the actual number of units withdrawn from the resource during the period.

Exhibit 4.1 presents disclosures applicable to depreciable assets. As can be seen, disclosures include the cost of the assets, the amount of accumulated depreciation, and the methods of depreciation. Exhibit 4.2 provides illustrative disclosures for natural resources.

5
Long-Term Investment Disclosures

The large number of business combinations being consummated and the accounting and economic complexities inherent in these combinations have created the need for the accounting profession to devote significant time to developing accounting standards appropriate for these business combination transactions. The CAP, APB, and FASB all have currently applicable authoritative pronouncements that must be consulted when attempting to understand the accounting intricacies applicable to business combinations.

While several forms of business combinations (e.g., mergers, acquisitions, affiliations, etc.) have been evidenced in the recent past, all of these combinations are accounted for in one of two ways: (1) a pooling of interests or (2) a purchase. The purpose of this chapter is to summarize the classification and accounting rules for these business combinations and other long-term investments in stock and subsequent to acquisition.

POOLING OF INTERESTS—AT ACQUISITION

In order to be classified and accounted for as a pooling of interests, a business combination must meet twelve criteria applicable to characteristics of combining companies, combining interest, and planned transactions. These criteria are discussed in detail in APBO No. 16, entitled "Business Combinations." The five year limitation specified in paragraph 99 of APBO No. 16 related to classifying poolings of interest around the October 31, 1970, effective date of this opinion was eliminated in SFAS No. 10, entitled "Extension of 'Grandfather' Provisions for Business Combinations." All twelve of these criteria must be met before a business combination constitutes a pooling of interests; these characteristics are enumerated below.

Characteristics of Combining Companies

To be a pooling of interest, companies must be combining independent ownership interests in their entirety to continue previously separate operations. The APB specified two conditions that should be met in order to satisfy this combining characteristic:

1. Each of the combining companies should be autonomous and should not have been a subsidiary or division of another company within two years before the plan is initiated.

2. Each of the combining companies should be independent of the other combining companies. To operationalize this condition, at the dates the plan of combination is initiated and consummated, the combining companies should hold no more than 10 percent of the total outstanding voting stock of any combining company.

Characteristics of Combining Interests

The APB established seven pooling of interest criteria that, if met, should indicate a mutual sharing of risks and rights of ownership of the combining interests:

1. The combination should be effected in a single transaction or completed in accordance with a specific plan within one year after the plan is initiated. A combination completed in more than one year from the initiation date may still qualify for a pooling of interests if the delay is beyond the control of the combining companies because proceedings of a government authority or litigation prevent completing the combination.

2. A corporation offers and issues only common stock with rights identical to those of the majority of its outstanding voting common stock (i.e., the class of stock that has voting control) in exchange for substantially all of the voting common stock interest of another company at the date the plan of combination is consummated. Substantially all means 90 percent or more of the outstanding voting stock. This condition does not prohibit the purchase of shares for cash or other consideration except that shares acquired other than by the required stock-for-stock exchange do not count in applying the 90 percent test. To operationalize this complex characteristic, the purpose is to issue voting common stock in exchange for 90 percent or more of the voting common stock of another combining company that is outstanding at the date the combination is consummated. These stock-for-stock exchanges are included in the 90 percent test only to the extent that they occur between the initiation and consummation dates of a business combination. Thus, excluded from the 90 percent test will be those shares of a combining company (1) acquired before and held by the issuing corporation and its subsidiaries at the date the plan of combination is initiated, regardless of the consideration surrendered to obtain the shares; (2) acquired by the issuing corporation and its subsidiaries after the date the plan of combination is initiated other than by

issuing the required voting common stock; and (3) outstanding after the date the combination is consummated.

3. None of the combining companies should change the equity interest of the voting common stock in contemplation of effecting the combination either within two years before the plan of combination is initiated or between the initiation and consummation dates. Examples of changes that would preclude a business combination from qualifying as a pooling of interest may include distributions to stockholders, exchanges, and retirements of securities.

4. Each of the combining companies reacquires shares of voting common stock only for purposes other than business combinations. No company should reacquire more than a normal number of shares between the initiation and consummation dates.

5. The ratio interest of individual common stockholders to other stockholders should not be modified as a result of the business combination.

6. The voting rights incident to ownership of common stock used to effect the business combination should be exercisable. Stockholders should neither be deprived of nor restricted in exercising those rights for a period of time.

7. The combination should be resolved as of the consummation date and no provisions of the plan relating to issue of securities or other consideration are pending.

Absence of Planned Transactions

There should exist no planned transactions that if implemented would counteract the effect of combining stockholder interest. The APB listed three conditions that should not exist if a business combination is to qualify as a pooling of interests:

1. The combined corporation does not agree directly or indirectly to retire or reacquire all or part of the common stock issued to effect the combination.

2. The combined corporation does not enter into other financial arrangements for the benefit of former stockholders of a combining company (e.g., guaranteeing loans).

3. The combined corporation does not intend or plan to dispose of a significant part of the assets of the combining companies within two years after the combination is consummated. This condition does not preclude disposals in the ordinary course of business and the disposals of duplicate facilities or excess capacity.

Applying the Pooling of Interests Method

Under a pooling of interests, there is a presumption that no resources were exchanged between the combining interests; rather, it is assumed that the combination is effected by exchanges of shares among the shareholders. Thus, since no purchase or sale has been consummated, the recorded assets and liabilities of the combining companies generally become the recorded assets and liabilities of the combined company. No goodwill should be recorded in a business combination accounted for as a pooling of interests.

Regardless of the number of shares issued to effect a pooling of interest, the investment in the combining company will be the sum of the net assets (equity) of the combining company or the issuing company's percentage of those net assets. Pooling of interests accounting is applied retroactively throughout the period of acquisition (the so-called "instant earnings problem") and prior periods. Thus, at the consummation date, the objective is to record the total net assets of the combining company to be added to the net assets of the issuing company for combined net assets.

An exception to this general rule would exist if the amount of outstanding shares of stock of the combined company at par or stated value exceeded the amount of capital stock of the separate combining companies. This excess should be deducted first from other contributed capital and then from combined retained earnings.

Since a pooling of interests recognizes neither the acquiring of assets nor the obtaining of capital, costs incurred to effect such combinations should be expensed as incurred.

To the extent that the combined corporation generates a profit or incurs a loss resulting from the disposal of a significant part of the assets of the previously separate companies, that profit or loss should be disclosed separately if (1) the profit or loss is material in relation to net income of the combined corporation and (2) the disposition is within two years after the combination is consummated. Such profit or loss should be disclosed as an extraordinary item.

Financial statements of the combined enterprise should disclose that a pooling of interest has occurred during the period. The basis of current presentation and restatements of prior periods may be disclosed in the body of the financial statements or by references to notes. For the period in which the pooling of interest is consummated, notes to the financial statements should include

1. Name and brief description of the companies combined, except a corporation whose name is carried forward to the combined company
2. Mention that the pooling of interests method is being utilized
3. Description and number of shares issued to effect the combination
4. Details of results of operations of the previously separate companies for the period before the combination is consummated that are included in combined net income
5. Descriptions of the nature of adjustments of net assets of the combining companies to adopt the same accounting practices and of the effects of the

changes on income reported previously by the separate companies and now presented in comparative statements

6. Details of an increase/decrease in retained earnings from changing the fiscal year of a combining company

7. Reconciliations of amounts of revenue and earnings previously reported by the company that issues the stock to effect the combination with the combined amounts currently presented in financial statements and summaries

8. All the above disclosures also disclosed on a pro-forma basis in information given to stockholders of the combining companies.

THE PURCHASE METHOD—AT ACQUISITION

Business combinations not meeting all the criteria for a pooling of interests must be accounted for as a purchase; part purchase, part pooling accounting no longer is acceptable under GAAP. Since purchase acquisitions involve a transfer of economic resources between enterprises or stockholders, these business combinations should be accounted for pursuant to the general principles of historical cost accounting; i.e., the enterprise purchased should be accounted for based on the fair value of consideration surrendered or fair value of consideration received, whichever is more clearly determinable.

The cost incurred to purchase all or part of another enterprise should be allocated to the net assets of the acquired enterprise based on relative fair values of the assets acquired. Exceptions to this general rule involve goodwill and deferred income taxes previously recorded by an acquired company, which should not be recorded by the acquiring enterprise. Any difference between the sum of the assigned costs of identifiable tangible and intangible net assets and the actual costs of the group of net assets should be designated goodwill.

In implementing this assignment of costs, first, all identifiable net assets should be assigned a portion of the cost of the acquired company (normally equal to fair values). Second, any excess actual cost over assigned cost should be designated goodwill. If the assigned cost exceeds actual cost in a purchase combination, any values otherwise assignable to noncurrent assets (other than long-term investments in marketable securities) should be reduced proportionately to determine assigned costs. A deferred credit (negative goodwill) should not be recorded unless those noncurrent assets are reduced to zero value.

The cost of a company acquired in a business combination accounted for as a purchase includes direct costs of acquisition. However, costs of registering and issuing equity securities should be accounted for as a reduction in the otherwise determinable fair value of the securities (i.e., charged to paid-in capital). Any indirect and general expenses related to acquisitions should be deducted in determining income as incurred.

Some purchase combinations may involve contingent consideration based on earnings or security prices. When a contingency based on earnings (i.e., maintaining or achieving specified future earnings) is resolved and additional consideration is distributable, the acquiring company should record the current value of the additional consideration issued or issuable as an increment to cost of the acquired company. This additional cost, usually assigned to goodwill, should be amortized over the remaining life of the asset.

If additional consideration is based on the maintenance or achievement of a specified security price, securities issued unconditionally to effect the business combination should be recorded at the specified price. Thus, the cost of an acquired company includes contingent consideration based on security prices. When additional consideration becomes distributable, based on the resolution of a security price contingency, the acquiring company should record the current fair value of the additional consideration but simultaneously should reduce the previously recorded consideration.

Notes to the financial statements should disclose the following in the period in which a business combination accounted for as a purchase has been effected:

1. The name and a brief description of the acquired company.
2. The method of accounting for the business combination (the purchase method).
3. The period for which results of operations of the acquired company are included in income of the acquiring company. Such income of the acquired company should be included in income of the acquiring company only after the date of acquisition and should be adjusted to reflect the acquiring company's cost of generating those earnings (see Post-Acquisition Accounting below).
4. The cost of the acquired company.
5. Description of the plan of amortization of recorded goodwill, the amortization method, and period. Per APBO No. 17, "Intangible Assets," such goodwill should be amortized systematically and rationally over a period not to exceed 40 years.
6. Any contingent payments, options, or commitments specified in the combination agreement and the proposed accounting treatment.
7. Supplementary pro-forma disclosures also should be made applicable to results of operations for the current and immediately preceding period.

POST-ACQUISITION ACCOUNTING

In ARB No. 51, entitled "Consolidated Financial Statements," the CAP concluded that it should be presumed, in the absence of evidence to the contrary, that consolidated financial statements are more meaningful to statement users than individual financial statements. Thus, consolidated financial statements should be presented when one enterprise has a (direct or indirect) "controlling financial interest" in another enterprise. The general rule for this controlling financial interest is ownership of a majority voting interest, i.e., over 50 percent, in the outstanding voting shares of another company.

There are exceptions to this general rule of consolidation. For example, subsidiaries should not be consolidated where control is likely to be temporary or where control does not exist with the majority shareholders (e.g., where the subsidiary is in legal reorganization or bankruptcy). Also, minority interest in the subsidiary may be so large that separate financial statements would be more meaningful.

A difference in fiscal periods of a parent and a subsidiary does not within itself justify exclusion of a subsidiary from consolidation. Typically, it is feasible for the subsidiary to prepare (for use in the consolidation process) statements for a period that closely corresponds to the reporting period of the parent. However, where the difference in reporting period endings is not more than about three months, it usually is acceptable to use in the process of consolidation the subsidiary's statements for its fiscal period (proper disclosure of this fact should be made).

In APBO No. 18, entitled "Equity Method for Investments in Common Stock," the APB concluded that the equity method (one-line consolidation) also should be used by investors who exercise "significant influence" over operating and financial policies of an investee even though the percentage investment in outstanding voting stock is 50 percent or less. The ability to exercise significant influence over an investee could be evidenced in several ways, including representation on the board of directors, participation in policymaking processes, material intercompany transactions, interchange of managerial personnel, and technological dependency.

Another important consideration in attempting to assess the degree of influence exercised over an investee is the extent of ownership by an investor in relation to shareholdings by other investors. In attempting to achieve some degree of uniformity, the APB concluded that in the absence of evidence to the contrary, an investment (direct or indirect) of 20 percent or more of the voting stock of an investee should lead to the presumption that the investor exercises significant influence over the investee. Conversely, when an investment consists of less than 20 percent of the voting stock of an investee, it should be presumed, in the absence of evidence to the contrary, that the investor does not exercise significant influence over the investee.

When the equity method is appropriate, it should be applied in consolidated financial statements and in parent–company financial statements prepared for issuance to stockholders as the financial statements of the primary reporting entity. Exhibit 5.1 illustrates when financial statements should be prepared on each of the bases.

Under the cost method, an investor should record the investment in stock at cost and recognize in income only dividends that are received from earnings generated subsequent to acquisition. Dividends received in excess of post-acquisition earnings constitute a return of the investment cost and should be deducted from the carrying amount of the investment as opposed to being recognized as income. A series of operating losses of an investee or other factors may indicate that a decline in value of the investment is other than temporary; in these cases, a realized loss should be recognized and the investment carrying amount should be reduced.

Under the equity method, an investor initially should record the investment at cost. But the investor should adjust the carrying amount of the investment to recognize a proportionate share of investee earnings as these earnings are generated by the investee. This adjustment to the investment account should be included in determining income of the investor after the income of the investee has been adjusted for intercompany transactions and to amortize any difference between investor cost and the underlying book value of assets acquired by the investor. Dividends received from an equity method investee constitute a return of investment and should not be included in income. Similar to the cost method, declines in investment value that are deemed to be other than temporary should be recognized immediately as a realized loss and reduction in investment carrying value.

In applying the equity method, an investor's share of investee losses

Exhibit 5.1
Relationship Between Consolidated Financial Statements,
Equity Method Investees, and Cost Method Investees

Controlling Interest (more than 50 percent ownership of outstanding voting shares)	Consolidated financial statements are appropriate.
Significant Influence	Equity method of accounting is appropriate.
1. Ownership of 20 percent or more of outstanding voting shares	
2. Personnel interrelationships	
3. Technological dependency	
4. Material intercompany transactions	
5. Participation in policy decisions	
6. Represented on board of directors	
Lack of Significant Influence (see above tests for significant influence)	Cost method of accounting is appropriate.

may equal or exceed the carrying amount of the investment. In most of these cases, the investor should discontinue applying the equity method when the investment account reaches a zero balance and should not provide for additional losses unless the investor has guaranteed obligations of the investee or is otherwise committed to provide further financial support to the investee. An exception to this general rule results, and additional losses should be recognized, when the "imminent return to profitable operations" by an investee appears reasonably assured; i.e., a material, nonrecurring loss of an isolated nature caused the investment account reduction, while future earning capacity of the investee is unimpaired. If application of the equity method is suspended, the investor should not resume application of the method until the investor's share of net income equals the losses previously not recognized by the investor.

The investor also should discontinue applying the equity method when events or transactions (e.g., purchase of more shares of investee stock) indicate that the investor no longer exercises significant influence over the operating and financial policies of the investee. The carrying value of the investment should not be adjusted in these cases, but should remain as the cost basis for the investment under the cost method.

Conversely, events or transactions may indicate that an investment previously accounted for under the cost method now should be accounted for under the equity method. In these cases, the equity method should be adopted retroactively as if the equity method had been appropriate from the date of initial investment.

MARKETABLE EQUITY SECURITIES

Prior to 1976, there was considerable diversity between enterprises in accounting for marketable securities held at cost. Some enterprises were accounting for marketable securities at cost, some at market (or variations of market), and some at LCM, and some were applying more than one of these methods to different classes of securities. In an attempt to unify practices related to accounting for marketable securities, the FASB in December 1975 issued SFAS No. 12, "Accounting for Certain Marketable Securities."

Applicability of Provisions and Interpretations of SFAS No. 12

The "certain" marketable securities to which SFAS No. 12 applies are marketable equity securities. A marketable equity security is any instrument of ownership, or right to acquire or dispose of ownership, where the sales, bid, or ask price of the instrument is currently available on a national securities exchange or on the over-the-counter market. The term "marketable equity securities" does not encompass preferred stock that by its terms either, must be redeemed by the issuing enterprise or is redeemable at the option of the investor, nor does it include treasury stock or convertible bonds.

In addition, SFAS No. 12 applies only to investments in marketable equity securities that are not appropriately accounted for by the equity method. It does not apply to not-for-profit organizations, such as mutual life insurance companies, or employee benefit plans. However, in FASBIN No. 10, entitled "Applicability of FASB Statement No. 12 to Personal Financial Statements," the FASB ruled that SFAS No. 12 applies to personal financial statements prepared in conformity with GAAP. The cost column in these statements should reflect marketable equity securities at aggregate LCM, and the estimated value column should show these securities at market.

Certain industries such as investment companies, brokers and dealers in securities, stock life insurance companies, and fire and casualty insurance companies apply specialized industry accounting practices with respect to marketable securities. SFAS No. 12 does not alter any industry specialized accounting practices except for the following:

1. Entities carrying marketable equity securities at cost must now carry these securities at the lower of aggregate cost or market, as defined in SFAS No. 12,
2. Declines in market value that are deemed to be other than temporary for securities included in the noncurrent portfolio or in an unclassified balance sheet should be accounted for as previously discussed,
3. Income tax implications also should be applied as previously discussed.

Current/Noncurrent Status of Securities

If the financial statements of an entity include a classified balance sheet, marketable equity securities should be grouped into either a current or a noncurrent portfolio. The determination of the current/noncurrent classifications is based on the intent of management. If management intends to dispose of the security within the normal operating cycle or one year, whichever is longer, the security should be classified as current and accounted for in the current portfolio. Conversely, if management does not intend to dispose of the security within this time period, the security should be classified as noncurrent and placed in the noncurrent portfolio. Finally, if an entity issues financial statements that do not include a classified balance sheet, all marketable equity securities should be considered noncurrent assets.

The Lower of Cost or Market Rule

The amount at which a portfolio of marketable equity securities is reflected in the financial statements of an enterprise (carrying amount)

Exhibit 5.2
Investments in Affiliated Companies: Hanna Mining Company

ASSETS	1980	December 31	1979
Current Assets			
Cash	$ 1,880,777		$ 1,575,934
Short-term securities	19,171,212		46,826,796
Receivables:			
Trade	38,950,918		59,396,675
Other	14,104,562		12,230,324
	53,055,480		71,626,999
Inventories:			
Finished products	38,936,172		9,583,955
Supplies	17,547,720		15,971,836
	56,483,892		25,555,791
Total current assets	130,591,361		145,585,520
Property, Plant and Equipment			
Mineral and oil lands and leases	18,183,137		13,774,411
Plants and equipment	126,263,835		121,059,531
	144,446,972		134,833,942
Less allowances for depreciation and depletion	97,148,201		89,255,992
Total property, plant and equipment	47,298,771		45,577,950
Other Assets			
Working assets — Interests in associated companies	331,053,921		297,511,907
Interests in other companies	68,903,097		68,689,594
Sundry assets and deferred charges	10,927,683		8,159,092
Total other assets	410,884,701		374,360,593
	$588,774,833		$565,524,063
LIABILITIES AND STOCKHOLDERS' EQUITY			
Current Liabilities			
Trade payables	$ 50,130,081		$ 56,113,800
Accrued expenses	21,478,874		16,451,419
Federal income taxes	11,568,429		15,493,800
Current portion of long-term debt	514,405		34,307
Total current liabilities	83,691,789		88,093,326
Long-Term Liabilities			
Long-term debt	53,689,242		52,463,128
Deferred income taxes	28,457,300		24,014,900
Other	6,360,310		3,807,831
Total long-term liabilities	88,506,852		80,285,859
Stockholders' Equity			
Common Stock, par value $1 a share: Authorized 13,500,000 shares;			
Issued 8,945,050 shares (8,942,550 in 1979)	8,945,050		8,942,550
Capital surplus	23,802,251		23,735,201
Retained earnings	420,060,536		399,186,272
Unrealized loss on long-term investment	(35,678,682)		(34,166,182)
Cost of treasury stock (36,500 shares)	(552,963)		(552,963)
Total stockholders' equity	416,576,192		397,144,878
	$588,774,833		$565,524,063

(continued)

should be the lower of its aggregate cost or market value determined at the balance sheet date. Cost refers to the original cost of a marketable equity security unless a new cost basis has been assigned based on recognition of an impairment of value that was deemed other than temporary or as a result of a transfer between current and noncurrent classifications (both discussed later). In such cases, the new cost basis will be the cost for purposes of applying SFAS No. 12. Market value refers to

Exhibit 5.2 (continued)

Interests in Associated and Other Companies

	Percent Owned	Income (Loss) 1980	1979	1978	Dividends Received 1980	1979	1978	Carrying Value 1980	1979
					(amounts in thousands)				
Working assets—associated companies:									
Carried at equity:									
Iron Ore Company of Canada	26.77	$21,775	$25,594	$ 81	$21,950	$ —	$ —	$111,158	$111,333
WellTech, Inc.	50.0	5,251	2,040	—	—	—	—	74,204	68,867
St. John d'el Rey Mining Co., Ltd. (Brazil)	66.41	8,319	2,761	202	1,323	1,321	1,505	30,859	23,861
Alcoa Aluminio S.A. (Brazil)	31.97	4,848	6,041	3,840	—	1,106	1,012	27,945	22,927
Domestic Iron Ore Companies		(5,213)	6,235	6,030	—	5,275	5,498	17,294	22,539
Coal Companies		(2,206)	(3,692)	(3,663)	589	—	—	34,799	21,126
Vessel Companies		3,325	1,202	367	157	218	232	6,451	3,133
Insurance Companies		977	164	105	265	10	—	1,787	1,075
Other		16	88	(53)	253	—	71	1,870	977
Carried at cost:									
Exmibal (Guatemala)	20.0	—	—	—	—	—	—	8,323	8,323
Cerro Matoso S.A. (Colombia)	17.5	—	—	—	—	—	—	5,857	5,748
Other		—	34	—	—	34	—	10,507	7,603
								$331,054	$297,512
Other companies:									
Carried at equity:									
Labrador Mining and Expl. Co., Ltd. (Canada)	20.0	3,973	11,516	1,617	1,788	1,666	3,507	$ 33,446	$ 31,261
Other		719	1,350	851	1,145	1,524	754	1,822	1,983
Carried at cost:									
National Steel Corporation (cost $63,316,182)	5.9	2,585	2,860	2,750	2,585	2,860	2,750	27,637	29,150
Unipar (Brazil)	15.1	512	922	634	512	922	634	5,990	5,990
Other		140	193	268	140	193	268	—	298
		45,021	57,308	13,029	$30,707	$15,129	$16,231	$ 68,903	$ 68,690
Less dividend income of non-equity companies		3,237	4,009	3,652					
Income of companies carried at equity		$41,784	$53,299	$ 9,377					

Iron Ore Company of Canada:

Following is a summary of financial information of Iron Ore Company of Canada, owned 26.77% by Hanna:

	1980	1979	1978
	(in thousands)		
Net current assets	$115,570	$115,096	
Investments and other assets	13,837	15,261	
Property, plant and equipment — net	632,612	658,474	
Long-term debt and liabilities	(338,735)	(364,891)	
Net assets	$423,284	$423,940	
Sales and operating revenues	$693,218	$727,419	$421,263
Net income	$ 81,321	$ 95,608	$ 299

WellTech, Inc.:

In 1979, Hanna and one of the Bechtel group of companies each purchased 50% of the outstanding shares of WellTech, Inc. for approximately $59,000,000 and advanced $8,000,000 for acquisitions made by WellTech. The allocation of the aggregate purchase price has been recorded on the financial statements of WellTech, with the resulting goodwill being amortized over 40 years.

Following is a summary of financial information of WellTech, Inc., oil well servicing company owned 50% by Hanna:

	1980	1979
	(in thousands)	
Net current assets	$ 15,312	$ 12,302
Property, plant and equipment — net	117,926	93,036
Goodwill and other	88,282	85,788
Long-term debt and liabilities	(72,438)	(52,546)
Net assets	$149,082	$138,580
Revenues (1979 eight months)	$120,213	$ 46,742
Net income (1979 eight months)	$ 10,502	$ 4,080

the aggregate of the market price times the number of shares or units of each marketable equity security in the portfolio.

Temporary Declines in Market Value

Whenever there is a decline in market value below cost that is judged to be "temporary," its impact is assessed on an aggregate portfolio basis

Exhibit 5.2 (continued)

St. John d'el Rey Mining Co., Ltd.:

Following is a summary of financial information of St. John d'el Rey Mining Co., Ltd., owned 66.41% by Hanna. St. John owns 49% of MBR, Brazilian iron ore company:

	1980	1979	1978
		(in thousands)	
Net current assets	$ 997	$ 1,263	
Investment in MBR	51,854	37,451	
Deferred income taxes	(8,225)	(4,624)	
Net assets	$ 44,626	$34,090	
Net income	$ 12,567	$ 4,200	$ 365

MBR's iron ore sales amounted to $218,050,000 in 1980, $197,242,000 in 1979 and $171,929,000 in 1978 and MBR's debt amounted to $96,210,000 at December 31, 1980.

Alcoa Aluminio S.A.:

Following is a summary of financial information of Alcoa Aluminio S.A., Brazilian aluminum producer owned 31.97% by Hanna:

	1980	1979	1978
		(in thousands)	
Net current assets	$ 26,283	$ 647	
Property, plant and equipment — net	152,275	114,173	
Other assets and deferred charges	16,402	19,728	
Long-term debt and liabilities	(107,268)	(62,552)	
Net assets	$ 87,692	$ 71,996	
Net sales	$144,811	$114,639	$ 87,083
Net income	$ 15,696	$ 19,450	$ 13,691

Coal Companies:

Following is a summary of combined financial information of Colowyo Coal Company and H-G Coal Company, Colorado coal producers owned 50% and Rapoca Energy Company and Terry Eagle Coal Company, eastern coal producers owned 47.5% by Hanna:

	1980	1979	1978
		(in thousands)	
Net current assets	$ 19,208	$ 7,392	
Property, plant and equipment — net	176,093	112,440	
Other assets and deferred charges	9,014	3,881	
Long-term debt and liabilities	(133,252)	(81,263)	
Net assets	$ 71,063	$ 42,450	
Sales	$ 85,063	$ 31,376	$ 16,800
Loss before income taxes	$ 4,402	$ 7,193	$ 7,316

Domestic Iron Ore Companies:

Following is a summary of combined financial information of the Butler Taconite Project, National Steel Pellet Company, and Pilot Knob Pellet Company, iron ore producers owned 37.5%, 15% and 50% respectively by Hanna:

	1980	1979	1978
		(in thousands)	
Net current assets	$ 71,051	$ 76,415	
Property, plant and equipment — net	287,140	306,854	
Other assets and deferred charges	4,492	5,170	
Long-term debt and liabilities	(259,566)	(265,058)	
Net assets	$103,117	$123,381	
Sales	$187,685	$351,607	$302,540
(Loss) income before closing costs and income taxes	$ (15,779)	$ 24,653	$ 19,735

Included in the Company's equity in the loss for 1980 is a $4,700,000 pre-tax write-off resulting from the permanent closing of the Pilot Knob iron ore mine and pellet plant.

Labrador Mining and Exploration Company, Limited:

Following is a summary of financial information in Canadian dollars of Labrador Mining and Exploration Company, Limited, owned 20% by Hanna:

	1980	1979	1978
		(in thousands)	
Net current assets	$ 15,325	$ 7,176	
Note receivable	168,786	168,786	
Investments			
Iron Ore Company of Canada	10,804	10,804	
Norcen Energy Resources Limited	381,708	77,720	
Other assets	10,657	6,884	
Long-term debt and liabilities	(398,103)	(99,048)	
Net assets	$189,177	$172,322	
Royalty income on iron ore	$ 40,923	$ 41,072	$ 22,973
Net income	$ 27,255	$ 68,402	$ 13,855

Included in the 1979 net income is $45,459,000 relative to the sale of shares of Noranda Mines, Limited.

Translation and Exchange Gains and Losses:

The Company's share of translation and exchange gains and losses of companies carried on the equity method amounted to a gain of $2,113,000 in 1979 and losses of $6,909,000 in 1980 and $9,202,000 in 1978.

by comparing aggregate market value with aggregate cost. The portfolio is then written down by the amount that cost exceeds market so that it is reflected in the balance sheet at market value. If there are subsequent recoveries in the market value of the securities, the portfolio is written up, but only to the extent of its cost basis. Thus, for temporary declines, historical cost remains the same and is used for all comparisons of cost and market.

For the noncurrent portfolio, the net unrealized loss is reflected in the

Exhibit 5.3

Balance Sheet Disclosures of Marketable Equity Securities: Chicago Pneumatic Tool Company

	December 31, 1982	January 1, 1982*
ASSETS		
Current Assets:		
Cash	$ 8,194,000	$ 8,623,000
Accounts and notes receivable (net)	60,865,000	80,140,000
Inventories	141,508,000	169,664,000
Prepaid expenses	1,847,000	2,246,000
Refundable income taxes	11,737,000	–
Marketable equity securities	284,000	–
Deferred income taxes	4,154,000	1,585,000
Total current assets	228,589,000	262,258,000
Investments in Companies Not Consolidated:		
Finance Subsidiary	8,852,000	5,797,000
Affiliates	2,345,000	2,294,000
Long-Term Receivables	2,257,000	803,000
Property, Plant and Equipment (Net)	59,620,000	63,921,000
Other Assets	13,238,000	13,264,000
Total Assets	$314,901,000	$348,337,000
LIABILITIES AND STOCKHOLDERS' EQUITY		
Current Liabilities:		
Short-term debt	$ 8,508,000	$ 9,988,000
Accounts payable	31,265,000	32,878,000
Payroll, taxes and other accrued expenses	32,653,000	35,980,000
U.S. and foreign income taxes	5,417,000	6,237,000
Total current liabilities	77,843,000	85,083,000
Long-Term Debt	85,009,000	94,306,000
Pension Liability	6,081,000	3,914,000
Deferred Income Taxes	4,373,000	2,741,000
Other Liabilities	3,002,000	2,875,000
Minority Interests	2,053,000	1,621,000
Total Liabilities	178,361,000	190,540,000
Stockholders' Equity:		
Preferred stock (without par value)		
Authorized 1,000,000 shares –		
none issued to date		
Common stock ($8 par value)		
Shares authorized 12,000,000		
Issued 5,586,521 shares	44,692,000	44,692,000
Additional paid-in capital	9,345,000	9,345,000
Retained earnings	120,196,000	133,662,000
	174,233,000	187,699,000
Less: Cumulative translation effect	17,203,000	9,153,000
Treasury stock at cost (698,970 shares)	20,490,000	20,490,000
Unrealized loss on marketable equity securities	–	259,000
Total Stockholders' Equity	136,540,000	157,797,000
Total Liabilities and Stockholders' Equity	$314,901,000	$348,337,000

*Reclassified for comparative purposes.
The accompanying Notes to Financial Statements are an integral part of this statement.

stockholders' equity section of the balance sheet below retained earnings.

Declines in Market Value Other than Temporary

Whenever there is a market decline below cost for an individual security included in noncurrent assets or in an unclassified balance sheet,

Exhibit 5.4
Illustrative Disclosures for Marketable Equity Securities: Chicago Pneumatic Tool Company

Marketable Equity Securities

Marketable equity securities are carried at the lower of cost or market. At December 31, 1982 the aggregate cost of the marketable equity securities included in current assets was $476,000 and the aggregate market was $284,000. To reduce the carrying amount of these securities to market, an unrealized loss of $192,000 was charged to income in 1982.

At December 31, 1982 the aggregate cost of marketable equity securities included in other noncurrent assets was $135,000 (1981–$598,000) and the aggregate market value was $135,000 (1981–$339,000). A valuation allowance of $259,000, representing the excess of cost over market of these securities, was included in stockholders' equity at January 1, 1982. Sales of marketable equity securities resulted in a net realized gain of $145,000 in 1981. There were no realized gains or losses from the sale of marketable equity securities in 1982 or 1980.

Property, Plant & Equipment

Property, Plant, & Equipment

(In thousands)	1982	1981
Major classes at year end:		
Land	$ 3,615	$ 3,756
Buildings	44,621	44,713
Machinery & equipment	76,812	77,477
	125,048	125,946
Less accumulated depreciation	65,428	62,025
Property, Plant & Equipment (Net)	$ 59,620	$ 63,921

Leases and Lease Commitments

Capitalized Leases

(In thousands)	1982	1981
Property, plant and equipment at year end include the following amounts for capitalized leases:		
Buildings	$2,912	$3,073
Machinery & equipment	2,222	2,164
Total capitalized	5,134	5,237
Less accumulated depreciation	2,209	1,768
Capitalized leases (net)	$2,925	$3,469
Lease obligations included in short-term and long-term debt:		
Short-term debt	$ 725	$ 751
Long-term debt	2,444	3,064
Total	$3,169	$3,815

The Company is committed in the normal course of operations to make rental payments under non-cancellable operating leases relating to buildings and machinery and equipment, including certain office equipment. Rental expense under these leases amounted to $3,456,000 in 1982, $3,690,000 in 1981 and $2,624,000 in 1980.

Future minimum rental commitments of the Company under all leases with terms of one year or more are shown below. This data reflects existing leases and does not include future replacement upon their expiration.

this decline is judged to be temporary or other than temporary. If the decline is judged to be other than temporary, the cost basis of the individual security should be written down to a new cost basis and the amount of the writedown should be accounted for as a realized loss, even though the securities have not been sold. The new cost basis should not be changed for subsequent recoveries in market value.

Disclosures for Marketable Equity Securities

The following information with respect to marketable equity securities should be disclosed by an investor in the body of the financial statements or in the accompanying notes:

1. The aggregate cost and market value as of the balance sheet date. If a classified balance sheet is presented, the securities should be segregated between current and noncurrent portfolios.

2. Gross unrealized gains and losses as of the date of the latest balance sheet presented, segregated between current and noncurrent portfolios.

3. The net realized gains and losses, basis for determination of the gains and losses, and changes in valuation allowances for each period for which an income statement is presented.

Exhibits 5.2 through 5.4 provide illustrative disclosures of the matters discussed in this chapter. Exhibit 5.2 concentrates on investments not accounted for as marketable equity securities per SFAS No. 12. Exhibit 5.3 illustrates the disclosures applicable to marketable equity securities. Exhibit 5.4 combines both types of disclosure. Particularly, Exhibit 5.4 shows the effect of a net unrealized loss on noncurrent marketable equity securities on total stockholders' equity (a reduction of $259,000 at January 1, 1982).

6
Intangible Asset Disclosures

THE NATURE OF INTANGIBLE ASSETS

Intangible assets generally exhibit all of the following characteristics:

1. They are long term in nature.
2. They have no physical existence.
3. The asset value is dependent on the rights that possession confers to the owner.
4. The economic life of the asset may be subject to a greater degree of uncertainty than other assets.

These characteristics may be seen more clearly with the use of a brief example. Assume that an enterprise acquires a patent for a new process that improves its production efficiency. The patent is expected to benefit the company's operations for several years. The right to use this new process has no physical existence, yet the firm will receive a valuable economic benefit. The economic life of the patent is subject to a higher degree of uncertainty than most assets in that it may be of substantial economic benefit to the enterprise for many years. Conversely, the patent may become worthless in a short time if new technological devices become available. Since the patent displays all of the characteristics listed above, it would be classified as an intangible asset. Other assets commonly classified as intangible assets include trademarks, tradenames, copyrights, franchises, goodwill, secret processes, and organizational costs.

Determining the Cost of Purchases of Intangible Assets

One of the major issues regarding intangibles prior to the issuance of APBO No. 17, "Intangible Assets," was when and under what conditions an intangible asset should be recorded on the books of an entity. In an attempt to resolve this issue, the APB divided intangibles between those that were acquired from external sources and those that were developed internally. For those intangibles acquired externally, the APB requires recognition of an asset on the books of the acquiring entity. This applies to all intangibles, including purchased goodwill. When an intangible asset is purchased separately and not as part of a group of assets, it should be recorded at cost at the date of acquisition. This cost, as with any asset, is measured by the fair market value of the consideration given or the fair market value of the consideration received, whichever is more clearly determinable. Generally, when assets are purchased as a group, they are allocated a portion of the cost based on the fair market values of the individual assets. This principle is also applicable where specifically identifiable intangibles are among the assets purchased.

Another issue resolved by the APB was under what conditions additions to intangibles or internal generation of goodwill would be capitalized on the books of the entity. The board responded by setting forth three conditions to be met before costs of developing, maintaining, or restoring intangible assets would be capitalized rather than being expensed immediately:

1. The cost must be related to a specifically identifiable asset.
2. The related asset must have a determinate life capable of reasonable estimation.
3. The related asset must not be inherent in a continuing business and not be related to an enterprise as a whole. (This criterion is meant to apply to those assets such as goodwill that would have no value except for their existence within a firm; thus, an enterprise would never reflect internally generated goodwill as an asset.)

Unless these three criteria are met, all such costs should be expensed immediately.

Balance Sheet Presentation of Intangible Assets

Intangible assets have been reported on the balance sheet under the captions of "intangibles," "deferred charges," and "other assets." If the intangible assets are material, they should be reported separately under an appropriate caption. Intangible assets are typically shown on the balance sheet at their "net of amortization amounts." Exhibit 6.1 illustrates the disclosures for intangible assets.

As can be seen, General Mills, Inc., has a material amount in intangible assets (predominantly goodwill) that are classified as "Other Assets." Further, their footnote disclosure indicates the basis of amortization of intangible assets as being straight line over no more than 40

Exhibit 6.1
Intangible Asset Disclosures: General Mills, Inc.

Assets

(In Millions)	May 25, 1980	May 27, 1979
Current Assets:		
Cash and short-term investments	$ 39.1	$ 97.0
Receivables, less allowance for possible losses		
of $10.9 in 1980 and $9.0 in 1979	374.2	313.4
Inventories (Notes 1-C and 3)	543.1	501.8
Prepaid expenses	29.6	24.2
Total Current Assets	986.0	936.4
Land, Buildings and Equipment, at cost (Note 1-B):		
Land	65.8	56.7
Buildings	389.2	347.6
Equipment	571.5	505.1
Construction in progress	97.3	65.6
	1,123.8	975.0
Less accumulated depreciation	(376.3)	(331.3)
Net Land, Buildings and Equipment	747.5	643.7
Other Assets:		
Goodwill and other intangible assets (Note 1-D)	179.1	179.5
Miscellaneous assets	99.8	75.6
Total Other Assets	278.9	255.1
Total Assets	$2,012.4	$1,835.2

See accompanying notes to consolidated financial statements.

D. Amortization Of Goodwill And Other Intangibles

Goodwill represents the difference between purchase prices of acquired companies and the related values of net assets acquired and accounted for by the purchase method of accounting. Any goodwill acquired after October, 1970, is amortized over not more than 40 years.

The costs of patents, copyrights and other intangible assets are amortized evenly over their lives by charges against earnings. Most of these costs were incurred through purchases of businesses.

Annually, the Board of Directors reviews goodwill and other intangibles and determines if the values are appropriate.

E. Research and Development

All expenditures for research and development are charged against earnings in the year incurred. The charges for fiscal 1980 and 1979 were $44.4 million and $37.3 million, respectively.

years. Finally, note that General Mills makes an annual assessment of the continuing value of the assets.

RESEARCH AND DEVELOPMENT COSTS

Prior to the issuance of SFAS No. 2, entitled "Accounting for Research and Development Costs," companies followed a wide variety of practices regarding R & D costs. Some capitalized some projects and expensed others. Owing to the significant amounts involved for many companies, the FASB moved to standardize the accounting for these costs. This resulted in the requirement that all R & D costs be expensed as incurred.

The first issue to be resolved by the FASB was a definition of R & D activities. This was done to reduce arbitrary determinations by the individual firms. The terms are defined as follows.

Research is planned search or critical investigation aimed at discovery of new knowledge, with the hope that such knowledge will be useful in developing a new product or service or a new process or technique or in bringing about a significant improvement to an existing product or process.

Development is the translation of research findings or other knowledge into a plan or design for a new product or process or for a significant improvement to an existing product or process whether intended for sale or use. R & D activities include (but are not limited to)

1. Laboratory research aimed at discovery of new knowledge
2. Conceptual formulation and design of possible product or process alternatives
3. Design, construction, and operation of a pilot plant that is not of a scale economically feasible to the enterprise for commercial production
4. Engineering activity required to advance the design of a product to the point that it meets specific functional and economic requirements and is ready for manufacture.

R & D activities do not include

1. Engineering follow-through in an early phase of commercial production
2. Routine on-going efforts to refine, enrich, or otherwise improve upon the qualities of an existing product
3. Adaptation of an existing capability to a particular requirement or customer's need as part of a continuing commercial activity
4. Legal work in connection with patent applications or litigation and the sale or licensing of patents.

Once it is determined that R & D activities have begun, the R & D costs to be expensed must be established. The general rule is that where costs are incurred for assets that have alternative future uses, only those costs directly related to the R & D activities are expensed currently. When assets acquired have no alternative future use, the entire cost is expensed currently as R & D costs.

Contractual R & D

In SFAS No. 2, the FASB did address the question of contractual R & D from the standpoint of the party paying for the contract services. This statement specifies that these costs are R & D and therefore should generally be expensed as incurred. However, as was noted earlier, this left unanswered the question of how the enterprise performing the contract services should account for the arrangement.

R & D Arrangements

The provisions of SFAS No. 68 are applicable to enterprises which are parties to an R & D arrangement whereby they can obtain the results of R & D that has been funded (either partially or totally) by other entities. Examples of these situations are a joint venture enterprise created by two (or more) petrochemical entities to perform R & D activities on new processes and a subsidiary enterprise established to develop new computer software packages. As can be seen, frequently a related party relationship exists. The disclosures applicable to related party transactions are specified in SFAS No. 57, "Related Party Disclosures." The accounting and disclosure requirements of SFAS No. 68 are in addition to the disclosures required by SFAS No. 57.

R & D Arrangements Representing Obligations

When an R & D arrangement representing obligations begins, the enterprise typically will receive funds from the other parties to finance all or part of the arrangement. At the time the funds are received, the enterprise must determine whether a liability is created by the receipt of the funds. The FASB requires that the assessment be predicated on the transfer of financial risk. Essentially, if the financial risk of the R & D project is transferred to the entity providing funds, the arrangement is essentially a contract agreement and accounting principles applicable to contract accounting should be used. If, however, the enterprise receiving funds retains some or all of the financial risk, it has a liability upon receipt of the funds.

Operationally, SFAS No. 68 makes this distinction primarily upon the likelihood that funds will have to be repaid. Thus, if the enterprise is obligated to repay any of the funds regardless of the outcome of the R & D project, it has retained financial risk. Accordingly, it must estimate the amount of required repayment and recognize a liability for that amount. This requirement is applicable regardless of the form of the repayment (e.g., cash, common stock, or other). Further, paragraph 6 of SFAS No.

68 requires this treatment regardless of the legal form of the commitment to repay. It is the substance that should dictate. Therefore, examples of situations where the enterprise is committed to repay (and, thus, have a liability) include the following:

1. A guarantee or contractual commitment assures repayment of the funds regardless of the outcome.
2. The other parties can require the enterprise to repurchase their interest regardless of the outcome.
3. The other parties will receive securities of the enterprise (either debt or equity) upon termination of the project regardless of outcome.
4. The agreement indicates it is probable (as defined in SFAS No. 5, "Accounting for Contingencies," this is construed as to be likely) that repayment will occur regardless of the outcome of the project (e.g., repayment will be necessary unless the R & D generates a predetermined amount of revenues).

As can be seen, the general presumption is that financial risk has not transferred entirely to the other parties and a liability will result. However, financial risk is deemed to have transferred to the other parties if repayment is based totally on the R & D project having future economic benefit (e.g., a project to develop a computer software package where the funds will be repaid only in the form of royalties on future sales of the software package). In these instances, a contract to perform R & D for others has been entered into and the enterprise should account for the funds as contract revenue.

If the enterprise has incurred a liability to repay all the funds provided in the R & D arrangement, all costs incurred on the R & D project are deemed to be R & D costs to the enterprise. As a consequence, the costs should be expensed as incurred according to the provisions of SFAS No. 2.

If the enterprise is obligated to repay part but not all of the funds provided (such as risk-sharing venture), the enterprise should expense only its portion of the R & D costs as the liability is incurred.

R & D Arrangement Is a Contract to Perform Services

If the financial risk has been transferred to the other parties, the enterprise has only a contract to perform R & D services. Therefore, in this instance, it initially should account for the funds as unearned revenue. As the services are performed, the unearned revenue should be recognized as it is earned.

Accounting for Loans or Advances to the Other Parties

In some instances, the enterprise may pay the parties providing the funds an advance (such as an advance against future royalties on the R

& D project). If repayment of the advance is based solely upon the R & D project generating future economic benefits, the advance is deemed to be a cost to the enterprise since (as with all R & D costs) at the time the costs are incurred, there is a significant doubt that the specific project will reach fruition. If the advance is for some other activity (e.g., advertising), it should be expensed according to the nature of the activity.

Issuance of Warrants

If the enterprise issues warrants or similar instruments upon receipt of the funds, it has generated paid-in capital. As a consequence, paid-in capital should be recorded for the fair value of the warrants at the date the R & D arrangement is entered into.

Disclosure of R & D Costs

Disclosure of the total R & D costs charged to expense is required for the period or for each period presented when comparative financial statements are provided. An additional examination of Exhibit 6.1 reveals that General Mills incurred and expensed $53.8 million in R & D costs for fiscal 1982. Further, all costs incurred for R & D during the reporting period were expensed in the period incurred.

7
Long-Term Bond Disclosures

Business organizations often use long-term obligations such as bonds and long-term notes and mortgages to finance the activities and acquisitions of the firm. Bonds and long-term notes and mortgages are reported on the balance sheet under long-term liabilities. They are recorded at the sum of the discounted present values of the face amount of the bond plus the series of cash payments to be made, each discounted at the market rate of interest in effect at the inception of the debt. This chapter will discuss the issuance and post-issuance accounting and disclosure for bonds.

ACCOUNTING FOR THE ISSUANCE OF DEBT AND AMORTIZATION OF INTEREST, BOND DISCOUNT, AND BOND PREMIUM

Bonds generally provide for periodic fixed interest payments at a rate written in the terms of the bond issue and ordinarily printed on the face of the bonds (the stated or nominal rate). If at issuance the market rate of interest for the particular type of bond is above the stated rate, the bonds are issued at a discount in order to yield the investor the market rate. If the stated rate is above the market rate at issuance, the bonds are issued at a premium. In either of these cases, the face amount of the bond will be different from the cash proceeds exchanged, and the difference between the face amount and the cash proceeds will be recorded as the bond discount or premium. The bond discount or premium must be amortized as interest over the period from the date of sale to the bond maturity date. The effective interest or interest method of amortization is required by APBO No. 21 unless the results of another approach are not materially different.

EARLY EXTINGUISHMENT OF DEBT

Early extinguishment is defined in APBO No. 26, entitled "Early Extinguishment of Debt," as the "reacquisition of any form of debt security or instrument before its scheduled maturity except through conversion by the holder, regardless of whether the debt is viewed as terminated or held as so-called 'treasury bonds'." All open market or mandatory reacquisitions of debt securities to meet sinking fund requirements are early extinguishments.

APBO No. 26 requires that the difference between the debt repurchase price and the net carrying amount of the debt be recognized as gain or loss in the period of extinguishment. With the exception of the gains and losses resulting from debt reacquisitions to meet sinking fund requirements, gains or losses on early extinguishment of debt should be treated as extraordinary items in accordance with SFAS No. 4, entitled "Reporting Gains and Losses from Extinguishment of Debt."

Reporting Gains and Losses from Extinguishment of Debt

SFAS No. 4 requires that gains and losses from the extinguishment of debt be aggregated and, if material, classified as an extraordinary item, net of related income tax effect. This treatment applies regardless of whether the extinguishment is early, at maturity, or after maturity. Gains and losses resulting from retirements to satisfy sinking fund requirements are exceptions to the general rule of SFAS No. 4. Such gains and losses are aggregated and reported as a separate line item in income from continuing operations.

Required disclosures for gains and losses classified as extraordinary items include (1) the source of funds used to extinguish the debt, (2) the income tax effect in the extinguishment period, and (3) the per share amount of gain or loss net of tax effect.

ACCOUNTING FOR CONVERTIBLE DEBT

APBO No. 14, entitled "Accounting for Convertible Debt and Debt Issued with Stock Purchase Warrants," identifies three types of debt securities that contain both debt and equity features: (1) convertible debt, (2) debt with nondetachable stock purchase warrants, and (3) debt with detachable stock purchase warrants.

The convertible debt securities discussed in APBO No. 14 are those debt securities that are convertible into common stock of the issuer or affiliated company at a specified price at the option of the holder and that are sold at a price or have a value at issuance not significantly in excess of the face amount.

Exhibit 7.1
Long-Term Debt Disclosures: Armstrong World Industries, Inc.

As of December 31	1980	1979
	(000)	(000)
Assets Current assets:		
Cash	$ 6,317	$ 13,185
Short-term securities	31,467	22,153
Accounts and notes receivable (less allowance for discounts and losses: 1980—$10,208,000; 1979—$9,622,000)	177,075	165,693
Inventories	217,409	235,813
Other current assets	13,248	10,419
Total current assets	445,516	447,263
Property, plant, and equipment (less accumulated depreciation and amortization: 1980—$379,370,000; 1979—$352,186,000)	436,404	419,418
Other noncurrent assets	9,593	9,631
	$891,513	$876,312
Liabilities and stockholders' equity Current liabilities:		
Payable to banks	$ 23,847	$ 22,858
Current installments of long-term debt	2,972	2,720
Accounts payable and accrued expenses	108,183	105,280
Income taxes	13,041	8,328
Total current liabilities	148,043	139,186
Long-term debt	103,813	125,754
Deferred income taxes	47,274	40,406
Minority interest in foreign subsidiary	3,824	3,309
Total noncurrent liabilities	154,911	169,469
Stockholders' equity:		
Preferred stock, $3.75 cumulative, no par value. Authorized 161,821 shares; issued 161,522 shares (at redemption price of $102.75 per share)	16,596	16,596
Voting preferred stock. Authorized 1,500,000 shares	—	—
Common stock, $1.00 par value per share. Authorized 60,000,000 shares; issued 25,939,455 shares	25,939	25,939
Capital surplus	47,066	47,066
Retained earnings	525,646	504,744
	615,247	594,345
Less treasury stock, at cost:		
Preferred stock, $3.75 cumulative—43,373 shares	3,986	3,986
Common stock—1,192,748 shares	22,702	22,702
	26,688	26,688
Total stockholders' equity	588,559	567,657
	$891,513	$876,312

(*continued*)

Exhibit 7.1 (continued)

Debt	1980	Average year-end Interest rate	1979	Average year-end Interest rate
	(000)	%	(000)	%
Payable to banks (Foreign: 1980—100%; 1979—63%)	$ 23,847	8.52	$ 22,858	13.15
Long-term debt: 8% sinking-fund debentures due 1996	$ 34,225	8.00	$ 37,495	8.00
8.45% notes due 1984	50,000	8.45	50,000	8.45
8³/₄% Swiss franc bonds due 1989	—	—	21,875	8.75
Capitalized leases	6,214	6.64	5,283	5.00
Mortgage loans and notes	11,320	7.50	9,902	6.82
Other	5,026	5.46	3,919	5.95
Total long-term debt	106,785		128,474	
Less current installments	2,972		2,720	
Net long-term debt	$103,813	7.97	$125,754	8.04

The 8% sinking-fund debentures are redeemable at the Company's option at 104.4% prior to May 15, 1981, and at declining prices thereafter. Sinking-fund payments sufficient to retire $2.5 million principal amount of the debentures are due annually. At December 31, 1980, bonds having a face amount of $5.8 million were being held in anticipation of future sinking-fund requirements. At December 31, 1979, those bonds held amounted to $5.0 million.

The 8.45% notes are redeemable at the Company's option beginning on November 15, 1981, at par. There are no sinking-fund requirements.

In October, 1980, utilizing the early redemption provision in its 8³/₄% Swiss franc bond agreement of 1974, the Company repaid the Sfr. 35.0 million obligation.

All obligations related to long-term debt have been satisfied through 1980.

Scheduled amortization of long-term debt

	(000)
1982	$ 2,308
1983	3,867
1984	54,416
1985	4,470
1986	4,485

The increased amortization of debt in 1984 represents scheduled redemption of the 8.45% notes maturing in that year.

Under a parallel loan agreement, the Company's British subsidiary borrowed £11.0 million in 1974 from an unrelated British financial institution, and the Company loaned $25.6 million (the approximate equivalent of £11.0 million on the original date) to a U.S. affiliate of the British financial institution, with a net annual interest cost of 2¹/₄%. Each loan matures in 1985 with a right to prepay without premium.

Under another parallel loan agreement, the Company borrowed £6.0 million in 1978 from the pension funds of an unrelated British company, and the Company loaned $11.0 million (the

approximate equivalent of £6.0 million on the original date) to the same pension funds, with a net annual interest cost of 1³/₈%. Each loan is to be repaid in equal installments in 1986, 1988, and 1990, with a right to prepay without premium.

For reporting purposes, the parallel loans are offset. When U.S. receivables are higher than the current dollar values of the pound sterling loans, differences are included in "Other noncurrent assets"; when U.S. receivables are lower, differences are included in "Other" long-term debt.

The Company presently has worldwide short-term lines of credit of approximately $190 million at about 25 banks. These lines are reviewed and renewed periodically by the Company and its banks and may fluctuate from time to time within a range of $150 to $200 million. Many of the credit lines are extended on an informal basis because the Company is maintaining balances in the banks to compensate for other services rendered. The Company maintains average compensating balances of less than 10% of the credit lines; these compensating balances are supported by book balances ranging between $6 and $12 million; however, there are no fixed restrictions on any cash balances.

The Company borrows from its banks generally at the lowest rates available to commercial borrowers and also issues short-term commercial notes supported by the lines of credit.

Litigation

Since 1970 the Company has been named as one of a number of defendants in lawsuits alleging injury to the health of individuals incurred in connection with the installation and removal of asbestos-containing products. Nearly all such suits against the Company allege exposure to asbestos-containing insulation products manufactured or sold by it. Approximately 3,850 suits have asserted claims on behalf of approximately 5,790 individual plaintiffs. As of December 31, 1980, about 3,290 of such suits involving approximately 5,200 individuals remain pending, an increase from the 1,900 suits involving approximately 2,700 individuals as of December 31, 1979. At year-end 1980, the Company had also received similar separate claims not arising out of litigation and involving approximately 60 individuals. Two suits assert claims in behalf of an unspecified number of individuals, one of which involves asbestos insulation products, and the other allegedly involves employees of a gasket fabricator. Most complaints in which damages are specified seek recovery against the defendants of $1,000,000 plus punitive damages. A substantial number of complaints seek much higher damages. Of the cases that have been fully litigated, the largest recovery against the Company was $8,250; of the cases that have been settled, higher amounts have been paid, but the average settlement has been lower than the $8,250 amount. The Company's products may not be involved in a number of these suits. The Company discontinued the sale of all asbestos insulation products in 1969. However, because of the time period prior to manifestation of injury resulting from exposure to asbestos fibers and the inability to determine the number of future cases claiming that such injury arose from exposure to the Company's products, the number of potential unasserted claims and the potential liability therefrom with which the Company may be involved in the future cannot reasonably be ascertained.

The extent of insurance coverage for the bulk of such lawsuits and potential unasserted claims is disputed by the insurance carriers of the Company. In 1980 the Company filed suit against its primary and excess carriers in a California state court to resolve the dispute concerning the carriers' obligations. Based upon a review of the coverage issues by counsel for the Company, the Company believes it has a substantial legal basis for establishing its rights to defense and indemnification, within provable periods of coverage, from its carriers in respect of substantially all such suits and claims. It is probable that resolution of this complex matter will take at least several years.

Even though the potential unasserted claims and liability therefrom cannot be ascertained and there is no assurance of prevailing in the dispute with the Company's insurance carriers, after consideration of the factors discussed above and the Company's experience with this litigation, the Company believes that its liability for these lawsuits and claims would not have a material adverse effect on the Company's financial position.

Usually, the terms of these securities include

1. A lower interest rate than the issuer could establish for ordinary debt
2. An initial conversion price greater than the market price of the common at the time of issuance
3. A conversion price that will only decrease in accordance with antidilution provisions.

Convertible debt is typically callable at a specified call price at the option of the issuer and is subordinated to nonconvertible debt.

Based on the inseparability of the debt and conversion features, the APB concluded in APBO No. 14 that convertible debt should be accounted for solely as debt and no portion of the proceeds from issuance of such debt should be attributed to the conversion feature. In accounting for convertible debt, the difference between the face amount of the debt and the cash proceeds from its sale should be rewarded as a premium or discount on the debt.

ACCOUNTING FOR DEBT WITH STOCK PURCHASE WARRANTS

Debt securities are sometimes issued with stock warrants that give the holder the option to purchase from the issuer (at a specified price and within a stated time period) a specified number of shares of common stock. If the two elements of the security exist independently (the detachable warrants trade separately from the debt instrument), APBO No. 14 requires that separate recognition be given to the value of the debt and the warrants. Under the provisions of this opinion, the proceeds of debt securities issued with detachable stock purchase warrants should be allocated to the debt and the warrants based on the relative fair market values of the debt and equity elements of the security. The portion of the proceeds allocatable to the warrants is treated as paid-in capital. Discount or premium resulting from the allocation process (proceeds allocated to debt minus face of debt equals discount or premium) should be amortized over the life of the debt using the effective interest method.

If debt issued with stock purchase warrants that are not detachable from the debt and the debt security must be surrendered in order to exercise the warrants, the security will be accounted for as if it were convertible debt.

Exhibit 7.1 provides an illustration of the disclosures applicable to long-term debt securities.

8
Lease Disclosures

A lease represents a contractual agreement between a lessor and a lessee that provides the lessee the right to use the property subject to lease for a specified time period in return for designated cash payments to be made to the lessor over the term of the lease. Several financial and operating advantages to leasing exist, such as

1. Securing the use of property without significant down payments
2. Maintaining technologically current equipment and thereby avoiding, or at least reducing, the risk of obsolescence
3. Obtaining a more flexible debt arrangement
4. Incurring a lease obligation that many times is not formalized in the financial statements; i.e., the lease obligation under certain leases need be disclosed only in the financial statement footnotes.

While this listing is by no means all inclusive, these advantages are indicative of why leasing has become increasingly popular throughout the last two decades.

Because the nature of lease agreements is so complex, authoritative rule-making bodies in accounting have devoted a significant amount of literature to explaining how to account for and disclose leases in financial statements.

DEVELOPMENT OF THE AUTHORITATIVE LEASE ACCOUNTING LITERATURE

Before 1964, leases were not considered capitalizable in most cases. Basically, the accounting treatment afforded lease agreements was to charge to expense the payments as accruable for the lessee and recognize revenue as receivable for the lessor. Then, the APB initiated the issuance of four lease accounting pronouncements that governed lease accounting until November 1976. These four documents were

1. APBO No. 5, "Reporting Leases in Financial Statements of Lessee"
2. APBO No. 7, "Accounting for Leases in Financial Statements of Lessors"
3. APBO No. 27, "Accounting for Lease Transactions by Manufacturer or Dealer Lessors"
4. APBO No. 31, "Disclosure of Lease Commitments by Lessees."

While these documents, in general, were theoretically sound, at least two major problems existed with them. First, there was a significant amount of what was termed "off balance sheet financing" available. Lease commitments, for whatever duration and regardless of cancelability, in many cases were being disclosed only in footnotes to financial statements [refer back to leasing advantage (4)], but these lease commitments were just as real as some obligations being termed liabilities on the balance sheet. Second, there existed inconsistencies in the four opinions primarily as related to classification. This latter problem has been labeled the "nonsymmetrical lease classification problem." The problem existed because the criteria outlined in APBO No. 5 for what constitutes a capital lease for lessees were not the same as the capital lease criteria for lessors in APBO No. 7. The result of these nonsymmetrical classification criteria was that lessees could analyze a lease agreement and determine that an asset and related obligation should not be established, whereas lessors could analyze the same agreement and conclude that substantially all the risks and rights of ownership applicable to the property subject to lease transferred to the lessee. Thus, in this case, the lessee would not establish the property as an asset but the lessor would write off the property as if sold and the property would not be reflected in the financial statements of either party. Conversely, the lease agreement classification could result in both lessee and lessor reflecting the same asset on two separate balance sheets.

Because of these and other problems in classifying and accounting for leases, the FASB issued SFAS No. 13, "Accounting for Leases," in November 1976 in an attempt to codify lease accounting into one document. The fundamental objective of SFAS No. 13 was that if substantially all the benefits and risks incident to ownership of the property subject to lease transfer from the lessor to the lessee, the lease agreement should be accounted for as the acquisition of an asset and incurrence of a liability by the lessee and as a sale or financing by the lessor (a capital lease). All other leases should be accounted for as operating leases. But implementing this fundamental notion has been difficult in practice, both from a classification and an accounting perspective, such that SFAS No. 13 has been amended and interpreted thirteen times; there now exists a total of fourteen promulgated pronouncements that govern lease accounting. The remainder of this chapter is devoted to explaining the technical classification, accounting, and disclosure provisions currently in effect applicable to leases.

LEASE CLASSIFICATION CRITERIA

Lessees should classify leases as either operating or capital in nature. Lessors should make the same distinction except that they should subclassify capital leases as sales type, direct financing, or leveraged.

Paragraph 7 of SFAS No. 13 itemizes four criteria, only one of which must be met before a lessee can capitalize an asset and obligation to reflect the substance of a lease agreement. All other leases would be operating leases. The last two criteria [paragraphs 7(c) and 7(d)] are not applicable if the beginning of the lease term falls within the last 25 percent of the total estimated economic life of the leased property. Paragraph 8 of SFAS No. 13 itemizes criteria from the lessor's perspective that are to be utilized in addition to the criteria in paragraph 7 in determining whether or not the lessor has a capital or operating lease. If at least one of the criteria in paragraph 7 and both of those in paragraph 8 are met, the lessor has a capital lease (either sales type, direct financing, or leveraged). All other leases would be operating leases.

The paragraph 7 criteria are summarized as follow (refer to Appendix 12A of the document for important definitions):

1. The lease transfers ownership of the property to the lessee by the end of the lease term.

2. The lease contains a bargain purchase option.

3. The lease term is equal to 75 percent or more of the estimated economic life of the leased property.

4. The present value at the beginning of the lease term of the minimum lease payments, excluding that portion of the payments representing executory costs such as insurance, maintenance, and taxes to be paid by the lessor, equals or exceeds 90 percent of the excess of the fair value of the leased property to the lessor at the inception of the lease over any related investment tax credit retained and expected to be realized by the lessor. A lessor should compute the present value of the minimum lease payments using the interest rate implicit in the lease. A lessee should compute the present value of the minimum lease payments using the lessee's incremental borrowing rate unless (a) it is practicable for the lessee to learn the implicit rate computed by the lessor and (b) the implicit rate computed by the lessor is less than the lessee's incremental borrowing rate. If both of these conditions are met, the lessee should use the rate of interest implicit in the lease.

The paragraph 8 criteria applicable to lessors are as follow:

1. Collectibility of the minimum lease payments is reasonably predictable.
2. No important uncertainties surround the amount of unreimbursable costs yet to be incurred by the lessor under the lease. Examples of such uncertainties might include commitments by the lessor to guarantee performance of the leased property in a manner more extensive than the typical product warranty or to effectively protect the lessee from obsolescence of the leased property. However, the necessity of estimating executory costs such as insurance, maintenance, and taxes to be paid by the lessor should not within itself constitute an important uncertainty under paragraph 8(b).

SFAS No. 27, entitled "Classification of Renewals or Extensions of Existing Sales-Type or Direct Financing Leases," provides that a renewal or extension of an existing sales-type or direct financing lease that otherwise qualifies as a sales type lease should be classified as a direct financing lease unless the renewal or extension occurs at or near the end of the original term specified in the existing lease, in which case the lease should be classified as a sales-type lease. A renewal or extension that occurs in the last few months of an existing lease is considered to have occurred at or near the end of the existing lease term. Changes in estimates or in circumstances should not give rise to lease reclassification for accounting purposes.

While both lessors and lessees should classify leases as capital or operating, capital leases from the perspective of lessors may take one of three forms:

1. A sales-type lease gives rise to manufacturer or dealer profit (or loss). Operationally, this means the fair value of the leased property at the inception of the lease is greater (or less) than the cost or carrying value of the property.
2. A direct financing lease is a capital lease agreement (other than a leveraged lease) that does not give rise to manufacturer or dealer profit (or loss). In such a case, the fair value of the leased property at the inception of the lease equals the cost or carrying value of the property.
3. A leveraged lease is a three-party lease agreement involving a lessee, a lessor, and a long-term creditor. The financing provided by the long-term creditor is sufficient to give the lessor substantial "leverage" in the transaction and is nonrecourse to the general credit of the lessor. The lessor's net investment declines during the early years of the lease (maybe even to a negative amount) once the investment has been completed and rises in subsequent years of the lease term. A leveraged lease meets all the characteristics listed below, provided the lessor chooses to defer any applicable investment tax credit and allocate it to income over the lease term. If the lease agreement meets the characteristics itemized below but the investment tax credit is not deferred and allocated to income over the lease term, the lease agreement

should be classified and accounted for as a direct financing lease with the nonrecourse debt shown as a liability in the balance sheet. All of the following characteristics must be met:

a. The lease agreement meets the criteria for classification as a direct financing lease (sales-type leases cannot be leveraged leases).
b. The lease involves a third-party, long-term creditor in addition to the lessee and lessor.
c. The financing provided by the long-term creditor is nonrecourse to the general credit of the lessor (although the creditor may have recourse to the property or related rentals) and is sufficient to provide the lessor with "substantial leverage" in the transaction.
d. The lessor's net investment in the leveraged lease declines during the early years once the investment has been completed and rises in later years of the lease; this pattern may occur more than once.

LESSEE ACCOUNTING AND REPORTING

This section summarizes the general accounting and disclosure requirements for lessees related to both capital and operating leases. Special categorizations of leases (e.g., real estate leases, subleases, and sale-leasebacks) will be discussed later in this chapter.

Capital Leases

For leases classified as capital in nature, lessees should record an asset and an obligation, at the inception of the lease, in the amount of the present value of the minimum lease payments to be made during the lease term. Executory costs such as insurance, maintanance, and taxes should be excluded from this computation and charged to expense as these costs become payable.

Capitalized assets and obligations should be segregated or separately identified in the balance sheet of the lessee or related footnotes. Lease obligations are subject to the same current/noncurrent classification status applicable to other liabilities. And, the lease obligation should be amortized through determining the appropriate periodic interest to be recognized under the effective interest method.

For leases capitalized per SFAS No. 13 as amended, lessees should, at a minimum, make the following disclosures:

1. The gross amount of the assets recorded as of the date of each balance sheet presented, in the aggregate and by major classes (by nature or function).
2. Minimum future payments required as of the date of the latest balance sheet presented, in the aggregate and for each of the five succeeding fiscal years (reduced by executory costs, which are expensed as incurred).
3. The total of minimum sublease rentals (discussed later in this chapter) to be received in the future under noncancelable subleases as of the date of the latest balance sheet presented.

4. Total contingent rentals actually incurred during each period for which an income statement is presented. Contingent rentals are not included in minimum lease payments, but rather are expensed as incurred (see glossary definition from SFAS No. 29).

5. A general description of the leasing arrangement, including the basis on which contingent rentals are determined, the existence and terms of renewal or purchase options and escalation clauses, and restrictions imposed by the lease agreements.

As can be seen in Exhibit 8.1, Horn & Hardart Company reported a total of $4,439,000 in gross assets capitalized under leases at December 31, 1977, segregated into those applicable to store facilities and equipment leases. Minimum future payments are disclosed for each of the five years after 1977 and aggregating to $5,786,000, of which $2,398,000 represents interest.

Further, Horn & Hardart disclosed that it received $478,000 from subleases and has no contingent rentals due. Footnote 11 begins with a general description of the leasing arrangements.

Operating Leases

In accounting for operating leases, lessees should not formalize either an asset or an obligation related to the leasing arrangement. Rather, lease (rent) expense should be recognized, normally on a straight-line basis, over the life of the lease. While the FASB states a preference for recognizing lease rentals on a straight-line basis, another "systematic and rational" approach may be used if the approach results in recognizing expenses that are more indicative of the benefits received under the lease.

For operating leases, lessees should make the following financial statement disclosures:

1. For leases with terms in excess of one year, minimum future payments required as of the date of the latest balance sheet, in the aggregate, and for each of the five succeeding fiscal years

2. For leases with terms in excess of one year, the total minimum rentals to be received in the future under noncancelable subleases as of the latest balance sheet date

3. For all leases, rental expense in each period for which an income statement is presented, with separate disclosure of minimum rentals, contingent rentals, and sublease rentals

4. For all leases, a general description of the leasing arrangement, including the basis on which contingent rentals are determined, the existence and terms of renewal or purchase options and escalation clauses, and restrictions imposed by the lease agreements.

Exhibit 8.1
Lessee Disclosure of Capital Lease: Horn & Hardart Company

HORN & HARDART COMPANY
Notes to Financial Statements

11. Leases

The Company conducts the major part of its operations from leased facilities. Most of the leases are operating leases, with some providing for additional rents based upon percentages of sales and/or increases in real estate taxes. Seven leases are classified as capital leases and expire in 12 to 15 years. They each provide five 15-year renewal options with specified minimum rentals. The properties held under these leases were formerly owned by the Company and leased back, as described below. All such capital leases are net leases and contain options under which the Company may repurchase the properties at specified increments above the prices at which they were sold. All capital leases cover premises on which the Company has constructed and operates Burger King restaurants.

In addition, the Company leases restaurant equipment under capital leases with terms varying from five to seven years and data processing equipment under an operating lease which expires in 1982.

During 1977 and 1976, the Company sold certain properties under sale-leaseback transactions. The gains realized on these transactions of $207,000 in 1977 and $2,165,000 in 1976 were deferred and are being amortized over the initial terms of the leases as reductions of applicable expense. Rental information applicable to properties leased back is included below. The building portions of the lease payments have been capitalized under the provisions of Statement No. 13 of the Financial Accounting Standards Board. The land portions are accounted for as operating leases.

The Company has adopted the policy of retroactively capitalizing these financing leases by recording the related assets and lease obligations on the accompanying balance sheet at December 25, 1976. The asset value of capital leases is amortized over the life of the lease using the straight-line method. The effect of the change upon net income for the years ended December 31, 1977 and December 25, 1976 is not material. Since all of the capital leases were entered into in 1976 and 1977, there is no cumulative effect of this change on net income for years prior to 1976.

• • • •

Capital Leases:

Classes of Property	Asset Balances At	
	Dec. 31, 1977	Dec. 25, 1976
Store facilities	$1,997,000	$ 915,000
Equipment leases (c)	2,352,000	1,908,000
	4,349,000	2,823,000
Less accumulated amortization..............	961,000	498,000
	$3,388,000	$2,325,000

Future minimum lease payments under capital leases together with the present value of the net minimum lease payments as of December 31, 1977:

Year Ending	
1978	$ 892,000
1979	840,000
1980	658,000
1981	500,000
1982	337,000
Later years	2,559,000
Total minimum lease payments (d)	5,786,000
Less amount representing interest (e)	2,398,000
Present value of net minimum lease payments (f)	$3,388,000

• • • •

(c) Capitalized lease obligations are collateralized by leased equipment. In addition, capitalized lease obligations of $272,000 at December 31, 1977 are collateralized by notes receivable of $300,000, second mortgages of $50,000 each on two properties having a net book value of $1,478,000, and certificates of deposit of $29,000.

(d) Minimum payments have not been reduced by income from minimum sublease rentals of

(continued)

Exhibit 8.1 (continued)

$478,000 due in the future under noncancelable subleases. They also do not include contingent rentals which may become payable under certain leases on the basis of a percentage of sales in excess of stipulated amounts. There were no contingent rentals paid in 1977 or 1976.

(e) Amount necessary to reduce net minimum lease payments to present value calculated at the Company's incremental borrowing rate at the inception of the leases.

(f) Reflected in the balance sheet as current and noncurrent obligations under capital leases of $476,000 and $2,912,000 in 1977 and $320,000 and $1,778,000 in 1976.

Consolidated Balance Sheets

Assets	1977	1976
		(As restated. see Note 11)
Property (Notes 1, 2, 6, 7, 10, and 11):		
Land and land improvements	1,102	2,152
Building and building improvements	2,138	5,900
Furniture, fixtures and equipment	2,159	3,111
Assets held under capital leases	4,349	2,823
Leasehold improvements	5,980	7,577
Total—at cost	16,028	21,596
Less:		
Allowance for restaurant conversions or closings	(1,195)	(518)
Accumulated depreciation and amortization	(5,975)	(9,399)
Net property	8,858	11,649

In Exhibit 8.2, American Building Maintenance Industries disclosed aggregate minimum rentals under noncancelable leases for each of the five years after December 31, 1977 ($3,628,000 in 1978, for example), and aggregated into five year periods beyond that ($11,815,000 for 1983-1987, for example). The amount expensed for 1977 is disclosed as $5,487,000 including contingent rentals of $1,015,000. Footnote 8 begins with a general description of the leasing arrangements.

LESSOR ACCOUNTING AND REPORTING

The lease accounting and disclosure requirements applicable to lessors depend on the type lease that has been signed. Lessors should apply the classification criteria discussed earlier to determine whether the lease is capital or operating in nature and with capital leases, the specific categorization, i.e., sales type, direct financing, or leveraged. The accounting and disclosure requirements for these leases are discussed below.

Capital Leases—Sales Type

For sales-type leases, the lessor should record as a receivable the minimum rentals during the lease term plus the unguaranteed residual

Exhibit 8.2
Lessee Disclosure of Operating Lease:
American Building Maintenance Industries

Notes to Financial Statements

8. Rental Expense and Lease Commitments
The company is obligated under noncancelable leases which are principally for parking lots and garages. The leases are accounted for as operating leases and not financing leases as the terms of the leases are for less than 75 percent of the economic life of the properties and the leases do not have terms which assure the lessor a full recovery of the fair market value of the property at the inception of the lease plus a reasonable return on the use of the assets invested.

Leases entered into after December 31, 1976 have been classified as operating leases in accordance with Financial Accounting Standards Board statement number thirteen.

Rental expense for the years ended October 31, 1977 and 1976 is summarized as follows:

	1977	1976
Minimum rentals under noncancelable leases....................	$3,857,000	$4,068,000
Contingent rentals	1,015,000	856,000
Short-term rental agreements	615,000	535,000
	$5,487,000	$5,459,000

The contingent rentals are principally applicable to leases of parking lots and garages and are based on percentages of the gross receipts attributable to the related facilities.

Minimum rental commitments under noncancelable leases which expire between 1978 and 1998 are as follows:

1978	$ 3,628,000
1979	3,439,000
1980	3,099,000
1981	2,787,000
1982	2,553,000
1983–1987	11,815,000
1988–1992	6,932,000
1993–1997	1,568,000
Remainder	40,000

value accruing to the benefit of the lessor. The present value of the minimum rentals should be recorded as the sales price, while the cost or carrying value of the property (less the present value of any residual value plus any direct costs of negotiating and closing the lease) should be charged against income the same period. The difference between the receivable and the present value of that receivable should be recorded as unearned income. This unearned income should appear as a deduction from the receivable and amortized to income over the life of the lease to produce a constant rate of return.

The following disclosures are required for sales-type leases:

1. Minimum rents receivable as of the date of each balance sheet presented, with separate deductions from the total for amounts representing executory costs included in the minimum rentals and the accumulated allowance of uncollectible rentals

2. Unguaranteed residual values
3. Unearned income
4. Future minimum lease payments to be received for each of the five succeeding fiscal years
5. Contingent rentals included in income
6. A general description of the leasing arrangements.

In Exhibit 8.3, for example, Pullman Incorporated disclosed for their sales-type leases a gross lease payment receivable at December 31, 1977, or $73,520,000. Further unguaranteed residual values amounting to $8,047,000 are disclosed, as well as unearned interest of $36,931,000. The amounts to be received for each of the next five years are disclosed as well ($44,630,000 for 1978).

Capital Leases—Direct Financing

For direct financing leases, the lessor should record as a receivable the minimum rentals during the lease term plus any unguaranteed residual value accruing to the lessor. Any difference between this receivable and the cost or carrying amount of the property under lease should be recorded as unearned income and amortized to income over the life of the lease to produce a constant rate of return.

The following disclosures are required for direct financing leases:

1. Minimum rents receivable as of the date of each balance sheet presented, with separate deductions from the total for amounts representing executory costs included in minimum rentals and the accumulated allowance for uncollectible rentals
2. Unguaranteed residual values
3. Unearned income
4. Future minimum lease payment to be received for each of the five succeeding fiscal years
5. Total contingent rentals
6. Any amounts of unearned income included in income to offset initial direct costs charged against income for each period in which an income statement is presented
7. A general description of the leasing arrangements.

The disclosures for a direct financing lease are very similar to those made for a sales-type lease. In Exhibit 8.4, American Hoist & Derrick Company disclosed minimum lease payments to be received of $2,344,000 at December 31, 1977, reduced by unearned income of $447,694. Similar to the disclosures made previously, American Hoist & Derrick separated its payments due for each of the next five years and

Exhibit 8.3
Lessor Disclosure of Sales-Type Lease: Pullman Incorporated

LEASING AND FINANCING SUBSIDIARIES OF PULLMAN INCORPORATED
Notes to Financial Statements

4. Lease Information

Leasing operations consist principally of the leasing of railroad freight cars and highway truck trailers, nearly all of which are produced by Pullman. Substantially all of the railroad car leases are classified as operating leases and are generally for terms of 5 to 15 years. The truck trailer leases are for terms of 5 to 8 years and the major portion are classified as sales-type leases.

At December 31 equipment under operating leases consists of:

	1977	1976
	(Thousands of dollars)	
Railroad cars	$325,856	$311,148
Highway truck trailers	10,026	8,740
	335,882	319,888
Less accumulated depreciation	(85,214)	(70,665)
Leased equipment—net	$250,668	$249,223

Rentals under noncancelable operating leases subsequent to December 31, 1977 total $167,180,000 and during the next five years are as follows (thousands of dollars):

1978	$44,630	1981	$20,632
1979	35,831	1982	12,006
1980	27,493		

At December 31 the net investment in sales-type leases with unrelated parties entered into by Pullman and acquired by leasing and financing subsidiaries consists of:

	1977	1976
	(Thousands of dollars)	
Lease payments receivable	$73,620	$62,831
Estimated residual value	8,047	5,737
Less: Unearned finance charges	(36,931)	(32,677)
Unamortized discount from Pullman	(1,607)	(744)
Net investment in leases with unrelated parties	$43,129	$35,147

At December 31, 1977 the maturity schedule for the next five years of lease payments receivable for sales-type leases with unrelated parties is (thousands of dollars):

1978	$8,337	1981	$6,600
1979	7,719	1982	5,905
1980	7,100		

At December 31 the net investment in direct financing leases with Pullman relating to equipment purchased from and leased back to Pullman consists of:

	1977	1976
	(Thousands of dollars)	
Lease payments receivable	$ 29,048	$ 17,075
Estimated residual value	4,685	2,005
Less unearned finance charges	(11,687)	(5,528)
Net investment in leases with Pullman	$22,046	$13,552

(continued)

Exhibit 8.3 (continued)

At December 31, 1977, the maturity schedule for the next five years of lease payments receivable for financing leases with Pullman is (thousands of dollars):

1978	$4,939	1981	$4,038
1979	4,677	1982	3,515
1980	4,386		

Combined Balance Sheet

	December 31	
	1977	1976
	(Thousands of dollars)	(As restated)
Assets		
Leased equipment—net...............................	$250,668	$249,223
Installment contracts receivable—net.....................	155,401	134,096
Net investment in leases:		
With unrelated parties...............................	43,129	35,147
With Pullman..	22,046	13,552

began the footnote with a general description of the leasing arrangements.

Capital Leases—Leveraged Leases

A unique form of financing productive assets known as "leverage leasing" is increasingly being utilized in the business community. Its increasing use reflects the significant advantages to lessors in leveraged leasing:

1. A majority of the funds used to purchase the property subject to lease are supplied by a third-party creditor.
2. The loan from the creditor is nonrecourse to the general credit of the lessor.
3. During early years of the lease term, depreciation and interest deductions should exceed annual lease income, thereby providing excess deductions to be applied against other income.
4. The lessor receives the benefit of the investment tax credit.
5. The leased asset reverts back to the lessor at the end of the lease term.
6. No liability to the creditor is recorded in the liability section of the balance sheet to the lessor, thus enabling a better debt-to-equity ratio.

While this list of advantages may not be all inclusive, it does indicate why leveraged leasing is growing in popularity among lessors.

A lease agreement is classified as a leveraged lease when the lessor elects to deter recognition of any investment tax credit and allocate the

Exhibit 8.4
Lessor Disclosure of Direct Financing Lease:
American Hoist & Derrick Company

MACHINERY INVESTMENT CORPORATION SUBSIDIARY OF
AMERICAN HOIST & DERRICK COMPANY
Notes to Financial Statements

7. Leases:
   The companies lease various equipment generally manufactured by and purchased from the Parent Company. At November 30, 1977, the companies had approximately 45 leases of which 34 were accounted for as operating leases and 11 as direct financing leases. The equipment is generally leased for periods ranging from a few months to seven years with all executory costs paid by the lessee.
   The following presents the net investment in direct financing leases at November 30:

	1977	1976
Total minimum lease payments to be received...................	$2,344,000	$1,498,000
Less unearned income..	447,694	170,201
Net investment	$1,896,306	$1,327,799

The following is a schedule of minimum future rentals to be received under direct financing and operating leases in effect at November 30, 1977, for the periods ending November 30:

	Direct finance leases	Operating leases
1978...........	$ 646,000	$439,000
1979...........	532,000	
1980...........	447,000	
1981...........	288,000	
1982...........	219,000	
1983...........	137,000	
1984...........	75,000	
Total	$2,344,000	$439,000

credit to income over the lease term and when the following conditions are evident in the lease agreement:

1. The lease agreement contains criteria that indicate a direct financing lease has been negotiated. Sales-type leases cannot constitute leveraged leases in that no manufacturer of dealer profit may be recognized.
2. The lease agreement involves at least three parties: a lessee, a lessor, and a long-term creditor.
3. The financing provided by the long-term creditor must be nonrecourse to the general credit of the lessor (although the creditor may have recourse to the lease property and related rental payments). The financing should be sufficient to provide the lessor with "substantial leverage" in the transaction.
4. The lessor's net investment in the lease declines during early years of the lease once the investment has been completed and rises during later years of the lease. This investment pattern may occur more than once.

The "investment with separate phases" method should be used in determining positive and negative net investment periods (separate phases). Income then will be recognized at a constant rate of return on the net investment only in the periods in which the net investment is positive, thereby associating lease income with the unrecovered balance of the earning asset.

Lessor recovery of the net investment in the early years of the lease term is due to the inclusion in lease income of cash flows from the tax benefits of the investment tax credit, accelerated depreciation, and interest deductions. As a result of this cash flow stream, the net investment balance usually is negative during the middle years of the lease term and the lessor has temporary use of funds for reinvestment. It should be emphasized that earnings on these reinvested funds (secondary earnings) are considered separate from leveraged lease income and are reported in income only when realized.

In later years of the lease term, the cash flows are influenced by net tax liabilities; the investment tax credit will have been utilized and the tax benefits from depreciation and interest deductions diminish. In these years, the lessor has a net cash outflow since his tax obligations exceed any excess of rental receipts over debt interest and principal payments to the third-party creditor.

The lessor should record his investment in a leveraged lease, not the nonrecourse debt. The net of the following account balances represents the lessor's initial and continuing investment in a leveraged lease:

1. Rents receivable, less principal and interest applicable to the nonrecourse debt
2. A receivable for the amount of the investment tax credit to be realized
3. The estimated residual value of the leased property
4. Unearned and deferred income consisting of the estimated pre-tax lease income (or loss), after deducting initial direct costs, remaining to be allocated to income over the lease term plus any investment tax credit remaining to be allocated to income over the lease term.

The net income to be recognized under a leveraged lease is composed of three elements: (1) pre-tax lease income (or loss) allocated in proportionate amounts from unearned and deferred income, (2) investment tax credit allocated in proportionate amounts from unearned and deferred income, and (3) the related tax effect of any pre-tax lease income (or loss) recognized, which should be reflected in current period tax expense. In lease arrangements where projected net cash receipts are less than the lessor's initial investment, a loss for the difference should be recognized immediately at the inception of the lease.

Exhibit 8.5
Lessor Disclosure of Leveraged Lease: UGI Corporation

UGI CORPORATION
Notes to Financial Statements

1. Significant Accounting Policies
                            • • • •

Lease Accounting
The leveraged lease transactions are accounted for by recording as the net investment in each lease the aggregate of rentals receivable (net of principal and interest on the non-recourse loans) and estimated residual value of the equipment less the unearned income (including the investment tax credits). The unearned income from the lease transactions is recognized during the periods in which the net investment is positive.

7. Investment in Leveraged Leases:
A subsidiary of UGI is a lessor, either solely or in participation with others, of certain equipment under long term leveraged lease agreements with various parties. The Company did not enter into any new lease agreements during 1977. During 1976, the subsidiary's share of the cost of this equipment under new lease agreements ($35,024) was financed with equity investments by the subsidiary ($10,223) and non-recourse loans from other sources ($24,801). The loans are secured by first liens on the equipment which consists principally of commercial aircraft.

At the end of the lease terms the equipment is returned to the lessors. For income tax purposes, the subsidiary receives the investment tax credit, if any, and has the benefit of tax deductions for depreciation based on its proportionate ownership of the leased equipment. Also, the subsidiary may deduct the interest on the non-recourse debt for income tax purposes. Since, during the early years of a particular lease, the aforementioned deductions exceed the lease rental income substantial excess deductions are available to offset other taxable income of UGI and its subsidiaries. In the later years of a lease, rental income will exceed the deductions for income tax purposes and income taxes will be payable on the excess income generated by the particular lease. Deferred income taxes are provided to reflect these timing differences.

The investment in leveraged leases at December 31, 1977 and 1976 consists of the following:

	1977	1976
Rentals receivable (net of principal and interest on the non-recourse debt)	$14,337	$14,361
Estimated residual value of leased equipment	4,280	4,280
Less: unearned and deferred income	(3,701)	(5,150)
Investment in leveraged leases	14,916	13,491
Less: accumulated deferred income taxes arising from leveraged leases	(12,110)	(5,632)
Net investment in leveraged leases	$ 2,806	$ 7,859

Income recognized from the leveraged leases for financial reporting purposes during 1977 and 1976 was comprised of the following:

	1977	1976
Income (loss) before income taxes included in other income, net)	$1,145	$(244)
Income tax (provisions) benefits	(526)	182
	619	(62)
Investment tax credit recognized	295	815
Net income from leveraged leases	$ 914	$753

The accounting requirements applicable to leveraged leasing include disclosure standards peculiar to these agreements, as follow

1. In the balance sheet, deferred income taxes should not be netted against the investment in leveraged leases.

2. In the income statement, or related footnotes, net income from leveraged leases and its components are to be classified or separately disclosed as pre-tax income, investment tax credit recognized, and tax effects of pre-tax lease income.

3. When leveraged leasing is material to the lessor in terms of revenue, net income, or assets, the components of the net investment balance should be disclosed in the footnotes.

Exhibit 8.5 provides illustrative disclosures applicable to leveraged leases for UGI Corporation. As an example, in 1977, UGI recognized pre-tax income of $1,145,000, investment tax credit of $195,000, and tax expense of $526,000 on its leveraged leases. Additionally, their accounting policies applicable to leveraged leases are disclosed.

Operating Leases

For operating leases, the cost or carrying amount of the property under lease should be included in the property, plant, and equipment section of the lessor's balance sheet and should be depreciated or amortized in the normal manner. Rental receipts should be reported as income over the lease term on a straight-line basis unless another "systematic and rational" basis is more indicative of the leased property's finishing value.

For operating leases, the following financial statement disclosures should be made by the lessor:

1. As of the latest balance sheet date, the cost of the property held for leasing by major category of property less any related accumulated depreciation

2. Minimum future rentals on noncancelable leases as of the latest balance sheet presented, in the aggregate and for each of the five succeeding fiscal years

3. Total contingent rentals included in income for each period in which an income statement is presented

4. A general description of the leasing arrangements.

ACCOUNTING FOR SUBLEASES

Paragraphs 35 through 40 of SFAS No. 13 constitute the conclusions of the FASB concerning accounting and reporting for subleases and similar transactions. The following types of leasing transactions represent subleases:

1. The property subject to lease is re-leased by the original lessee and the lease agreement between the original lessor and the original lessee remains in effect.
2. A new lease is substituted under the original lease agreement. The ultimate lessee becomes the primary obligor under the agreement and the original lessee may or may not be secondarily liable.
3. A new lessee is substituted through a new agreement and the original lease agreement is canceled.

Accounting by the Original Lessor

In many sublease arrangements, the original lessor is unaffected by the agreement between the sublessor and ultimate lessee. When the sublessor enters into a sublease or if the original lease agreement is sold or transferred by the original lessee to a third party, the original lessor should not alter his accounting for the original lease.

However, if the original lease is replaced by a new agreement with a new lessee, the original lessor should account for the termination of the original lease and should classify and account for the new lease as a separate agreement. The lease termination should be accounted for by removing the net investment in the lease from the accounts, recording the leased asset at the lower of its original cost, present fair value, or present carrying amount, and the net adjustment should be charged to income of the period.

Accounting by the Original Lessee (Sublessor)

The major accounting and reporting problems of subleases relate to the original lessee. These problems concern the fact that an original lessee must address both lessee and lessor accounting issues.

When a new lease agreement is constructed such that the original lessee no longer is the primary obligor under the original lease, accounting for the termination of the original lease depends on the classification of the original lease. If the original lease was a capital lease, the asset and obligation related to that lease should be negated and any gain or loss should be recognized immediately in income. If the original lessee is secondarily liable under the new agreement, the loss contingency should be treated in accordance with SFAS No. 5, "Accounting for Contingencies." Any consideration paid or received upon termination of the original lease should be included in the determination of gain or loss to be recognized. If the original lease was an operating lease and the original lessee is secondarily liable under the new lease, the loss contingency should again be treated in accordance with SFAS No. 5.

When a new lease is agreed upon such that the original lessee is not relieved of the primary obligation under the original lease, original lessee accounting and reporting once again are dependent on how the original lease was classified. If the original lease contained a transfer of title or a bargain purchase option clause, the original lessee should classify the sublease agreement based upon all the criteria applicable to lessors in paragraphs 7 and 8 of SFAS No. 13. Notice that the original lessee as sublessor must now also meet the predictability tests in paragraph 8 of SFAS No. 13 above and beyond the lessee criteria initially applied to determine classification of the original lease. If the new lease meets the capitalization tests for lessors, the sublessor should classify the new lease as a sales-type or direct financing lease contingent on whether any manufacturer or dealer profit is evident. The unamortized balance of the leased asset under the original lease should be treated as the cost of property subject to the sublease. If the sublease does not qualify as a capital lease to the sublessor, the new lease should be considered an operating lease. In either case, the sublessor should continue to account for the obligation under the original lease as if the sublease had not transpired.

If the original lease met either the 75 or the 90 percent test of SFAS No. 13 but did not contain a transfer of title or a bargain purchase option, the sublessor should, with one exception, classify the new lease in accordance with the 75 percent and the lessor predictability tests only. If these tests are met, the sublease should be classified as a direct financing lease. This requirement precludes the use of the 90 percent test in classifying a sublease of this nature and also seemingly precludes the recognition of any manufacturer or dealer profit. In any event, the unamortized cost of the leased property to the sublessor should be treated as the cost of property subject to the sublease. If the sublease does not meet the capitalization requirements imposed for subleases, the new lease should be accounted for as an operating lease. In the case of either a capital lease or an operating lease, the sublessor should continue to account for the obligation under the original lease as before.

The exception to this general rule arises when the timing and other circumstances surrounding the sublease indicate that the new lease was intended as an integral part of an overall lease arrangement where the sublessor serves only as an intermediary. For these leasing transactions, the sublease should be classified according to the criteria relating to the 75 and 90 percent and the lessor predictability tests. In applying the 90 percent test, the fair value of the leased property should be the fair value of the property to the original lessor at the inception of the original lease.

If the original lease was considered an operating lease, the sublessor

Exhibit 8.6
Sublease Disclosure: Dow Chemical Company

H. LEASED PROPERTIES

Capital leases included with owned property in the balance sheet were:

	December 31	
	1979	1978
	(In thousands)	
Land	$ 522	
Land and waterway improvements	149	
Buildings	1,392	$ 250
Machinery and equipment	165,403	176,997
Office furniture and equipment	8,051	13,112
Total	175,517	190,359
Less — Accumulated depreciation	103,371	99,661
Net	$ 72,146	$ 90,698

Minimum lease commitments at December 31, 1979 were as follows:

	Capital Leases	Operating Leases
	(In thousands)	
1980	$ 24,992	$ 43,165
1981	20,586	32,575
1982	14,458	27,953
1983	11,536	24,372
1984	10,925	21,831
1985 and thereafter	100,036	141,352
Total minimum lease payments	182,533	$291,248
Less Estimated executory costs	446	
Net minimum lease payments	182,087	
Less — Amounts estimated to represent interest	70,281	
Present value of net minimum lease obligations ..	111,806	
Less — Current accounts payable	16,180	
Long-term capital lease obligations	$ 95,626	

Minimum operating lease commitments have not been reduced by minimum sublease rentals of $3.5 million due in the future under noncancelable subleases.

Rental payments under operating leases charged to expense were:

	1979	1978
	(In thousands)	
Minimum rentals	$ 92,060	$ 86,886
Contingent rentals	7,652	1,339
Less — Sublease rentals	(2,470)	(1,610)
Net	$ 97,242	$ 86,615

should account for the original lease and the sublease as an operating lease. The FASB in essence precludes the sublessor from transferring more property rights than indicated in the original lease.

To supplement the other lessee disclosures, when sublease rental receipts are significant, they should be separately shown for the five succeeding years and in the aggregate. This disclosure is illustrated in Exhibit 8.6 for Dow Chemical Company.

REAL ESTATE LEASES

Real estate leases may involve properties such as land, building, parts of buildings, and equipment included in a real estate lease package.

Leases Involving Land Only

If a lease agreement is applicable to land only, the lease should be considered a capital lease to the real estate lessee only if the lease transfers title to the lessee during the lease term or if the lease agreement contains a bargain purchase option (the 75 and 90 percent tests are not applicable to land leases from either the lessee's or lessor's perspective). If the lease contains either of these provisions, the real estate lessee should capitalize an asset and related obligation in the amount of the present value of the minimum lease payments to be made during the lease term. If the lease agreement contains neither a title transfer nor a bargain purchase option, the lessee accounts for the transaction as an operating lease and therefore charges rental payments against income as they are incurred.

Lessors should apply the same classification criteria to land lease agreements as lessees, but, in addition, before a lessor concludes that a lease agreement is a capital lease, the rent collectibility and cost uncertainty tests also must be met. Under capital leases related to land, the lessor should write off the property and substitute a receivable.

Leases Involving Land and Building

Land and building agreements that contain title transfer or bargain purchase option provisions must be accounted for by the lessee as capital leases. The land and building elements of the lease should be accounted for separately based on their relative fair values at the inception of the lease. Because both the land and the building are presumed to be owned by the lessee by the end of the lease term, the properties must be segregated so that the building may be depreciated and the land may be maintained at undepreciated cost. Since ownership of the building is presumed to transfer to the lessee, either through title transfer or bargain purchase option exercise, the building should be depreciated over its estimated economic life without regard to length of the lease term.

If the lease agreement contains neither a title transfer nor a bargain purchase option provision, the relative significance of the land element to the total value of the lease package must be assessed. The FASB has defined the materiality threshold in these situations to be 25 percent. When the fair value of the land is less than 25 percent of the aggregate fair value of the leased properties, the land element is presumed immaterial. Conversely, if the land element comprises 25 percent or more of the aggregate fair value of the leased properties, the land is presumed material. The FASB utilizes this materiality standard in operationalizing the requirements of SFAS No. 13.

Where the land portion of the lease is deemed immaterial and the lease term is 75 percent or more of the estimated economic life of the building or the present value of the minimum lease payments equals or exceeds 90 percent of the excess fair value of the leased property over any investment tax credit retained and expected to be realized by the lessor, the lease agreement is a capital lease and should be accounted for as a single lease unit. In these cases, the lessee in essence has the privilege of depreciating the cost of the land along with the cost of the building. While this approach lacks theoretical merit, it may be defended on grounds that the land element in the lease package is deemed immaterial. The cost of these properties should be amortized over the lease term since the overall estimated life of the property is not relevant to a lessee who does not gain ultimate title to leased properties.

In land and building agreements where the land portion is considered material, in applying the 75 and 90 percent tests, the land and building should be considered separately and the land element always should be considered an operating lease. If the building element meets either of these capitalization tests, the present value of the minimum lease payment associated with the building should be recorded as the initial value of the building to be depreciated over the lease term by the lessee. Otherwise, both the land and building constitute operating leases to the lessee.

Leases Involving Equipment and Real Estate

When a lease agreement involves real estate as well as equipment or machinery, the equipment element in the lease package should be considered separately by both the lessee and the lessor. If any one of the lessee capitalization tests is met, the lessee should consider the equipment portion of the lease package to be a capital lease regardless of whether the remaining properties meet the criteria. Similarly, the lessor should consider the equipment element a capital lease if any one of the four capitalization tests is met and the lessor predictability tests are met. All other equipment leases are operating leases. In essence, the FASB has concluded that the inclusion of equipment in a real estate lease package should not alter the accounting process specified for real estate transactions. Therefore, non-real estate properties are considered as if a separate lease document specified the agreements between the lessee and the lessor related to the equipment.

Leases Involving Only Part of a Building

It is commonplace to find lease agreements covering only part of a large facility, e.g., shopping mall locations. From the perspective of the lessee, if the fair value fo the leased space is objectively determinable, the classification and accounting provisions applicable to land and building leases should be followed. FASBIN No. 24, entitled "Leases Involving Only Part of a Building," specifies that for purposes of determining the fair market value of part of a building, reasonable estimates based upon objective independent appraisals or estimated replacement cost information may be utilized. This interpretation should allow more lease agreements to be considered capital leases, since the 90 percent test should be met more often. However, if the fair value of the leased property is not objectively determinable, but the lease agreement meets the 75 percent criterion, the lessee should capitalize the lease agreement using the estimated economic life of the building in which the leased property is located. If neither the 90 nor the 75 percent test is met, the lease agreement should be considered an operating lease.

From the perspective of the lessor, both the cost and the fair value of the leased property must be objectively determined before the land and building lease provisions are applicable since both these amounts must be utilized in lessor classification. FASBIN No. 24 is equally applicable to lessors in determining fair value. If the cost or fair value of the leased property is not objectively determinable, the lease agreement should be considered an operating lease.

Profit Recognition of Sales-Type Leases of Real Estate

SFAS No. 13 provides "predictability" criteria in paragraph 8 that require lessors to assess both collectibility of lease receivables and predictability of future costs prior to classifying a lease as a sales-type lease. But this statement provides little operational guidance in determining whether a lease receivable is, in fact, collectible. This problem is compounded by the fact that there exists a conflict in SFAS No. 13 as relates to SFAS No. 66 entitled *Accounting for Profit Recognition on Sales of Real Estate*.

SFAS No. 26, "Profit Recognition on Sales-Type Leases of Real Estate," provides that unless it meets the requirements of the aforementioned accounting guide for full and immediate recognition of profit, a lease should be accounted for as an operating lease.

For leases involving real estate, lessors and lessees should make the disclosures applicable to capital and operating leases as before. Howev-

Exhibit 8.7
Real Estate Lease Disclosure: Champion International Corporation

Note 5. Property, Plant, and Equipment:

Property, plant, and equipment is summarized by major classifications as follows:

December 31 (in thousands of dollars)	1981			1980		
	Total	Owned	Leased	Total	Owned	Leased
Land and land improvements	$ 105,681	$ 93,954	$ 11,727	$ 96,352	$ 86,049	$ 10,303
Buildings.............	501,764	449,683	52,081	517,910	465,158	52,752
Machinery and equipment......	2,175,073	1,884,678	290,395	2,073,988	1,781,927	292,061
Construction in progress......	190,701	190,701	–	95,676	94,955	721
	2,973,219	2,619,016	354,203	2,783,926	2,428,089	355,837
Less– Accumulated depreciation....	1,119,070	982,901	136,169	1,024,973	903,473	121,500
	$1,854,149	$1,636,115	$218,034	$1,758,953	$1,524,616	$234,337

Interest capitalized during 1981, 1980, and 1979 was $15,102,000, $18,987,000, and $24,289,000, respectively.

Note 9. Commitments:

At December 31, 1981, future minimum lease payments for all capitalized leases and non-cancellable operating leases (net of sublease income) are:

Period (in thousands of dollars)	Capitalized Leases	Non-Cancellable Operating Leases
1982..	$ 17,822	$12,848
1983..	20,296	10,528
1984..	21,332	7,550
1985..	21,391	4,903
1986..	22,233	3,489
Thereafter	350,772	6,104
Total Payments	453,846	$45,422
Less: Amount representing interest...............................	225,618	
Present value of capitalized lease payments ($3,698 current; $224,530 long-term)	$228,228	

Payments under non-cancellable and cancellable operating leases that were charged to rental expense in 1981, 1980, and 1979 were $26,444,000, $28,129,000, and $25,924,000, respectively.

The company has options, expiring in 1982, to acquire additional acreage of timberlands in Michigan and Wisconsin. If these options are exercised, the company will have to pay an additional $14,756,000.

Exhibit 8.8
Real Estate Lease Disclosure: Scovill Inc.

I. Leases The Company leases certain equipment and facilities for various periods up to 2008 and it is expected in the normal course of operations that the leases will be extended or replaced. Certain leases provide for contingent rentals based on additional usage of equipment and vehicles in excess of a specified minimum. Leases for real estate generally include options to renew for periods ranging from 1 to 40 years. Assets subleased are minor in amount.

Capitalized leases on continuing operations are as follows:

	1981	1980
Buildings and land	$19,804,000	$19,804,000
Equipment	7,973,000	8,572,000
Less allowances for amortization	(14,611,000)	(14,724,000)
	$13,166,000	$13,652,000

Lease amortization is included in depreciation expense.

Future minimum payments under capital leases and non-cancelable operating leases of continuing operations at December 27, 1981 are:

	Capital Leases	Operating Leases
1982	$ 3,672,000	$ 3,031,000
1983	3,328,000	2,142,000
1984	2,978,000	1,537,000
1985	1,693,000	1,169,000
1986	1,155,000	1,037,000
Thereafter	6,208,000	1,731,000
Total minimum lease payments	19,034,000	$10,647,000
Less amounts representing interest	(5,412,000)	
Present value of net minimum lease payments	$13,622,000	

Rental expense for all non-capitalized leases of continuing operations was $5,827,000 in 1981 (1980–$5,616,000; 1979–$5,553,000).

er, in the event that real estate is significant, these amounts should be segregated out. Exhibits 8.7 and 8.8 illustrate these disclosures for Champion International Corporation and Scovill Inc., respectively. Note especially in the exhibits that the disclosures indicate payments attributable to the real estate versus those applicable to the equipment.

ACCOUNTING FOR SALES WITH LEASEBACKS

SFAS No. 13 generally required treatment of a sale-leaseback as a single financing transaction in which any profit or loss on the sale was deferred and amortized by the seller/lessee. But operationlaizing this provision when the leaseback covers only a relatively small part of the property sold or when the leaseback is only for a short period of time has proven difficult. In some cases, the profit on the sale might exceed the total rentals under the leaseback, resulting in a negative rental if the provisions of SFAS No. 13 were followed. As a consequence, the FASB revised the accounting requirements applicable to sale-leasebacks with the issuance of SFAS No. 28, entitled "Accounting for Sales with Leasebacks."

Since a sale-leaseback involves both a sale of the property and a lease of the property, the seller/lessee must disclose the profit recognized and the substance of the lease provisions.

9
Pension Disclosures

Accounting by employers for the costs associated with pension plans has long been governed by the provisions of APBO No. 8, "Accounting for the Cost of Pension Plans." The APB took an income statement approach in reaching its conclusions in that APBO No. 8 provides guidance in determining the amount of the annual pension cost that should be expensed and the balance sheet amount is merely a residual account so that the entry will balance.

The enactment in 1974 of the Employee Retirement Income Security Act (ERISA) as well as the creation and reporting requirements of the Pension Benefit Guarantee Corporation (PBGC) significantly altered the environment for vesting and funding of pension plans. As a consequence, it has been argued that the accounting rules promulgated in APBO No. 8 do not adequately reflect the costs associated with pension plans in today's environment. Because of this perception, the FASB added the project to its agenda in 1976. After spending a significant period of time in deliberating the issues involved, the FASB promulgated its conclusions on the topic in December 1985 with the issuance of SFAS No. 87, "Employers' Accounting for Pensions," and No. 88, "Employers' Accounting for Settlements and Curtailments of Defined Benefit Pension Plans and for Termination Benefits." These documents represent a major milestone in the decade old FASB pension project and will provide financial statement users with increased information about enterprises' pension costs and liabilities. This additional information takes the form of (1) enhanced footnote disclosures of pension data and (2) the balance sheet recognition of at least a portion of organizations' unfunded pension liabilities.

In March 1980, the FASB issued SFAS No. 35, "Accounting and Reporting by Defined Benefit Plans." In this statement, the FASB concluded that the benefit plan itself should provide financial information that is useful in assessing the plan's present and future ability to pay benefits when due. This was deemed necessary because employees render service long before they receive the benefits to which they are entitled as a result of that service, and they are concerned with whether the plan will be able to pay their future benefits. The FASB determined specific guidelines as to what should be included in the financial statements of a defined benefit plan.

The FASB then issued SFAS No. 36, "Disclosure of Pension Information," in May 1980. In this document, the FASB discussed the need for comparability in financial statements of employers and statements of defined benefit plans. The disclosures for reporting pension plans in APBO No. 8 were revised in SFAS No. 36. The specific information of the official pronouncements above will be discussed in detail in this chapter.

ACCOUNTING FOR THE COST OF PENSION PLANS PER APBO NO. 8

To understand the requirements and mechanics of SFAS No. 87, it is first necessary to define some of the terms frequently referred to in the opinion. These definitions are located in Appendix B of APBO No. 8.

Actuarial assumptions: Factors that actuaries use in tentatively resolving uncertainties concerning future events affecting pension cost, e.g., expected mortality rate, employee turnover, compensation levels, investment earnings, etc.

Actuarial cost method: A particular technique used by actuaries for establishing the amount and incidence of the annual actuarial cost of pension plan benefits, or benefits and expenses, and the related actuarial liability

Normal cost: The annual cost assigned under the actuarial cost method in use, to years subsequent to the inception of a pension plan or to a particular valuation date

Vested benefits: Benefits that are not contingent on the employees continuing in the service of the employer.

While the provisions of SFAS No. 87 represent a major improvement in the reporting requirements applicable to pension plans, as will be seen, the wide diversity that can still result under the provisions of SFAS No. 87 have led the FASB to increase the footnote disclosures as an attempt to aid comparability among reporting entities.

The major changes from current accounting and reporting rules involve accounting for single-employer defined benefit pension plans. Further, additional disclosures would be called for by emolyers who participate in a multiemployer plan or who sponsor a defined contribution plan.

While there are significant changes from current accounting and reporting practices required by SFAS No. 87, the document does propose the retention of three fundamental aspects of present pension accounting: delaying recognition of certain events, reporting net cost, and offsetting liabilities and assets.

Within the three major areas of commonality with current practice discussed above, SFAS No. 87 does create three major changes that significantly affect current reporting practices. These are:

1. The provisions of SFAS No. 87 require a standardized method of measuring net periodic pension cost that is intended to improve comparability and understandability by recognizing the compensation cost of an employee's pension over that employee's approximate service period and by relating that cost more directly to the terms of the plan.

2. SFAS No. 87 requires that the reporting enterprise immediately recognize a liability (the minimum liability) in certain circumstances when the accumulated benefit obligation exceeds the fair value of the plan assets. SFAS No. 87 continues to delay recognition of the related charge to net periodic pension cost.

3. SFAS No. 87 requires expanded disclosures intended to provide more complete and more current information than can be practically incorporated in financial statements at the present time.

In specifying the accounting treatment accorded to pension plans, the FASB segregates pension plans into three basic types: (1) defined contribution plans, (2) multiemployer plans, and (3) single-employer defined benefit plans. In accounting for the plans, SFAS No. 87 requires that employers identify the types of plans in existence. To the extent that an employer sponsors different types of plans, it must account for the plans separately.

A defined contribution plan is one that provides pension benefits such that an individual account is established for each participant and the plan specifies the manner of determining the periodic contribution to the plan. As such, defined contribution plans are structured so that the employees can determine how much is contributed to the plan on their behalf rather than how much they can expect to receive at retirement. A typical defined contribution plan is structured such that the employer contributes a set percentage of the employees' salary to the plan annually (e.g., a contribution of 7% of salary annually). The plan may or may not be contributory (i.e., the employee also makes contributions to the plan).

A multiemployer plan is one in which two or more unrelated employers contribute to a plan, typically under the provisions of a collective-bargaining agreement. In these situations, the assets contributed by one employer may be used to pay benefits to employees of another company. The plan is administered by a trustee (or board of trustees) who is beyond the direct control of the employers. For example, a national labor union may have a pension plan for its employees funded by the companies that hire union employees (e.g., a pension plan for United Auto Workers members is funded by payments made by Ford, Chrysler, and General Motors, and Ford employees can receive retirement benefits from funds contributed by General Motors).

A single-employer defined benefit plan is one where the plan defines the amount an employee will receive upon retirement (e.g., 2% per year of service applied to the average of the last two years' income). In these plans, the amount of contribution should be actuarially computed in a manner that allows the plan to have sufficient assets to fund the retirement benefits as they come due.

In determining the net periodic pension cost in accordance with the provisions of SFAS No. 87, the reporting entity should account for its defined benefit plans separately. Thus, while the FASB allows the use of netting in accounting for an individual defined benefit plan, net pension liabilities of one plan may *not* be offset against net pension assets of another defined benefit plan sponsored by the same employer. The net pension cost of the reporting period is composed of the confluence of several elements:

1. Service cost
2. Interest cost
3. Actual return on plan assets
4. Amortization of unrecognized prior service cost
5. Amortization of gain or loss
6. Amortization of the unrecognized net obligation or asset existing at the date of initial application of SFAS No. 87.

The service cost component (or normal cost)—which is the cost attributed under the actuarial method to employee efforts performed in the current period—is included in the net pension cost in the period of service. This requirement is consistent with the principle of matching in that the sponsor receives the benefit of the employees' labor efforts in the current period and the pension costs attributable to those efforts are properly matched against income of the current period. The FASB requires that the company determine the service cost attributable to the current period by applying the actuarial method which is specified or implied in the pension agreement. The FASB argues that the actuarial method can significantly affect the computations. Therefore, in an effort to increase comparability among reporting entities, it has restricted the use of different actuarial methods such that it is only appropriate if the plan specifies or implies a different method.

Exhibit 9.1
Illustration of Pension Cost Relationships

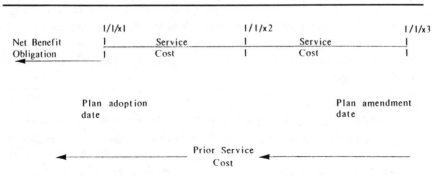

The interest cost component is, in reality, a financial item rather than a cost of employee compensation. The provisions of SFAS No. 87 require that the projected benefit obligation—actuarial present value of all benefits attributed to prior service including assumptions about future increases in salary levels, service periods, etc.—be computed at each balance sheet date. The projected benefit obligation will increase during the year partly because interest accrues on that obligation. The interest cost is computed by applying the assumed discount rate for the projected benefit obligation to the amount of projected benefit obligation at the beginning of the period.

To the extent that some or all of the plan is funded, the assets held by the plan should generate a return in the current period. The return is computed as the fair value of the plan assets at the end of the period minus the fair value of the plan assets at the beginning of the period plus the benefits paid during the period minus the contributions of the period. The fair value of the plan assets is computed based upon the selling price of investment assets in an unforced liquidation and the cost less accumulated depreciation for assets used in the operation of the plan (e.g., building and equipment). While the actual return on plan assets is computed as part of the net pension cost of the period, a portion of the gain or loss is deferred and amortized in subsequent periods. The expected return, like the interest cost component computed above, is a financial item and results from applying the expected return on plan assets to the beginning market-related value of the plan assets.

SFAS No. 87 treats increases or decreases in prior service costs that arise from plan amendments in a similar fashion to their treatment under APBO No. 8 in that they are amortized over future periods. Unlike APBO No. 8, however, SFAS No. 87 requires that these costs be amortized and specifies the amortization rate for this process. If most of the plan's participants are active, the unrecognized prior service cost must be amortized by assigning equal amounts to each expected future service period of the active employee group. This is computed on the basis of the closed group (i.e., no provisions are made for employees who join the group after the amendment date). Amortization is required only if the two amounts exceed a "corridor" amount. The corridor amount is 10% of the greater of the projected benefit obligation or fair value of plan assets. (This amount will usually be based on the projected benefit obligation.) Only if the amount exceeds the corridor is there any amortization of the gain or loss.

SFAS No. 87 requires that when a sponsor first adopts its provisions the projected benefit obligation and fair value of plan assets as of the beginning of that reporting period must be computed to provide a starting point. A net obligation exists if the projected benefit obligation exceeds the fair value of the assets while a net asset exists if the opposite is true. The net obligation or asset is required to be amortized straight-line over the average remaining service period of employees expected to receive benefits unless the expected service period is less than 15 years or most or all of the participants are inactive. If the average service period is less than 15 years, the 15 year period may be (but is not required to be) used to amortize the net obligation or asset. If most of the employees are inactive, their average life expectancy should be used in amortizing the net obligation or asset.

In addition to the computation of the net pension cost of the period, SFAS No. 87 requires that an additional minimum liability be recorded by the company if the *accumulated* benefit obligation exceeds the fair value of the plan assets at year end. The accumulated benefit obligation is an actuarial computation of the value of pension benefits attributed to periods worked *without* considering future salary increases or future service assumptions. Thus, this amount will be less than the projected benefit obligation. However, the FASB argues that when the accumulated benefit obligation exceeds the fair value of the plan assets, the sponsor has a minimum liability equal to that deficit. As such, the sponsor must accrue an amount necessary to result in a net liability equal to the excess of the accumulated benefits over the fair value of plan assets by recording the minimum liability and an intangible asset.

ACCOUNTING AND REPORTING BY DEFINED BENEFIT PENSION PLANS

In paragraph 16 of APBO No. 8, the APB determined that a company may limit its legal obligations by specifying that pensions shall by payable only to the extent of the assets in the pension fund. Such information concerning the assets in the pension plan would be beneficial to the employees in assessing the present and future ability of the plan to pay benefits when due. However, there were no promulgated standards for the accounting and reporting of annual financial statements of a defined benefit pension plan. After careful consideration, the FASB issued SFAS No. 35, "Accounting and Reporting by Defined Benefit Plans," in March 1980. SFAS No. 35 became effective for plan years after December 15, 1980, but earlier application was encouraged. However, SFAS No. 75, "Deferral of the Effective Date of Certain Accounting Requirements for Pension Plan of State and Local Government Units," indefinitely deferred the effective date of SFAS No. 35 for plans sponsored by state and local governments.

A defined benefit plan is a pension plan stating the benefits to be received by employees after retirement or the method of determining such benefits. The employer's contributions under such a plan are determined actuarially on the basis of the benefits expected to become payable. Since a defined benefit plan is for the employees' future benefit, the FASB concluded that the financial statements of such plans should provide useful information about the present and future benefits due to such employees and about the pension fund's ability to provide such benefits. It also determined that the contents of the financial statements of a defined benefit plan should focus on the participants. However, the statements also will be useful to others who have a direct or indirect interest in the pension plan, i.e., those who advise plan participants and creditors/investors of the employer.

SFAS No. 35 does not establish requirements for the preparation, distribution, or attestation of the financial statements for any plan. It does apply to defined benefit plans of state and local governmental units, as well as private enterprises and plans that are subject to ERISA. It does not apply to government sponsored Social Security plans or plans expected to be terminated.

The FASB agreed that the primary objective of the financial statements of a defined benefit plan is that they should provide the users (participants) with information that will help them assess the present future ability of the plan to pay benefits when due. This is accomplished by including all of the following in the financial statements:

1. The net assets available during the plan year
2. The changes in net assets during the plan year
3. The actuarial present value of accumulated plan benefits as of either the beginning or the end of the plan year
4. The effects of certain factors affecting the year-to-year change in the actuarial present value of accumulated plan benefits, if significant.

The statements of net assets available for benefits, of accumulated plan benefits, and of related changes may be presented either separately or in a combined format. Also the FASB had no preference concerning how the actuarial present value of accumulated plan benefits and year-to-year changes therein should be disclosed. Either or both of these disclosures may be made on the face of the financial statements or in related notes. But regardless of the disclosure format selected, each category of information should be disclosed entirely in one location. The FASB recognized the fact that comparative statements can provide more useful information in assessing the future ability of the plan to pay benefits when due. Also, it concluded that the statements alone do not provide all the necessary information for assessment.

The FASB is allowing pragmatic solutions to some difficult problems in developing these disclosures. For example, information regarding net assets should be developed under the accrual method of accounting with plan investments valued at fair value. But the FASB has excluded from the required fair value determination contracts with insurance companies where their complexity and wide variety present difficult measurement problems when these contracts represent plan assets. Since sufficient information was not available to the FASB to assess the implementation problems presented by such insurance company contracts, it selected the practical solution of requiring such contracts to be reported in plan financial statements in the same way they are reported, or would be reported, in annual reports required by ERISA to be filed with certain governmental agencies. The result of this requirement is that insurance contracts may not be valued at fair value.

A second example of FASB attempts to pragmatize SFAS No. 35 relates to the benefit information date. While the FASB states a preference that this date be at the end of the year, it allows the presentation of benefit information at either the beginning or the end of the year. This flexibility in determining the benefit information date is the result of several pragmatic facts, including the idea that determination of end-of-the-year benefit information on a timely basis was not feasible and would increase actuarial fees since actuarial valuations typically are performed during a plan year using beginning-of-the-year information. The FASB concluded that the costs of developing end-of-the-year data on a timely basis would outweigh the resultant benefits and therefore allows this either/or flexibility. However, the FASB does require that if a beginning-of-the-year benefit information date is used, net asset valuations also must be made at the beginning of the plan year; this continues the belief of the FASB that benefit and net asset information must be presented at the same date to allow analysis of the financial status of the pension plan.

Net Assets Available for Benefit

SFAS No. 35 requires information regarding net assets to be developed under the accrual method. This information should be in sufficient detail for the users to identify available plan benefits. The accrual basis requires that sales and purchases of securities be recorded on the basis of the trade date. However, if the settlement date is later than the trade date, accounting on the basis of settlement date is acceptable if both of the following are met: (1) The fair market value of the purchased or sold securities before the date of report does not significantly change from the trade to the reporting dates; and (2) The sales or purchases are not significant in the composition of the plan assets available for benefit. Operating assets should be valued at cost less accumulated depreciation. These assets encompass buildings, equipment, and furniture and fixtures. Investments should be recorded at fair value, which generally is measured by utilization of market prices. In the absence of an active market for applicable investments, a market for similar investments or estimates of discounted cash flow information may prove useful.

An exception to this fair value rule exists for contracts with insurance companies; these contracts should be valued in the same manner as they are or would be valued under the provisions of ERISA. Exhibit 9.2 summarizes the various components of the net assets available for benefits as well as their valuation assignments.

A statement of changes in net assets available for benefits also should be prepared. This statement should provide detailed information about significant changes during the year. As a minimum this statement should include discussion of

1. The net appreciation or depreciation in fair value for each significant class of investment. This includes realized gains and losses on investments that are bought and sold during the year.
2. Any investment income not included in (1) above.
3. Employer contributions, segregated between cash and noncash contributions. The noncash contributions should be recorded at fair value.
4. Participant contributions, including those transmitted by the sponsor.
5. Contributions from other identified sources, e.g., state subsidies or federal grants.
6. Benefits paid to participants during the year.
7. Payments to insurance companies to purchase contracts that are excluded from plan assets.
8. Administrative expenses.

Exhibits 9.3 and 9.4 illustrate the statement of net assets available for benefits and the statement of changes therein. Note that a beginning-of-the-year benefit information date is used. In this case, both statements include the details of the preceding year for comparison with the beginning-of-the-year benefit information. The statement of net assets avail-

Exhibit 9.2

Summary of Valuation Methods Applicable to Net Assets Available for Benefits

Asset Description per SFAS No. 35	Example of Assets Included	Valuation in Disclosures
Contributions receivable	Amounts due from employers (not necessarily pension provision in employer financial statements), participants, and other funding sources, e.g., state subsidies or federal grants	Amounts committed to plan
Investments	Debt or equity securities, real estate, or contracts with insurance companies	Fair value at the reporting date except for contracts with insurance companies that should be valued as per ERISA
Operating assets	Buildings, equipment, furniture and fixtures, and leasehold improvements	Cost less accumulated depreciation or amortization

able for benefits records investments at fair value. These investments are divided into major categories. The receivables include accrued interest and dividends from the investments. The liabilities of the plan are subtracted from the total assets to determine the net assets available for benefits.

The statement of changes in net assets includes the minimum disclosures as detailed earlier. The net appreciation (depreciation) in fair value of investments is shown first. It is followed by other investment income. The contributions from the employer are all cash. If there were noncash contributions, they would be shown separately and recorded at fair value. The total deductions are subtracted from the total additions to determine the net increase (decrease) in net assets for the year. Then the net assets available for benefits at both the beginning and the end of the year are detailed. The net increase (decrease) should be the difference between the beginning- and end-of-the-year net asset amounts.

Present Value of Accumulated Plan Benefits

The FASB defined accumulated plan benefits as those future benefit payments that are attributable under the plan's provisions to employees' service rendered to the benefit information date. Therefore, the statement of accumulated plan benefits should provide useful information

Exhibit 9.3
Defined Benefit Pension Plan Disclosures: M & R Company

Statement of Net Assets Available for Benefits

	Year Ended December 31	
	19X2	19X1
Investment Income		
Net appreciation (depreciation) in fair value		
of investments	($ 10,000)	$ 20,000
Interest	250,000	200,000
Dividends	100,000	80,000
Rent	50,000	35,000
	$390,000	$335,000
Less investment expenses	40,000	35,000
	$350,000	$300,000
Contributions		
Employer	$800,000	$750,000
Employees	400,000	380,000
	$1,200,000	$1,130,000
Total Additions	$1,550,000	$1,430,000
Benefits paid to participants	$ 800,000	$ 750,000
Purchase of annuity contracts	200,000	180,000
	$1,000,000	$ 930,000
Administrative expenses	$ 50,000	$ 48,000
Total Deductions	$1,050,000	$ 978,000
Net increase	$ 500,000	$ 452,000
Net assets available for benefits		
Beginning of year	$5,100,000	$4,648,000
End of year	$5,600,000	$5,100,000

Statement of Changes in Net Assets Available for Benefits

	December 31	
	19X2	19X1
Assets:		
Investments at fair value		
Common stock	$4,000,000	$3,500,000
Corporate bonds and debentures	600,000	550,000
Mortgages	500,000	480,000
Real Estate	300,000	270,000
	$5,400,000	$4,800,000

(*continued*)

Exhibit 9.3 (continued)

	December 31	
	19X2	19X1
Receivables		
Employers Contributions	$ 50,000	$ 40,000
Securities Sold	100,000	80,000
Accrued Interest and Dividends	90,000	80,000
	$ 240,000	$ 200,000
Cash:	$ 200,000	$ 300,000
Total Assets	$5,840,000	$5,300,000
Liabilities:		
Accounts Payable		
Securities purchased	$ 100,000	$ 50,000
Other	$ 60,000	50,000
	$ 160,000	$ 100,000
Accrued Expenses	$ 80,000	$ 100,000
Total Liabilities	$ 240,000	$ 200,000
Net Assets Available for Benefits:	$5,600,000	$5,100,000

concerning employee earned benefits to be paid to (1) present employees or their beneficiaries, (2) deceased employees' beneficiaries, and (3) retired or terminated employees or their beneficiaries. The statement of accumulated plan benefits may be presented with either a beginning- or an end-of-the-plan-year benefit information date, although the end-of-the-year date is considered preferable. If the beginning of the plan year is used as the benefit information date, net asset information at that date also must be disclosed as well as a statement of changes in net assets for the preceding plan year.

The provisions of the pension plan itself should be used in measuring the accumulated plan benefits. Some plans specify benefit amounts for each year of service. If the amounts are not specified or clearly determinable in the provisions of the plan, then the benefits will accumulate in proportion to: (1) in the case of vested benefits, the number of years service completed to benefit information date divided by the number of years service for benefits to fully vest; and (2) in the case of nonvested benefits, the number of years service completed to benefit information date divided by the total projected service years. Factors for measuring plan benefits include (1) employees' history of pay and service, (2) projected years of service, and (3) automatic benefit increases. Factors not included in measuring plan benefits are (1) Contracts excluded from

Exhibit 9.4
Pension Plan Sponsor Disclosure: Armstrong World Industries, Inc.

Employee compensation cost summary	1980	1979	1978
	(000)	(000)	(000)
Wages and salaries, including vacations and holiday pay	**$366,452**	$369,303	$334,710
Social security and other payroll taxes	**28,939**	29,418	26,405
Pension costs	**19,107**	19,612	15,205
Medical, hospitalization, accident, life insurance, and other benefit costs	**22,259**	22,461	17,707
Total	**$436,757**	$440,794	$394,027

Average total employment of 22,645 in 1980 compares with 23,835 in 1979 and 23,876 in 1978.

Pension costs

The Company and most of its subsidiaries have pension plans covering substantially all employees. Pension costs charged to operations totaled $19.1 million in 1980, $19.6 million in 1979, and $15.2 million in 1978. Costs decreased between 1980 and 1979 primarily because of experience factors better than actuarially assumed. This reduction was partially offset by increases in member earnings and a full year's cost of increased benefits to retirees. The 1979 costs were higher than those of 1978 due to the effects of a full year's funding of 1978 plan enhancements, increases in member earnings, and increases in benefits to retirees.

Pension costs consist of actuarially determined current service costs and amounts necessary to amortize prior service obligations over periods ranging up to 30 years. The Company generally funds these pension costs currently.

A new requirement of the Financial Accounting Standards Board (Statement No. 36) calls for a comparison of the market value of plan net assets with the actuarially determined present value of "accumulated benefits." In contrast to previous benefit calculations, which included only vested amounts for active employees and for those no longer actively employed, "accumulated benefits" under this method also include nonvested amounts earned.

The table below compares the market value of plan net assets with the actuarially determined present value of liabilities under the two methods separately defined above. The table covers only the United States-based employees, as the Company's foreign pension plans are not required to report to governmental agencies pursuant to ERISA. Management believes that there are no substantial unfunded liabilities in the foreign plans under either method described above.

Comparative pension information	Financial Accounting Standards Board (Statement No. 36) requirement	Previous benefit calculations (APB No. 8)	
At January 1	1980	1980	1979
	(000)	(000)	(000)
Plan net assets at market value	$234,513	$234,513	$200,611
Actuarially computed present value of:			
Vested benefits based on 1979 method (APB No. 8)	—	243,874	228,245
Vested benefits based on SFAS No. 36	244,496	—	
Nonvested benefits	8,074	—	—
	252,570	243,874	228,245
Excess of present value of benefits over plan net assets	$ 18,057	$ 9,361	$ 27,634

Note:
Present value amounts are based on an assumed rate of return of 6%.

plan assets for which payments have been made to insurance companies, (2) plan amendments adopted after the benefit information date, and (3) increases in benefit levels or wage basis pursuant to the Social Security law.

Accumulated plan benefits should be disclosed as computed by an actuarial present value method. In determining these present value numbers, future benefits should be discounted to adjust for the time value of money and for the probability that payments ultimately will be made, e.g., to reflect the likelihood that the employee will not survive until retirement. In most cases, assumptions will have to be made related to such matters as future rates of return on plan assets, expected rates of inflations, and future administrative expenses. These assumptions should be made under the presumption that the pension plan is a going concern, and they should be realistic and internally consistent.

With insurance contracts, the FASB allows a simplified alternative. Assumptions that are inherent in the cost (at the benefit information date) of insurance contracts that would provide participants with their accumulated plan benefits may be used. Other necessary assumptions that are not included in the estimated cost of such contracts still must be made.

The statements of accumulated plan benefits should include the total actuarial present value of benefits as of the benefit information date. These benefits should be segregated into (1) vested benefits of participants currently receiving payments, (2) other vested benefits, and (3) nonvested benefits. A statement of changes in accumulated plan benefits also should be prepared to identify at the minimum the effects of the plan amendments and of changes in the nature of the plan and in actuarial assumptions. Other factors causing significant effects in the changes of the accumulated plan benefits may be included: (1) benefits accumulated and (2) the increase in interest due to a decrease in the discount period and paid benefits. If a statement format is selected, benefits paid and additional benefits accumulated during the year being reported on must be included in the statement. Changes in actuarial assumptions should be shown currently and prospectively as are other changes in accounting estimates; prior year restatements or pro-forma presentations should not be made.

Additional Required Disclosures

The additional disclosures required in SFAS No. 35 are as follow:

1. Per APBO No. 22, "Disclosure of Accounting Policies," information about the methods and significant assumptions used in assessing fair values or other reported values of plan investments and the actuarial present value of accumulated benefits
2. Provisions of the plan agreement
3. Amendments in the plan during the year
4. The priority of claims upon termination of the plan and benefits guaranteed by the Pension Benefit Guaranty Corporation
5. Funding policies and, for contributory plans, methods of determining employee contributions
6. Whether minimum funding as required by ERISA has been accomplished
7. The plan's federal income tax status

8. The identity of individual investments that constitute at least 5 percent of plan net assets available for benefits

9. Significant transactions between the plan and the sponsor, employer, or employee organizations

10. Any unusual or infrequent events or transactions that occurred after the benefit information date but prior to the issuance of the statement that might be significant to its usefulness.

Exhibit 9.3 provides an illustration of financial statements that may be prepared by a defined benefit plan in compliance with the provisions of SFAS No. 35. As can be seen, the M & R Company uses four statements to disclose the required information.

RELATIONSHIP OF SFAS NO. 35 TO ERISA

SFAS No. 35 allows certain information to be measured and reported in the same manner in the plan financial statements as for ERISA reporting. As such, there is a significant amount of overlap between ERISA and SFAS No. 35.

ERISA requires the employer and plan administrator to file certain plan information with the Department of Labor. Information included in this filing comprises (1) financial statements audited by an independent certified public accountant, (2) an actuarial report, (3) plan descriptions, (4) material changes in the plan, and (5) other detailed plan information. In addition, ERISA requires that the plan administrator provide each participant and beneficiary certain audited financial information that fairly summarizes the results of the latest annual reporting period.

With respect to a defined benefit plan, ERISA requires that the following summary information be provided to the plan participants and beneficiaries: (1) a statement of assets and liabilities, (2) a statement of changes in net assets available for plan benefits (including details of revenues and expenses), and (3) other disclosures about the plan in the notes to the financial statements. As can be seen from the foregoing discussion, SFAS No. 35 has provided the profession with the measurement and reporting principles necessary to meet the external reporting requirements of ERISA.

DISCLOSURES OF PENSION INFORMATION BY THE EMPLOYER

For defined contribution plans, the employer is required by SFAS No. 87 to accrue a net pension cost equal to the contribution necessary to meet the provisions of the plan in that period. Thus, to the extent the employer funds its contributions annually, the amount of net pension cost will be equal to the amount funded. If the plan requires the employer to make contributions for periods after the retirement or termination of an employee, the estimated cost should be accrued during the service period of the employee.

For defined contribution plans, the employer should disclose the following information:

1. A description of the plan(s), the employee group(s) covered, the basis for determining contributions, and the nature and effect of significant items affecting comparability among the reporting periods presented.
2. The amount of cost recognized during the period.

If the employer sponsors more than one defined contribution plan, these disclosures may be aggregated; however, the disclosures applicable to defined contribution plans **must** be made separately from those for defined benefit plans.

The accounting requirements for a multiemployer plan are similar to those for a defined contribution plan in that the required contribution for the period is recognized as the amount of the net pension cost. To the extent the amount is unpaid, it should be accrued as a liability.

The sponsor should make disclosures for any multiemployer plans separately from its single-employer plans. Specifically, the sponsor should disclose the following for its multiemployer plans:

1. A description of the multiemployer plan(s), the employee group(s) covered, whether the benefits provided to employees are defined benefit or defined contribution, and the nature and effect of significant items affecting comparability among the reporting periods presented.
2. The amount of cost recognized during the reporting period.

For defined benefit plans, the sponsor must disclose:

1. A description of the plan including employee group(s) covered, type of benefit formula, funding policy, types of assets held and significant nonbenefit liabilities, and the nature and effect of significant matters affecting comparability of information for all periods presented.
2. The amount of net pension cost recorded for the period as well as separate disclosure of the amount of service cost, interest cost, actual return on assets, and the net of the other components for the period.
3. A schedule reconciling the funded status of the plan with amounts reported in the employer's statement of financial position that separately discloses: (a) The fair value of plan assets; (b) The projected benefit obligation identifying the accumulated benefit obligation and the vested benefit obligation; (c) The amount of unrecognized prior service cost; (d) The amount of unrecognized net gain or loss (including asset gains and losses not yet reflected in market-related value); (e) The amount of any remaining unrecognized net obligation

or net asset existing at the date of initial application of the requirements of SFAS No. 87; (f) The amount of any additional liability recognized to record the minimum liability; (g) The amount of net pension asset or liability reported in the balance sheet.

4. The discount rate and salary rate increase used to compute the projected benefit obligation and the expected long-term rate of return on plan assets.

5. The amounts and types of securities held and the amount of annual benefits of employees and retirees covered by annuity contracts as well as any alternative amortization methods used.

Exhibit 9.4 provides an illustrative disclosure for Armstrong World Industries. This includes vested benefits of $244,496,000 and excess of present value of benefits over plan net assets of $18,057,000 at January 1, 1980 (assuming a 6 percent return on plan assets).

10
Income Taxes Disclosures

Accounting income is measured in accordance with GAAP. Taxable income, however, is determined in accordance with prescribed tax regulations and rules under provisions of the U.S. Internal Revenue Code. As a result, the basic objective of measuring accounting income is different from those objectives used to measure taxable income. The amount of tax actually payable to the government for a period does not necessarily represent the amount of income tax expense to be recognized for accounting purposes. The APB attempted to narrow the divergence that existed in practice when it promulgated APBO No. 11, "Accounting for Income Taxes."

The principal problems in accounting for income taxes arise from the fact that some transactions affect the determination of net income for financial accounting purposes in one reporting period and the computation of taxable income and income taxes payable in a different reporting period. The amount of income taxes determined to be payable for a period does not, therefore, necessarily represent the appropriate income tax expense applicable to transactions recognized for financial accounting purposes in that period. A major problem is thus the measurement of the tax effects of such transactions and the extent to which the tax effects should be included in income tax expense in the same periods in which the transactions affect pre-tax accounting income.

Further, the U.S. Internal Revenue Code permits a "net operating loss" of one period to be deducted in determining taxable income of other periods. This leads to the question of whether the tax effects of an operating loss should be recognized for financial accounting purposes in the period of loss or in the periods of reduction of taxable income.

In addition to the problems of measuring the provision for income taxes, there were questions of how to disclose the tax provision. Certain items includable in taxable income receive special treatment for financial accounting purposes, even though they are reported in the same period in which they are reported for tax purposes (e.g., extraordinary items). A question exists, therefore, as to whether the tax effects attributable to discontinued operations, extraordinary items, cumulative effect of a change in accounting principle, adjustments of prior periods (or of the opening balance of retained earnings), and direct entries to other stockholders' equity accounts should be associated with the particular items for financial reporting purposes. Additionally, guidelines were needed for balance sheet and income statement presentation of the tax effects of timing differences, operating losses, and similar items.

The basic principles for accounting for the tax effects of timing differences, net operating losses, extraordinary items, discontinued operations, and other items requiring intraperiod allocation are provided by APBO No. 11. However, the APB deferred a decision on determining the tax consequences of certain special transactions. It promulgated accounting treatment for these special areas in APBO Nos. 23, "Accounting for Income Taxes—Special Areas," and 24, "Accounting for Income Taxes—Investments in Common Stock Accounted for by the Equity Method (Other than Subsidiaries and Corporate Joint Ventures)."

In addition to the rules established for the determination of taxable income, the U.S. Internal Revenue Code allows enterprises to take an investment tax credit (ITC) on qualifying assets as a direct deduction from the taxes otherwise payable. The accounting treatment applicable to ITC is promulgated by the APB in APBO Nos. 2, "Accounting for the 'Investment Credit'," and 4, "Accounting for the 'Investment Credit'." The FASB has interpreted APBO Nos. 2 and 4 in FASBIN Nos. 25, "Accounting for an Unused Investment Tax Credit," and 32, "Application of Percentage Limitations in Recognizing Investment Tax Credit," to provide further clarification when accounting for an unused ITC.

DEFINITION OF TERMS

Terminology relating to the accounting for income taxes has varied; some terms have been used with different meanings. Definitions of certain terms used in this chapter are provided as a point of departure.

Income taxes: Taxes based on income determined under provisions of the U.S. Internal Revenue Code and foreign, state, and other taxes (including franchise taxes) based on income.

Income tax expense: The amount of income taxes (whether or not currently payable or refundable) allocable to a period in the determination of net income.

Pre-tax accounting income: Income or loss for a period, exclusive of related income tax expense.

Taxable income: The excess of revenues over deductions or the excess of deductions over revenues (exclusive of deductions arising from net operating loss carrybacks or carryforwards) to be reported for income tax purposes for a period.

Timing differences: Differences between the periods in which transactions affect taxable income and the periods in which they enter into the determination of pre-tax accounting income. Timing differences originate in one period and reverse or "turn around" in one or more subsequent periods. Some timing differences reduce income taxes that would otherwise be payable currently; others increase income taxes that would otherwise be payable currently.

Permanent differences: Differences between taxable income and pre-tax accounting income arising from transactions that, under applicable tax laws and regulations, will not be offset by corresponding differences or "turn around" in other periods.

Tax effects: Differentials in income taxes of a period attributable to (1) revenue or expense transactions that enter into the determination of pre-tax accounting income in one period and into the determination of taxable income in another period, (2) deductions or credits that may be carried backward or forward for income tax purposes, and (3) adjustments of prior periods (or of the opening balance of retained earnings) and direct entries to other stockholders' equity accounts that enter into the determination of taxable income in a period but that do not enter into the determination of pre-tax accounting income of that period. A permanent difference does not result in a "tax effect" as that term is used here.

Deferred taxes: Tax effects that are deferred for allocation to income tax expense of future periods.

Interperiod tax allocation: The process of apportioning income taxes among periods.

Tax allocation within a period. (Intraperiod tax allocation): The process of apportioning income tax expense applicable to a given period between income from continuing operations, results of discontinued operations, income before extraordinary items, extraordinary items, and cumulative effects of a change in accounting principle and of associating the income tax effects of adjustments of prior periods (or of the opening balance of retained earnings) and direct entries to other stockholders equity accounts with these items.

GENERAL CONCEPTS APPLICABLE TO ACCOUNTING FOR INCOME TAXES

Certain general concepts and assumptions were recognized by the APB to be essential in considering the problems of accounting for income taxes.

1. The operations of an entity subject to income taxes are expected to continue on a going concern basis, in the absence of evidence to the contrary, and income taxes are expected to continue to be assessed in the future.
2. Income taxes are an expense of business enterprises earning income subject to tax.

3. Accounting for income tax expense requires measurement and identification with the appropriate time period and therefore involves accrual, deferral, and estimation concepts in the same manner as these concepts are applied in the measurement and time period identification of other expenses.

4. Matching is one of the basic processes of income determination; essentially it is a process of determining relationships between costs (including reductions of costs) and (a) specific revenues or (b) specific accounting periods. Expenses of the current period consist of those costs that are identified with the revenues of the current period and those costs that are identified with the current period on some basis other than revenue. Costs identifiable with future revenues or otherwise identifiable with future periods should be deferred to those future periods. When a cost cannot be related to future revenues or to future periods on some basis other than revenues, or it cannot reasonably be expected to be recovered from future revenues, it becomes, by necessity, an expense of the current period (or of a prior period).

Of the general concepts accepted by the APB, item (2) is crucial to the conclusions adopted. The entire concept of interperiod tax allocation rests on the presumption that income taxes are an expense of doing business. It is that concept that is the basis for the requirements of APBO No. 11.

TIMING DIFFERENCES

Timing differences result because some transactions affect the determination of net income for financial accounting purposes in one reporting period and the computation of taxable income in a different reporting period. Timing differences always originate in one or more accounting periods and reverse or "turn around" in one or more subsequent periods. Just as importantly, deferred taxes are defined as the tax effects of timing differences. Thus, by assigning the applicable tax rate to the originating timing differences, deferred taxes are created.

There are four types of transactions that can give rise to timing differences:

1. Revenues or gains are included in taxable income later than they are included in pre-tax accounting income. (e.g., the use of the installment sale method to recognize income for tax purposes and recognize the sale immediately for accounting purposes).

2. Expenses or losses are deducted in determining taxable income later than they are deducted for determining pre-tax accounting income (e.g., estimated warranty costs are recognized for accounting purposes in the current period, but such costs are reported for tax purposes in the period paid).

3. Revenues or gains are included in taxable income earlier than they are included in pre-tax accounting income (e.g., rents collected in advance must be recognized in the period of receipt for tax purposes but should be deferred for accounting purposes until they are earned).

4. Expenses or losses are deducted in determining taxable income earlier than they are deducted in determining pre-tax accounting income (e.g., recording depreciation on an accelerated basis for tax purposes and recording depreciation on a straight-line basis for accounting purposes).

METHOD OF INTERPERIOD TAX ALLOCATION

Prior to the issuance of APBO No. 11, three distinct methods of interperiod tax allocation had developed in practice: the deferred method, the liability method, and the net-of-tax method. The APB rejected the liability and net-of-tax methods, concluding that the deferred method provides the most useful and practical approach to interperiod tax allocation and the presentation of income taxes.

Under the deferred method, the tax effects of current timing differences are deferred currently and allocated to income tax expense of future periods when the timing differences reverse. The deferred taxes are determined on the basis of the tax rates in effect at the time the timing differences originate and are not adjusted for subsequent changes in tax rates or to reflect the imposition of new taxes. The tax effects of transactions that reduce taxes currently payable as the timing differences originate are deferred tax credits; the tax effects of transactions that increase taxes currently payable as the timing differences originate are deferred tax changes.

Amortization of these deferred taxes to income tax expense in future periods is based upon the nature of the transactions producing the tax effects and upon the manner in which these transactions enter into the determination of pre-tax accounting income in relation to taxable income. Thus, originating timing differences that gave rise to deferred tax credits will reduce those same deferred tax credits as they reverse. Likewise, originating timing differences that created deferred tax charges will reduce deferred tax charges as they reverse. Thus, under the deferred method, only originating timing differences create deferred taxes. Reversing timing differences do not create deferred taxes, but rather they eliminate deferred taxes that were previously created. Further, the deferred taxes are eliminated using the same tax rate that was in effect when the timing differences originated.

In addition to requiring the use of the deferred method of interperiod tax allocation, APBO No. 11 requires that the deferred method be applied on a comprehensive basis. With comprehensive allocation, income tax expense should be based on the tax effects of transactions entering into the determination of pre-tax accounting income for the period, regardless of whether the taxes will be paid in a different period. Therefore, income tax expense should include any accrual, deferral, or estimation necessary to adjust the amount of income taxes payable for the period to measure the tax effects of those transactions included in pre-tax accounting income for that period. The tax effects so determined are allocated to the future periods in which the differences between pre-tax accounting income and taxable income reverse.

PERMANENT DIFFERENCES

Permanent differences result from events or transactions that are recognized but are not reflected in the computation of pre-tax accounting income. Likewise, a permanent difference arises when an event or transaction is reflected in taxable income but not in pre-tax accounting income. Thus, a permanent difference is an item that will be reflected in either pre-tax accounting income or taxable income but not in both.

Some permanent differences arise from statutory provisions under which specified revenues are exempt from taxable income (e.g., interest received on municipal obligations, premiums paid on officers' life insurance, and amortization of goodwill). Other permanent differences arise from items entering into the determination of taxable income that are not components of pre-tax accounting income in any period (e.g., the special deduction for certain dividends received and the excess of statutory depletion over cost depletion).

Since permanent differences do not enter into the computation of either pre-tax accounting income or taxable income, permanent differences do not have tax effects associated with them. Thus, deferred taxes are created only when timing differences originate, not when permanent differences occur.

DISCLOSURES

Once the provision for income taxes has been determined, APBO No. 11 requires disclosures to be made for the balance sheet and income statement and in the notes regarding the provision for income taxes.

Balance Sheet Disclosures

Balance sheet accounts related to tax allocation are of two types: (1) deferred tax charges and deferred tax credits relating to timing differences, and (2) refunds of past taxes or offsets to future taxes arising from the recognition of tax effects of carrybacks and carryforwards of operating losses and similar items.

Deferred tax charges and deferred tax credits relating to timing differences represent the cumulative recognition given to their tax effects and as such do not represent receivables or payables in the usual sense. They should be classified in two categories: one for the net current amount and the other for the net noncurrent amount. This presentation is consistent with the customary distinction between current and noncurrent categories and also recognizes the close relationship among the various deferred tax accounts, all of which bear on the determination of income tax expense.

Per SFAS No. 37, "Balance Sheet Classification of Deferred Income

Taxes," deferred tax charge or credit is related to an asset or liability if reduction of the asset or liability causes the timing difference to reverse. A deferred tax charge or credit that is not related to an asset or liability because (1) there is no associated asset or liability or (2) reduction of an associated asset or liability will not cause the timing difference to reverse (i.e., the deferred tax charge or credit is related to more than one asset or liability) should be classified based on the expected reversal date of the specific timing difference. Such classification disregards any additional timing differences that may arise and is based on the criteria used for classifying other assets and liabilities.

Deferred taxes represent tax effects recognized in the determination of income tax expense in current and prior periods; therefore, they should be excluded from retained earnings and from any other account in the stockholders' equity section of the balance sheet. Exhibit 10.1 provides an illustrative disclosure of deferred tax amounts made by Dow Chemical Company in its consolidated balance sheet. As can be seen, Dow had net current deferred tax charges amounting to $135,345,000 at December 31, 1979. Additionally, it had net noncurrent deferred tax credits of $581,876,000 at that date.

Finally, refunds or past taxes or offsets to future taxes arising from recognition of the tax effects of operating loss carrybacks or carryforwards should be classified as either current or noncurrent. The current portion should be determined by the extent to which realization is expected to occur during the current operating cycle.

Income Statement Disclosures

In reporting the results of operations, the components of income tax expense for the period should be disclosed as taxes estimated to be currently payable, tax effects of timing differences, and tax effects of operating losses. These amounts should be allocated to the income components on the income statement (intraperiod allocation) and may be presented as separate items in the income statement or alternatively as combined amounts with disclosure of the components parenthetically or in a note to the financial statements.

Tax effects attributable to adjustments of prior periods (or of the opening balance of retained earnings) and direct entries to other stockholders' equity accounts should be presented as adjustments of such items with disclosure of the amounts of the tax effects.

Other Disclosures

In addition to the balance sheet and income statement disclosures discussed above, other disclosures also should be made. They include:

1. Amounts of any operating loss carryforwards not recognized in the loss period, together with expiration dates (including separately amounts which, upon recognition, would be credited to deferred tax accounts);

Exhibit 10.1

Balance Sheet Disclosure of Deferred Taxes: Dow Chemical Company

ASSETS	December 31	
	1979	1978
	(In thousands)	
Current Assets		
Cash	$ 42,307	$ 57,622
Marketable securities and interest-bearing deposits		
(at cost, approximately market)	209,400	340,905
Accounts and notes receivable:		
Trade, (less allowance for doubtful receivables—		
1979, $53,113; 1978, $44,392)	1,572,905	1,290,851
Miscellaneous....................................	480,246	357,099
Deferred income tax benefits	135,345	70,245
Inventories:		
Finished and in process	856,812	629,255
Materials and supplies	456,293	370,293
	3,753,308	3,116,270
Investments		
Capital stock—at cost plus equity in		
accumulated earnings:		
Banking and insurance subsidiaries	185,931	154,203
Associated companies (50% owned)................	598,743	333,966
20%-49% owned companies	71,788	80,828
Other—at cost (less reserves—1979, $856; 1978, $1,260)	69,732	59,083
Noncurrent receivables (less reserves—		
1979, $268; 1978, $726)	96,135	96,465
	1,022,329	724,545
Plant Properties	8,909,244	8,037,638
Less—Accumulated depreciation	3,672,840	3,275,509
	5,236,404	4,762,129
Goodwill	106,892	84,039
Deferred Charges and Other Assets	132,704	102,137
TOTAL	$10,251,637	$8,789,120

2. Significant amounts of any other unused deductions or credits, together with expiration dates;

3. Reasons for significant variations in the customary relationships between income tax expense and pre-tax accounting income, if they are not otherwise

Exhibit 10.1 (continued)

LIABILITIES	December 31 1979	1978
	(In thousands)	
Current Liabilities		
Notes payable	$ 528,321	$ 386,024
Long-term debt due within one year	72,728	74,451
Accounts payable	1,173,893	836,613
United States and foreign taxes on income	266,659	163,305
Accrued and other current liabilities	573,501	490,586
	2,615,102	1,950,979
Long-Term Debt	3,054,979	2,937,264
Other Liabilities		
Minority interests in subsidiary companies	39,514	49,165
Deferred employee benefits	63,528	45,339
Deferred income taxes	581,876	411,679
	684,918	506,183
Stockholders' Equity		
Common stock	501,387	497,705
Capital surplus.....................................	479,878	447,036
Retained earnings	3,364,873	2,859,554
	4,346,138	3,804,295
Less—Treasury stock at cost	449,500	409,601
	3,896,638	3,394,694
TOTAL	$10,251,637	$8,789,120

apparent from the financial statements or from the nature of the entity's business.

Exhibit 10.2 illustrates the footnote disclosures necessary for the provision for income taxes for Dow. As can be seen, Dow has broken down the provision for income taxes in 1979 by federal, state, local, and

Exhibit 10.2
Footnote Disclosure of Income Taxes: Dow Chemical Company

L. TAXES ON INCOME The provision for taxes
on income consisted of:

(In millions)	Federal	State and Local	Foreign	Total
1979				
Current	$250.8	$ 14.9	$143.6	$409.3
Deferred	33.5		72.2	105.7
Total	$284.3	$ 14.9	$215.8	$515.0
1978				
Current	$192.1	$ 17.7	$102.3	$312.1
Deferred	54.5		17.3	71.8
Total	$246.6	$ 17.7	$119.6	$383.9

The current tax provision was reduced by investment tax credits of $98.1 million in 1979 and $79.2
million in 1978.

Deferred tax provisions related to the following:

	1979	1978
	(In millions)	
Excess of depreciation and depletion claimed for tax purposes over book amounts	$113.4	$49.1
Doubtful accounts and other losses in excess of those deductible currently for tax purposes	(5.3)	(4.3)
Undistributed earnings of foreign subsidiaries deemed not to be permanently invested	10.5	7.4
Income of export companies	2.5	11.4
Intercompany profit eliminated in consolidation	(6.9)	1.5
Use of LIFO method in countries where it is not allowed for tax purposes	(39.5)	3.2
Other — net	31.0	3.5
Total	$105.7	$71.8

Effective consolidated tax rates for 1979 and 1978
were 39.2% and 39.7%, respectively. Major differences between these rates and the United States
statutory rate were:

	Percent	
	1979	1978
Statutory rate	46.0	48.0
U.S. investment credits	(6.3)	(7.0)
Taxes on income of foreign operations at tax rates different from U.S. statutory rate	0.7	1.5
Untaxed equity in income of companies whose accounts are not consolidated	(3.5)	(4.6)
State and local income taxes (net of federal tax)	0.6	1.0
Other	1.7	0.8
Effective rate	39.2	39.7

Unremitted earnings of subsidiary and 50%-owned
companies which are deemed to be permanently
invested amounted to approximately $1.2 billion
and $1.0 billion at December 31, 1979 and 1978,
respectively.

Income tax returns filed in the United States
through 1973 have been settled.

foreign taxes. Additionally, the current and deferred amounts are segregated. Further, Dow has disclosed the minor timing differences (e.g.,
depreciation of $113,400 for 1979) and also the causes for the difference
between the effective and the statutory tax rate (e.g., investment
credits).

SPECIAL AREAS

APBO No. 11 states that a number of other transactions have tax
consequences somewhat similar to those discussed for timing differences. These transactions result in differences between taxable income and pre-tax accounting income in a period, and therefore create a
situation in which tax allocation procedures may be applicable in the
determination of results of operations. These transactions are also char-
acterized by the fact that the tax consequences of the initial differences
between taxable income and pre-tax accounting income may not reverse
until an indefinite future period, or conceivably some may never reverse. In addition, each of these transactions has certain unique aspects

that create problems in the measurement and recognition of their tax consequences.

Thus, the APB deferred action until further study was completed on the following special areas:

1. Undistributed earnings of subsidiaries
2. Intangible development costs in the oil and gas industry
3. "General reserves" of stock savings and loan associations
4. Amounts designated as "policyholders' surplus" by stock life insurance companies
5. Deposits in statutory reserves funds by U.S. steamship companies.

APBO Nos. 23 and 24 and SFAS No. 19, "Financial Accounting and Reporting by Oil and Gas Producing Companies," established the proper accounting treatment of topics (1) to (4) above. Further, SFAS No. 31, "Accounting for Tax Benefits Related to U.K. Tax Legislation Concerning Stock Relief," discussed the proper accounting treatment of tax benefits related to stock (inventory) relief in the United Kingdom.

Undistributed Earnings of Subsidiaries—The Indefinite Reversal Criteria

A domestic or foreign subsidiary remits earnings to a parent company after the parties consider numerous factors, including the following:

1. Financial requirements of the parent company
2. Financial requirements of the subsidiary
3. Operational and fiscal objectives of the parent company, both long term and short term
4. Remittance restrictions imposed by governments
5. Remittance restrictions imposed by lease or financing agreements of the subsidiary
6. Tax consequences of the remittance.

Remittance of earnings of a subsidiary may sometimes be indefinite because of the specific long-term investment plans and objectives of the parent company. Even in the absence of long-term investment plans, the flexibility inherent in the U.S. Internal Revenue Code may permit a parent company to postpone income taxes on the earnings of a subsidiary for an extended period or may permit the ultimate distribution to be taxed at special rates applicable to the nature of the distribution. Other circumstances may indicate that the earnings will probably be remitted in the foreseeable future. However, the parent company may control the events that create the tax consequences in either circumstance.

APBO No. 23 asserts that including undistributed earnings of a subsidiary in the pre-tax accounting income of a parent company, either through consolidation or accounting for the investment by the equity method, may result in a timing difference, in a difference that may not reverse until indefinite future periods, or in a combination of both types of differences, depending on the intent and actions of the parent company. It requires that the general presumption be that all undistributed earnings of a subsidiary included in consolidated income or in the parent company income under the equity method should be treated as a timing difference. This presumption can be overcome only if the "indefinite reversal criteria" are met.

APBO No. 23 also states that the presumption that all undistributed earnings will be transferred to the parent company may be overcome, and that no income taxes should be accrued by the parent company, if sufficient evidence shows that the subsidiary has invested or will invest the undistributed earnings indefinitely or that the earnings will be remitted in a tax-free liquidation. A parent company should have evidence of specific plans for reinvestment of undistributed earnings of a subsidiary, which demonstrate that remittance of the earnings will be postponed indefinitely. Experience of the companies and definite future programs of operations and remittances are examples of the types of evidence required to substantiate the parent company's representation of indefinite postponement of remittances from a subsidiary.

APBO No. 24 further states that the tax effects of differences between taxable income and pre-tax accounting income attributable to an investor's share of earnings of investee companies (other than subsidiaries and corporate joint ventures) accounted for by the equity method in accordance with APBO No. 18, "The Equity Method of Accounting for Investments in Common Stock," are related either to probable future distributions of dividends or to anticipated realization on disposal of the investment and therefore have essential characteristics of timing differences. Further, the ability of an investor to exercise significant influence over an investee differs significantly from the ability of a parent company to control investment policies of a subsidiary, and only control can justify the conclusion that undistributed earnings may be invested for indefinite periods.

The FASB was asked to clarify two issues with regard to APBO Nos. 23 and 24. First, in FASBIN No. 22, "Applicability of Indefinite Reversal Criteria to Timing Differences," the FASB addressed the question of whether the indefinite reversal criteria could be applied to timing differences other than those identified in APBO No. 23. It concluded that the indefinite reversal criteria apply only to the special area addressed in APBO No. 23.

Second, the FASB was asked to clarify the reporting of income tax benefits realized by an investor from the disposition of an investment in certain subsidiaries and other investees. Losses of a subsidiary or other investees that have been included in the investor's financial statements may create a difference between the accounting basis and the tax basis of the investment in the subsidiary or other investee because the investor cannot deduct those losses for income tax purposes. No recognition is given to the tax effect relating to the difference between the accounting basis and the tax basis in the years prior to disposition of the investment if realization of the tax benefit is not assured beyond any reasonable doubt. Upon disposition of the investment, a question arose as to whether tax benefits realized on disposition of the investment relating to a difference between the accounting basis and the tax basis of the investment in the subsidiary or other investee should be reported in the investor's financial statements as an extraordinary item or as a reduction of income taxes on continuing operations.

In FASBIN No. 29, "Reporting Tax Benefits Realized on Disposition of Investments in Certain Subsidiaries and Other Investees," the FASB concluded that the accounting for the effect of a difference between taxable income and pre-tax accounting income as stated in APBO Nos. 23 and 24 applies to an investor's accounting for the operating losses and the related tax benefits of operating loss carrybacks or carryforwards that may be realized by a subsidiary, a corporate joint venture, or other investee under applicable tax laws and regulations, and does not apply to tax benefits that may be realized by the investor from disposition of the related investment. An investor should classify tax benefits realized on disposition of an investment relating to a difference between the accounting basis and the tax basis of the investment in the subsidiary or other investee in the same manner as the classification accorded the gain or loss on disposition of the investment.

Intangible Development Costs in the Oil and Gas Industry

SFAS No. 19 requires that interperiod tax allocation be provided on timing differences for oil and gas producers. Some costs incurred in an enterprise's oil and gas producing activities enter into the determination of taxable income and pre-tax accounting income in different periods. A principal example is intangible drilling and development costs, which are deductible in determining taxable income when incurred but which, for successful exploratory wells and for all development wells, are capitalized and amortized for financial accounting purposes under the provisions of SFAS No. 19. As another example, some G & G costs,

which are charged to expense when incurred under the provisions of
SFAS No. 19, are deferred and deducted in subsequent periods for income tax purposes.

Comprehensive interperiod income tax allocation by the deferred
method should be followed by oil and gas producing companies for
intangible drilling and development costs and other costs incurred that
enter into the determination of taxable income and pre-tax accounting
income in different periods.

In applying comprehensive interperiod income tax allocation, the possibility that statutory depletion in future periods will reduce or eliminate
the amount of income taxes otherwise payable should not be taken into
account. That is, the so-called interaction of book/tax timing differences
with any anticipated future excess of statutory depletion allowed as a tax
deduction should not be recognized in determining the appropriate periodic provision for income taxes. Therefore, the excess of statutory
depletion over cost depletion for tax purposes should be accounted for
as a permanent difference in the period in which the excess is deducted
for income tax purposes; it should not be anticipated by recognizing
interaction.

"General Reserves" of Stock Savings and Loan Associations

Regulatory authorities require both stock and mutual savings and loan
associations to appropriate a portion of earnings to general reserves and
to retain the reserves as a protection for depositors. Provisions of the
U.S. Internal Revenue Code permit a savings and loan association to
deduct an annual addition to a reserve for bad debts in determining
taxable income, subject to certain limitations. This annual addition per-
mitted by the code generally differs significantly from the bad debt
experience upon which determination of pre-tax accounting income is
based. Thus, taxable income and pre-tax accounting income of an association usually differ.

Although a general reserve determined according to requirements of
the regulatory authorities is not directly related to a reserve for bad debts
computed according to provisions of the U. S. Internal Revenue Code,
the purposes and restrictions of each reserve are similar. Amounts of
bad debt deductions for income tax purposes are includable in taxable
income of later years only if the bad debt reserves are used subsequently
for purposes other than to absorb bad debt losses.

After considering these differences, the APB concluded in APBO No.
23 that a difference between taxable income and pre-tax accounting income attributable to a bad debt reserve that is accounted for as part of
the general reserves and undivided profits of a savings and loan association may not reverse until indefinite future periods or may never re-

verse. The association controls the events that create the tax consequence and is required to take specific action before the initial difference
reverses. Therefore, a savings and loan association should not provide
income taxes on this difference. However, if circumstances indicate that
the association is likely to pay income taxes, either currently or in later
years, because of known or expected reductions in the bad debt reserve,
income taxes attributable to that reduction should be accrued as a tax
expense of the current periods; the accrual of those income taxes should
not be accounted for as an extraordinary item.

"Policyholders' Surplus" of Stock Life Insurance Companies

The U.S. Internal Revenue Code provides for the exclusion from taxable income of a stock life insurance company of amounts determined
under a formula and the allocation of those amounts to policyholders'
surplus until the total policyholders' surplus equals a specified maximum. The amounts excluded from taxable income and designated as
policyholders' surplus are includable in taxable income of later years if
the company elects to (1) distribute policyholders' surplus to stockholders as dividends, (2) transfer amounts from policyholders' surplus
to shareholders' surplus designated for tax purposes as available for any
business purpose, or (3) take, or if it fails to take, certain other specified
actions (none of which usually occurs).

Thus, APBO No. 23 provides that a difference between taxable income
and pre-tax accounting income attributable to amounts designated as
policyholders' surplus of a stock life insurance company may not reverse
until indefinite furture periods or may never reverse. The insurance
company controls the events that create the tax consequences, and the
company is generally required to take specific action before the initial
difference reverses. Therefore, a stock life insurance company should
not accrue income taxes on the difference between taxable income and
pre-tax accounting income attributable to amounts designated as policyholders' surplus. However, if circumstances indicate that the insurance company is likely to pay income taxes, either currently or in later
years, because of known or expected reductions in policyholders' surplus, income taxes attributable to that reduction should be accrued as a
tax expense of the current period; the accrual of those income taxes
should not be accounted for as an extraordinary item.

Stock Relief in the United Kingdom

The FASB was asked to clarify the accounting for income taxes relating
to changes in the U.K. tax law with respect to "stock relief" (in the
United Kingdom, inventory is called "stock") for enterprises reporting
in conformity with U.S. GAAP. The U.K. "stock relief" legislation per-

mits enterprises to deduct, for the purpose of determining taxable income, increases in the carrying amount of inventories. The reversal increases taxable income, thereby resulting in the recapture of previously granted tax benefits. This recapture is known in the United Kingdom as the "clawback provision." In July 1979, the United Kingdom adopted legislation to limit the timing and the amount of tax that could be recaptured. Under the new legislation, the potential for recapture of tax benefits in 1973–74 and 1974–75 fiscal years was eliminated, effective from the beginning of an enterprise's 1979–80 fiscal year. The legislation also provides that the potential for recapture of the "stock relief" tax benefit received in a year will terminate if it has not been recaptured during a six year period. Thus, for an enterprise with a December year-end, any "stock relief" for the year ended December 31, 1975 (1975–76), not recaptured by December 31, 1981 (1981–82), will not be subject to recapture after January 1, 1982.

In SFAS No. 31, the FASB concluded that because of the potential recapture of "stock relief," the tax benefit related thereto should be deferred unless it is probable that the tax benefit will not be recaptured prior to the end of the relevant six year recapture period. If the tax benefit related to "stock relief" has been deferred and circumstances subsequently change indicating that it is probable that the tax benefit will not be recaptured prior to the end of the relevant six year recapture period, the tax benefit previously deferred should be recognized by a reduction of income tax expense in the period in which circumstances change. If the tax benefit related to "stock relief" has not been deferred and circumstances subsequently change, the tax benefit attributable to that "stock relief" should be deferred to the extent appropriate by a change to income tax expense of the period in which circumstances change.

To illustrate the disclosures called for on the "special areas," consider Exhibit 10.3. In this exhibit, Champion International Corporation disclosed that it had not provided for taxes on undistributed earnings of subsidiaries aggregating to $221 million at December 31, 1981. As shown in Exhibit 10.4, H. J. Heinz Company reported that it had tax benefits amounting to $19 million in 1974 applicable to the U.K. stock relief.

ACCOUNTING FOR TAX BENEFITS OF NET OPERATING LOSSES

If a company incurs a net operating loss for a period, the treatment of such a loss is determined by provisions of the U.S. Internal Revenue Code. An operating loss arises when, in the determination of taxable income, deductions exceed revenues. Operating losses may be carried back for a specified period and the remainder may be carried forward for a specified period to be applied against taxable income to reduce taxes

Exhibit 10.3
Disclosure of Indefinite Reversal Criteria Applied to Undistributed Earnings: Champion International Corporation

Note 14. Income Taxes:

The provision for income taxes includes the following components:

Years Ended December 31 (in thousands of dollars)	1981	1980	1979
Provision for income taxes currently payable:			
Federal	$ (5,927)	$ 5,416	$ 26,365
State and local	1,143	4,216	10,494
Foreign	19,679	8,069	23,616
	14,895	17,701	60,475
Provision for deferred income taxes:			
Federal	19,275	6,682	31,089
State and local	3,512	3,791	4,572
Foreign	(1,848)	13,447	9,567
	20,939	23,920	45,228
	$ 35,834	$ 41,621	$105,703

The company has reflected as of December 31, 1981, in "Receivables," $11,377,000 of refundable income taxes, which includes the current tax benefit associated with discontinued operations.

Domestic and foreign income before income taxes are as follows:

Years Ended December 31 (in thousands of dollars)	1981	1980	1979
Domestic	$103,924	$166,262	$278,616
Foreign	51,556	57,779	74,207
	$155,480	$224,041	$352,823

Principal reasons for the variation between the effective rate and the statutory Federal income tax rate were as follows:

	1981	1980	1979
At statutory rate	46.0%	46.0%	46.0%
Income taxed at capital gains rate	(11.3)	(14.1)	(10.9)
Investment credit	(12.0)	(15.2)	(11.3)
State and local taxes, net of Federal tax effect	1.6	1.9	2.3
All other–net	(1.3)	–	3.9
Effective income tax rate	23.0%	18.6%	30.0%

Deferred income taxes result from timing differences in income and expense between financial and taxable income, as follows:

Years Ended December 31 (in thousands of dollars)	1981	1980	1979
Excess of tax over financial depreciation and cost of timber harvested	$ 14,890	$ 14,792	$ 23,997
Capitalization of interest and deferral of preoperating and start-up costs (net)–deductible for tax purposes as incurred	2,317	6,352	20,529
Provision for accrued liabilities–deductible for tax purposes when paid	1,654	(1,530)	(3,889)
All other–net	2,078	4,306	4,591
	$ 20,939	$ 23,920	$ 45,228

Approximately $46,701,000 of investment tax credit recognized in current and prior years as a reduction of the financial income tax provision is available to offset income taxes to be paid in future years. The company expects to utilize these credits prior to their statutory expiration.

It is the company's intention to reinvest undistributed earnings of certain of its subsidiaries and thereby indefinitely postpone their remittance. Accordingly, no provision has been made for Federal or State income taxes on these undistributed earnings of $221,000,000 at December 31, 1981.

Exhibit 10.4
Disclosure of U.K. Stock Relief: H. J. Heinz Company

6. INCOME TAXES

The following constitutes the provisions for Federal, State,
U.S. Possessions and foreign taxes on income for 1980 and
1979.

	1980	1979
Current:		
Federal, State and		
U.S. Possessions	$45,066,000	$36,745,000
Foreign	7,027,000	25,002,000
	52,093,000	61,747,000
Deferred:		
Federal, State and		
U.S. Possessions	6,740,000	6,811,000
Foreign	2,103,000	4,321,000
	8,843,000	11,132,000
	$60,936,000	$72,879,000

The current provision includes taxes on income for the company's United Kingdom subsidiary, which are payable in the
second following year, as provided by United Kingdom tax
regulations. The current provision for Federal taxes in 1980
includes a reduction for the investment tax credit amounting
to $5,760,000 ($9,094,000 in 1979). The deferred provision
represents principally the taxes on differences between depreciation deducted for income tax purposes and for financial statement reporting. The company files consolidated Federal income tax returns, and such returns have been settled for all
years through 1973.

During the current year, the United Kingdom adopted tax
legislation that resulted in the permanent forgiveness of certain
previously deferred United Kingdom taxes of $19,423,000
applicable to 1973 and 1974. The payment of taxes was previously postponed in accordance with inventory tax relief provisions of the United Kingdom, and this tax legislation eliminated the potential for subsequent payment of the remaining
portion of those deferred taxes applicable to 1973 and 1974.
The effect of this forgiveness was reflected as a reduction in the
current provision for foreign taxes on income.

payable to the government. As such, tax benefits are obtained either (1)
from refunds of taxes paid in prior profitable years or (2) as reductions of
taxes otherwise payable in future profitable years. When an operating
loss is applied to reduce taxes otherwise paid or payable, pre-tax accounting income and taxable income will differ for the period to which
the loss is applied.

Since refunds of taxes paid in prior years arising from carrybacks of
operating losses are currently realizable, the tax benefits of such

Exhibit 10.4 (continued)

On April 25, 1980, a new income tax treaty between the United States and the United Kingdom became effective. The treaty grants partial relief from the double taxation on dividends from United Kingdom subsidiaries by providing for a refund to United States parent companies of a portion of the Advanced Corporation Tax previously paid on those dividends. The effect of this treaty, which was reflected in the fourth quarter of the current fiscal year, was a reduction in the current provision for foreign taxes on income of $4,969,000.

The provisions for taxes on income for 1980 were 41.9% of pretax income before the United Kingdom tax adjustments and 29.9% after those adjustments. The provision for taxes on income for 1979 was 39.8% of pretax income. The following reconciles the United States statutory rate with the effective rates. The company's United States statutory rate for 1980, based on statutory rates currently in effect, was 46%. The United States statutory rate for 1979, based on the company's fiscal year, was 47.3%.

	1980	1979
United States statutory tax rate	46.0%	47.3%
Investment tax credit	(2.8)	(5.0)
Income of foreign subsidiaries taxed at foreign tax rates	4.7	1.4
Income of U.S. Possessions subsidiaries taxed at possession tax rates	(7.0)	(5.0)
State income taxes (net of Federal income tax benefit)	1.3	1.3
Foreign currency adjustments without tax effects	(2.4)	(0.5)
Other	2.1	0.3
	41.9	39.8
Prior-year United Kingdom tax adjustments	(12.0)	—
	29.9%	39.8%

amounts carried back should be recognized in the loss year. This is required to achieve proper matching since current realization of the refund is assured. To the extent that these refunds have not been collected, they should be reflected in the balance sheet as current assets.

The accounting treatment applicable to a loss carryforward differs from that of a loss carryback. The existence of a carryforward is an indication that a company has incurred operating losses that exhausted benefits available from carrybacks. As a result, these benefits can be realized only as a loss carryforward. In APBO No. 11, the position is taken relative to loss carryforwards that the realization concept should take precedence over the matching concept. Loss carryforward benefits usually should be recognized only when realized through subsequent profitable operations, the only exception to this being a situation in which realization is assured beyond any reasonable doubt in the loss period.

Exhibit 10.5
Disclosure of Tax Effects of Net Operating Losses: U.S. Steel

	(In millions)	
	1979	1978
SALES	$12,929.1	$11,049.5
OPERATING COSTS		
Cost of sales (excludes items shown below)	10,705.3	9,046.4
Selling, general and administrative expenses	423.5	372.4
Pensions, insurance and other employee benefits	769.4	693.6
Wear and exhaustion of facilities	531.5	435.6
State, local and miscellaneous taxes	237.9	215.4
	12,667.6	10,763.4
OPERATING INCOME *(Excludes items shown below—Note 23)*	261.5	286.1
Interest, dividends and other income *(Note 18)*	196.0	155.3
Interest and other financing costs *(Note 18)*	(184.0)	(191.4)
INCOME BEFORE UNUSUAL ITEMS, TAXES ON INCOME AND CUMULATIVE EFFECT ON PRIOR YEARS OF CHANGES IN ACCOUNTING PRINCIPLES	273.5	250.0
UNUSUAL ITEMS		
Estimated provision for costs attributable to shutdown of facilities *(Note 19)*	(808.6)	–
Estimated provision for occupational disease claims *(Note 20)*	(88.1)	–
Revaluation of other investments *(Note 3)*	(53.2)	–
	(949.9)	–
INCOME (LOSS) BEFORE TAXES ON INCOME AND CUMULATIVE EFFECT ON PRIOR YEARS OF CHANGES IN ACCOUNTING PRINCIPLES	(676.4)	250.0
Provision (credit) for estimated United States and foreign income taxes *(Note 16)*		
Current	(6.3)	6.7
Deferred	(286.7)	1.3
	(293.0)	8.0
INCOME (LOSS) BEFORE CUMULATIVE EFFECT ON PRIOR YEARS OF CHANGES IN ACCOUNTING PRINCIPLES	(383.4)	242.0
Cumulative effect on prior years of changes in accounting principles *(Note 21)*	90.4	–
INCOME (LOSS)	$ (293.0)	$ 242.0
INCOME (LOSS) PER COMMON SHARE (in dollars) *(Note 13)*		
Primary:		
Income (loss) before cumulative effect on prior years of changes in accounting principles	$ (4.46)	$ 2.85
Cumulative effect on prior years of changes in accounting principles	$ 1.05	$ –
Income (loss)	$ (3.41)	$ 2.85
Fully diluted:		
Income (loss) before cumulative effect on prior years of changes in accounting principles	$ (4.46)	$ 2.78
Cumulative effect on prior years of changes in accounting principles	$ .98	$ –
Income (loss)	$ (3.41)	$ 2.78
PRO FORMA AMOUNTS ASSUMING ACCOUNTING CHANGES WERE APPLIED RETROACTIVELY		
Income (loss)	$ (383.4)	$ 256.5
Income (loss) per common share (in dollars)		
Primary	$ (4.46)	$ 3.02
Fully diluted	$ (4.46)	$ 2.94
INCOME REINVESTED IN BUSINESS		
Balance at beginning of year	$ 3,518.8	$ 3,412.7
Income (loss)	(293.0)	242.0
	3,225.8	3,654.7
Less—Dividends on common stock $1.60 and $1.60 per share	137.5	135.9
Balance at end of year	$ 3,088.3	$ 3,518.8

Exhibit 10.5 (continued)

16. TAX PROVISION—The provision (credit) for estimated United States and foreign taxes on income was:

	(In millions)	
	1979	1978
Currently payable (refundable):		
U. S. Federal		
Current year	$ .2	$ 20.8
Operating loss carryback effects	(26.7)	(34.9)
Adjustment of prior years	(4.1)	(1.9)
	(30.6)	(16.0)
U. S. State and Local	9.9	8.0
Foreign	14.4	14.7
Total	(6.3)	6.7
Deferred:		
U. S. Federal	(294.5)	(1.3)
U. S. State and Local	1.2	2.0
Foreign	6.6	.6
Total	(286.7)	1.3
Total provision (credit)	$(293.0)	$ 8.0

The components of the deferred tax provision (credit) resulting from timing differences were:

	(In millions)	
	1979	1978
Depreciation	$ 130.5	$ 107.3
Investment credit	(10.6)	(119.9)
Interest costs	.2	24.7
Unremitted earnings of foreign consolidated subsidiaries	15.7	2.3
Intercompany profit in inventory	2.1	3.9
Estimated provision for shutdown of facilities	(354.1)	—
Estimated provision for occupational disease claims	(49.3)	—
Revaluation of other investments	(14.2)	—
Reduction of deferred taxes resulting from operating loss	(20.0)	—
Adjustment of prior years	2.4	(24.5)
Other	10.6	7.5
Total deferred tax provision (credit)	$(286.7)	$ 1.3

The primary reasons that the provision (credit) for income taxes differs from the amount computed by applying the basic Federal income tax (FIT) rates to Income (Loss) Before Taxes On Income And Cumulative Effect On Prior Years Of Changes In Accounting Principles are as follows:

	(In millions)	
	1979	1978
U. S. statutory rate (1979—46%; 1978—48%) applied to income (loss) before tax	$(311.1)	$120.0
Investment credit	—	(81.2)
Excess wear and exhaustion	(44.3)	(26.3)
Unremitted earnings of certain foreign subsidiaries	4.3	9.8
Minimum income tax	1.0	12.1
Foreign income taxes	5.8	5.6
State and local income taxes after FIT benefit	6.0	5.6
Adjustment of prior years	(1.7)	(26.4)
Operating loss limitation	45.6	—
Other	1.4	(11.2)
Total provision (credit)	$(293.0)	$ 8.0

As a result of an operating loss, $3.0 million of investment credit recognized in previous years was reversed in 1979 and in addition, $66.4 million of current year investment credit was unused in determining the tax provision for 1979. The unused investment credits expire in 1985 and 1986, respectively.

The 1979 tax provision includes a $46.8 million deferred tax credit offset to the tax effect on prior years changes in accounting principles as a result of the 1979 loss carryback.

At December 31, 1979, for financial reporting purposes, U. S. Steel had an unused operating loss carryforward of $113 million and for tax reporting purposes, there was an unused 1979 net operating loss carryforward of $142 million which expires in 1986.

The U. S. income tax liabilities for all tax years prior to 1964 have been paid except for an additional $15.6 million assessment applicable to 1957-1960 involving an issue which has been appealed to the U. S. Court of Appeals for the Second Circuit. The government has also filed an appeal for those years, which would increase the assessment to $18.5 million. A suit for refund of $20.0 million in taxes and interest has been filed with the U. S. Court of Claims for the years 1962-1963 on an issue on which the Corporation expects a favorable decision. The tax years 1964-1975 are in various stages of audit or administrative review. The Corporation believes it has made adequate provision for income taxes and any interest which may become payable on account of those years not yet settled.

U. S. income taxes have not been provided on unremitted earnings of a foreign subsidiary, as these earnings are considered to be permanently invested by the subsidiary. On a consolidated basis, the earnings totaled $93.4 million through 1979.

Realization of the tax benefits of net operating loss carryforwards can be considered to be assured beyond a reasonable doubt only if two conditions are met: (1) The loss is the result of an identifiable, isolated, and nonrecurring event and the enterprise has been continuously profitable over a long period of time or has suffered only occasional losses that were more than offset by taxable income in subsequent years and (2) future taxable income is virtually certain to be large enough to offset the loss carryforward, and such income will occur soon enough to provide realization during the carryforward period.

In the usual case of a loss carryforward, in which realization is not assured beyond any reasonable doubt, tax benefits can be recognized

Exhibit 10.6
Disclosure of ITC: Hanna Mining Company

INCOME TAXES
Income taxes consist of the following:

	1980	
	Current	Deferred
Federal (credit)	$(5,221)	$2,892
Foreign	485	1,550
State	1,594	—
	$(3,142)	$4,442

Income before income taxes of $39,990,000 in 1980, $60,933,000 in
1979 and $31,819,000 in 1978 includes $22,570,000, $23,935,000 and
$7,642,000, respectively, attributable to associated and other com-
panies incorporated in foreign countries.

Deferred income tax expense results from the following:

	1980	1979	1978
	(in thousands)		
Undistributed income of companies carried at equity	$6,893	$8,415	$1,841
Depreciation	(1,697)	(588)	(399)
Other.	(754)	135	56
	$4,442	$7,962	$1,498

only during subsequent years as they are realized. When these benefits
are recognized, in full or in part, in subsequent periods, they should be
reported in the results of operations of those periods as extraordinary
items.

In the unusual case, where realization is assured beyond any reasonable doubt, tax benefits would be recognized in the year of the loss. In
those rare situations in which operating loss carryforwards are expected
to be realized beyond any reasonable doubt, the potential tax benefits
should be reflected in the balance sheet as assets. Such assets should be
classified as current or noncurrent depending on the extent to which
realization is expected to occur within the current operating cycle.

Exhibit 10.5 illustrates the disclosures applicable to tax effects of net
operating losses. In 1979, U.S. Steel had a net loss. It recognized a tax
benefit of $293 million for amounts to be carried back. Footnote 16 fur-
ther amplifies on the nature of the tax benefit that was recognized in
1979.

ACCOUNTING AND DISCLOSING INVESTMENT TAX CREDITS

When ITCs were allowed by the Internal Revenue Code as a direct reduction of taxes currently payable, a question arose as to the proper accounting for them. Two methods developed in practice. The flow-through method provides for immediate recognition of the ITC in the income statement. The deferral method calls for initial deferral of the ITC and recognition of the ITC in income over the life of the asset giving rise to it.

A controversy arose as to which method should be used. The APB addressed the matter in APBO Nos. 2 and 4. Its conclusions were that while the deferral method is preferable, both methods are acceptable. As a consequence, the entry must disclose the method used and the amount of ITC recognized in the current period.

In Exhibit 10.6, for example, the Hanna Mining Company reported ITCs of $875,800 recognized in income in 1980. Further, the company used the flow-through method to recognize its ITCs.

11
Other Long-Term Liabilities Disclosures

DISCLOSURE OF LONG-TERM OBLIGATIONS

Changing economic conditions in today's business environment have led to the introduction of new forms of financing. Examples of these are the following:

Project financing arrangements: The financing of a major capital project in which the lender looks principally to the cash flows and earnings of the project as the source of funds for repayment and to the assets of the project as collateral for the loan. The general credit of the project entity is usually not a significant factor, either because the entity is a corporation without other assets or because the financing is without direct recourse to the owner(s) or the entity.

Take-or-pay contracts: Agreements between a purchaser and a seller that provide for the purchaser to pay specified amounts periodically in return for products or services. The purchaser must make specified payments periodically in return for products or services. The purchaser must make specified minimum payments even if it does not take delivery of the contracted products or services.

Throughout contracts: Agreements between a shipper or processor and the owner of a transportation facility, such as an oil or natural gas pipeline or a ship or a manufacturing facility, that provide for the shipper or processor to pay specified amounts periodically in return for the transportation or processing of a product. The shipper or processor is obligated to provide specified minimum quantities to be transported or processed in each period and to make cash payments even if it does not provide the contracted quantities.

Other unconditional purchase obligations: Typically associated with project financing arrangements.

The arrangements and contracts may or may not give rise to an asset and obligation formalized on the balance sheet under current GAAP, depending on the circumstances surrounding the agreement. If not recognized on the balance sheet, they are often disclosed in the notes to the financial statements. If disclosed, the disclosure sometimes quantifies the enterprise's rights and obligations.

The FASB was asked to consider accounting for project financing arrangements. The particular inquiries related to whether the unconditional purchase obligations and indirect guarantees of indebtedness of others typical of project financing arrangements result in participants acquiring ownership interests and obligations to make future cash payments that should be recognized as assets and liabilities in their balance sheets.

However, the FASB also had on its agenda three topics that are part of the conceptual framework for financial accounting and reporting that pertained to the request:

1. Accounting recognition criteria for elements that address the types of transactions, events, and circumstances that should lead to recognition in financial statements of items that qualify as assets, liabilities, revenues, expenses, etc., under the definitions of elements of financial statements
2. Measurements of the elements of financial statements that consider how assets, liabilities, and other elements should be measured
3. Funds flows, liquidity, and financial flexibility, which determine the kinds of information that should be reported to facilitate assessment of the enterprise's flow of funds, liquidity, and ability to obtain cash to adapt to unexpected difficulties or opportunities.

Because of these pending projects, the FASB decided to defer action on the measurement questions raised. However, existing disclosures of unconditional purchase obligations and indirect guarantees of indebtedness of others associated with the financing arrangements were inconsistent among enterprises and often failed to satisfy the financial reporting objective of paragraphs 40 and 41 of SFAC No. 1, entitled "Objectives of Financial Reporting by Business Enterprises."

As an interim measure pending a decision on whether the obligations should be recognized on purchasers' balance sheets, the FASB decided that disclosures of unconditional purchase obligations and indirect guarantees of indebtedness of others associated with financing arrangements should be expanded and standardized to satisfy the objectives of financial reporting. Thus, in March 1981 the FASB issued SFAS No. 47, entitled "Disclosure of Long-Term Obligations," and FASBIN No. 34, entitled "Disclosure of Indirect Guarantees of Indebtedness of Others."

PURCHASE OBLIGATIONS REQUIRING DISCLOSURE

SFAS No. 47 states that unconditional purchase obligations associated with financing arrangements should be disclosed and quantified. The FASB also concluded that entities should disclose future cash payments in a manner similar to existing disclosures of capital lease obligation. The unconditional purchase obligation is an obligation to transfer funds in the future for fixed or minimum amounts or quantities of goods or services at a fixed or minimum price (for example, as in take-or-pay contracts or throughput contracts). An unconditional purchase obligation must be disclosed if it meets all of the following conditions:

1. If it is noncancelable or cancelable only
   a. On the occurrence of some remote contingency or
   b. With permission of the other party or
   c. If a replacement agreement is signed between the same parties or
   d. Upon payment of a penalty in an amount such that continuation of the agreement appears reasonably assured.
2. It was negotiated as part of arranging financing for the facilities that will provide the contracted goods or services (e.g., carrying costs for contracted goods).
3. It has a remaining term in excess of one year.

Future minimum lease payments under leases having these characteristics need not be disclosed in accordance with SFAS No. 47 if they are presently disclosed in accordance with SFAS No. 13, entitled "Accounting for Leases."

Also, if a capital project to which an unconditional obligation relates qualifies for the capitalization of interest in accordance with the provisions of SFAS No. 34, entitled "Capitalization of Interest Cost," the rate of interest on the unconditional obligation should be reflected (if related to the project financing arrangement) in computing the rate of interest to be used in the determination of the interest cost to be capitalized in the capital project.

Unrecorded Obligations

SFAS No. 47 requires that an unconditional purchase obligation be disclosed in the notes to the financial statements if it meets the three conditions set forth above. At minimum, the disclosure should include the following:

1. The nature and the term of the obligation(s)
2. The amount of the fixed and determinable portion of the obligation(s) as of the date of the latest balance sheet presented in the aggregate and, if determinable, for each of the five succeeding fiscal years
3. The nature of any variable components of the obligation(s)
4. The amounts purchased under the obligation(s) (e.g., the take-or-pay or throughput contract) for each period for which an income statement is presented.

Disclosures of similar or related unconditional purchase obligations may be combined. These disclosures may be omitted only if the aggregate commitments for all such obligations not disclosed are immaterial.

Disclosure of the amount of imputed interest necessary to reduce the unconditional purchase obligation(s) to present value is encouraged but not required. The discount rate should be the effective initial interest rate of the borrowings that financed the facility (or facilities) that will provide the contracted goods or services, if known by the purchaser. If the asset qualifies for interest capitalization, the interest rate used to captalize the interest may be the appropriate rate. If the purchaser cannot determine this rate, the purchaser's incremental borrowing rate (defined as the rate that, at the inception of an unconditional purchase obligation, the purchaser would have incurred to borrow over a similar term the funds necessary to discharge the obligation) may be used as the discount rate.

Recorded Obligations and Redeemable Stock

Certain unconditional purchase obligations under present GAAP are recorded as liabilities on the purchaser's balance sheets with the related assets recognized. SFAS No. 47 does not alter that accounting treatment or the treatment of future unconditional purchase obligations that are substantially the same as those obligations already recorded as liabilities with related assets, nor does it suggest that disclosure is an appropriate substitute for accounting recognition if the substance of an arrangement is the acquisition of an asset and the incurrence of a liability. SFAS No. 47 is intended as an interim document, specifying disclosure principles only.

Disclosure of information regarding recorded obligations and redeemable stock is required for each of the five years following the latest balance sheet date and in the aggregate. At a minimum, the following information must be disclosed if the amounts are material:

1. The aggregate amount of payments for unconditional purchase obligations that meet the three conditions presented earlier and that have been recognized on the purchaser's balance sheet
2. The combined aggregate amount of maturities and sinking fund requirements for all long-term borrowings
3. The amount of redemption requirements for all issues of capital stock that are redeemable at fixed or determinable dates, separately by issue or combined.

ACCOUNTING FOR TROUBLED DEBT RESTRUCTURING

A troubled debt restructuring occurs, according to SFAS No. 15, "Accounting by Debtors and Creditors for Troubled Debt Restructurings," when the creditor, for economic or legal reasons related to the debtor's financial difficulties, grants a concession to the debtor that would not otherwise be considered. SFAS No. 15 identifies treatment for the following types of troubled debt restructurings:

1. Transfers from debtors to creditors of receivables from third parties, real estate, or other assets to satisfy a debt
2. Granting of an equity interest to the creditor by the debtor to satisfy or partially satisfy a debt unless the equity interest is granted pursuant to existing terms for convertibility of debt to equity interest
3. Modification of debt terms, such as reducing the applicable interest rate over the remaining original debt term or extending the maturity date(s) of debt obligations at an interest rate lower than the current market rate for similar obligations
4. Granting of an equity interest to the creditor by the debtor and modification of the debt terms.

The existence of financial difficulties does not, in itself, indicate that a debt agreement alteration constitutes a troubled debt restructuring. In order to constitute a troubled debt restructuring, the creditor must make a concession to the debtor that would otherwise not be made. Examples of situations that do not constitute troubled debt restructurings include

1. The transfer of assets from the debtor to the creditor to fully satisfy a debt when the fair market value of the assets transferred is at least equal to the creditor's recorded investment in the receivable or the debtor's carrying amount of the payable
2. The reduction of the interest rate applicable to the debt solely to reflect a general decline in market interest rates
3. The refunding of debt by issuing new marketable debt with an effective interest rate approximately equal to the current market interest rate of similar debt issues of nontroubled debtors.

The accounting and reporting requirements of the various types of troubled debt restructuring identified in SFAS No. 15 are described below.

Transfer of Assets

If a troubled debt is to be settled fully by a transfer of assets from the debtor to the creditor, the fair market value of the transferred asset must be determined. The difference between the derived fair market value and the carrying value of the assets to the debtor should be recognized as a gain or loss to the debtor. The classification of this gain or loss should be made in accordance with the criteria of APBO No. 30, entitled "Reporting the Results of Operations." The amount by which the carrying value of the debtor's payable, or the creditor's recorded investment in the receivable, exceeds the fair market value of the transferred assets should be recognized as a gain to the debtor, and the creditor will ordinarily charge the excess against the appropriate allowance account. These restructuring gains should be aggregated and, if material, classified as an extraordinary item in accordance with SFAS No. 4.

If the debtor transfers assets to the creditor in partial satisfaction of a debt, the carrying amount of the payable, or the recorded investment in the receivable, should be reduced by the fair value of the assets transferred. The debtor should recognize a gain or loss on disposition of assets as in a full settlement transfer of assets; no restructuring gain or loss should, however, be recognized unless the remaining balance of the debt exceeds the total future cash payments specified in the new agreement. Subsequent interest income and expense, if applicable, should be determined using the effective interest method.

Granting of an Equity Interest

If the debtor grants the creditor an equity interest on satisfaction of a debt obligation, an estimate of the fair value of the equity interest surrendered is necessary in order to measure separately the consideration received for the equity interest and the restructuring gain.

The FASB determined that inclusion of restructuring gains on equity interests in contributed capital would violate the principle of recording stock issuances at the fair value of the consideration received.

Thus, when a debtor grants a creditor an equity interest, as in asset transfers, the excess of the fair value of consideration surrendered must be segregated into its component parts.

If a debtor grants a creditor an equity interest in partial satisfaction of an existing obligation, the accounting requirements are identical to those when assets are transferred. The carrying amount of the payable, or the recorded investment in the receivable, should be reduced by the fair value of the assets transferred. No restructuring gains or losses should be recognized unless the remaining balance of the debt exceeds the total future cash payments specified in the new agreement. Subsequent interest income and expense, if applicable, should be determined using the effective interest method.

Modification of Terms

The FASB concluded that debt restructurings with only a modification of debt agreement terms do not involve a transfer of resources or obligations and are continuations of existing debt. In most cases, the creditor's primary objective in these restructurings is to recover the investment in the receivable by reducing the effective interest between restructuring and maturity dates. Such restructurings should be accounted for on a prospective basis by both the debtor and the creditor.

If the amount of the existing debt is less than or equal to the aggregate future principal interest specified in the new debt agreement, the carrying amount of the payable and the recorded investment in the receivable should not be adjusted; rather, the effects of the changes should be reflected in future periods, with interest expense and interest income determined using the effective interest method. To the extent that the recoverability of the creditor's investment is not affected, no gain or loss on the restructuring should be recognized.

If the amount of the existing debt is greater than the aggregate future principal and interest specified in the new debt agreement, the debtor should recognize a gain equal to the excess of the carrying amount of the payable over the stipulated future cash payments. These restructuring gains of the debtor should be aggregated and, if material, classified as extraordinary items per SFAS No. 4. The creditor should recognize a loss to the extent that the recorded investment in the receivable at the time of restructuring exceeds the total future cash receipts specified in the new debt agreement. As a practical matter, most of these restructuring losses will be charged against an appropriate allowance account, but to the extent that these losses are charged against income, they should be classified according to the guidelines stipulated in APBO No. 30. After this type of debt restructuring, all cash receipts and disbursements, whether designated as principal or interest, should reduce the carrying amount of the payable and the recorded investment in the receivable, with no interest being recognized.

Disclosure Requirements

SFAS No. 15 requires that debtors make the following disclosures applicable to troubled debt restructurings consummated after December 31, 1977 (December 24, 1977, for companies utilizing a 52 to 53 week fiscal year):

1. For each restructuring, or class of restructurings, a description of changes in the debt agreement, the primary characteristics of the settlement, or both

2. The aggregate gain on restructuring of payables along with related tax implications

3. The per share amount of the aggregate gain on restructuring, net of the related tax effect

4. The aggregate gain or loss recognized during the period attributable to asset transfers

5. The extent to which any contingent payments are included in the carrying amount of restructured payables.

Troubled debt restructurings must be disclosed by creditors for fiscal years after December 15, 1977, and include receivables whose terms were modified in earlier restructurings but have been excluded from the prospective accounting provisions of SFAS No. 15. The amount of any commitments to lend additional funds to debtors whose terms have been modified in troubled debt restructurings must be disclosed as of the date of each balance sheet presented. For outstanding receivables whose terms have been modified in troubled debt restructurings by major category, the following disclosures are also required as of that date:

1. The aggregate recorded investment
2. Gross interest income that would have been recognized during the period if the receivables had been current in accordance with their original terms and had been outstanding during the period
3. Gross interest income on receivables recorded during the period.

12
Stockholders' Equity Disclosures

THE NATURE OF STOCKHOLDERS' EQUITY TRANSACTIONS

The stockholders' equity of a corporation represents the total amount of equity held by the business for its owners. Equities are accounted for and classified in accordance with their source of contribution and the type of security issued. The two basic sources for equities are contributions by investors and profits accumulated and retained in the business. The basic accounting issue is the classification of funds into the two types; neither gain nor loss is recognized in accounting for stockholders' equity transactions.

Capital stock transactions apply to both public and nonpublic enterprises. Several classifications and types of securities may exist depending upon the articles of incorporation and the corporate charter for a given firm.

Contributed capital may be divided into two types for each security. One account represents legal capital, which is the amount of capital required to remain in the business by statutory law. The amount of legal capital equals the par or stated value of the stock times the number of shares issued and outstanding. The second account holds the amount of capital contributed in excess of legal capital.

Contributed funds are evidenced through stock certificates held by investors. These rights may be transfered freely, and hold specific ownership privileges. The most common privileges are

1. The right to participate in management through votes equal to the number of shares held
2. The right to participate in the profits of the business through dividends

3. The right to share in corporate distributions upon liquidation

4. The right to purchase additional shares of stock in proportion to ownership held in the event of subsequent distributions

Ownership share may be represented by both common and preferred stock. Differences between the two include the nature and amount of dividends paid and their voting privileges. In all cases, preferred dividends must be paid before distributions are made available to common shareholders. Preferred dividends may be cumulative, in which case dividends in arrears on preferred stock must be paid before dividends on common stock.

A unique characteristic of a shareholder's interest is limited liability. An investor is liable only for the amount of funds paid in, and cannot be held responsible for the obligations of the corporation in excess of this amount.

TERMS AND DEFINITIONS

Authorized capital stock: The number of issuable shares of each class of stock as specified in the corporate charter

Contributed capital: Includes all of the following:
  1. Legal capital associated with common and preferred stock
  2. Additional paid-in capital in excess of par or stated value
  3. Contributed capital from treasury stock and stock requirement transactions
  4. Donations of assets from others.

Issued capital stock: The number of outstanding shares held by investors and the corporation's treasury stock

Outstanding capital stock: Shares issued and held by investors

Subscribed stock: Unissued shares set aside to meet future requirements of investors

Treasury stock: Shares issued yet subsequently acquired by the corporation; the difference between issued and outstanding shares

Unissued capital stock: The difference between the number of shares authorized and issued

DISCLOSURE OF PAID-IN CAPITAL

Disclosure requirements for paid-in capital include

1. For each class of stock authorized
   a. The amount authorized
   b. Amounts issued and outstanding
   c. Amounts held as treasury stock
   d. Any changes in amounts for the period
2. Amounts of legal capital, shown separately from other contributed capital amounts

3. Per share and aggregate amounts of cumulative preferred dividends in arrears

4. Shown in the aggregate or on a per share basis, the amounts that preferred shares may be called, and amounts subject to redemption through sinking fund arrangements

5. Aggregate amounts of the liquidation preference of preferred stock.

In addition, registrants with the SEC, in accordance with ASR No. 218, "Presentation in Financial Statements of Redeemable Preferred Stock," must disclose three general classes of securities: (1) preferred stock subject to mandatory redemption when the control is outside of management's hands; (2) nonredeemable preferred stock, or preferred stock redeemable at the option of management; and (3) common stocks. Further, the corporation must disclose for its redeemable preferred stocks the redemption terms, five year maturity data, and any changes in redeemable preferred stocks.

STOCK RIGHTS AND OPTIONS

Stock rights represent an option whereby the holder can purchase a specified number of shares at a predetermined price. The rights are evidenced by papers called "warrants." Each warrant may represent one or more rights. The purpose of stock rights is to disperse more capital to the shareholders while raising capital for the corporation. The rights normally have an associated value and may be traded in the open market. The company must disclose the number of rights outstanding and the number of potential shares issuable.

Stock Issued to Employees

Capital stock is often made available to employees for several reasons and in several ways. In accounting for these plans, the terms involved and the amount of expense applicable to the issuing corporation must be examined. The cost involved determines the nature of the plan, which may be either compensatory or noncompensatory. Definitions and accounting treatment of each follow.

In a compensatory plan, the issuing company incurs additional cost as shares are offered at a price below the fair value of the stock. This amount is amortized to expense over the compensation period. The main thrust of a compensatory plan is that an individual receives extra compensation above his salary for services rendered to the corporation. An accountant is faced with measuring and deferring the added cost to the corporation.

In a noncompensatory plan, stock is offered to employees at no additional cost to the issuing corporation. The employee does not receive additional compensation as a result of the warrants.

Many accounting differences exist for each type of plan, and the complexities will be discussed separately.

Stock Option Plans

The main complexity in a compensatory plan is the measurement of compensation cost and the subsequent amortization of this cost to the accounting period affected.

To determine if a plan is compensatory, the accountant must examine the terms of the plan and apply the rules governing a noncompensatory plan. A noncompensatory plan is defined by APBO No. 25, "Accounting for Stock Issued to Employees," as one having all of the following:

1. Almost all employees meeting limited employment requirements may participate in the plan.
2. Stock is offered equally to the employees or on a pro-rata basis, depending on salary or wages earned.
3. The option period is limited to a reasonable length of time.
4. The discount of the fair market value of the stock over the option price is no greater than the amount that would be offered to shareholders.

If the plan meets all of the above tests, then it will be noncompensatory. All other plans failing to meet one or more of the tests will be compensatory.

The first step in accounting for compensatory plans is to measure the compensation as determined at the "measurement date" at the amount equal to the fair market value of the rights in the hands of the employee. The compensation cost then must be deferred and matched to the accounting periods affected by the plan.

Many times, the date of grant and the measurement date differ. The measurement date is the earliest date when both the number of shares offered and the option price are known. This date may be either the date of grant or a subsequent date. Often a contingency exists involving either the number of shares to be offered or the option purchase price. In this case, the measurement date will fall after the date of grant.

Compensation cost is measured on the measurement date, and equals the market price per share less the option price per share times the number of shares offered. The cost is recognized on the balance sheet and amortized over the periods that benefit from the employee's service. The time period may be stated in the plan or inferred through the terms of the plan.

If the measurement date falls after the date of grant, the accountant is faced with the problem of estimating the compensation cost as of the date of grant. The estimated cost is assigned to the periods affected based on the market price of the stock at the end of each period. On the measurement date, any changes in terms or prices will be treated currently and prospectively as in a change in estimate.

The compensation cost is deferred to an account titled "deferred compensation" and is reported as a reduction of total stockholders' equity. The deferred cost is then charged to expense through straight-line amortization. Under no circumstances should compensation cost be charged to expense before the date of grant.

ACCOUNTING FOR TREASURY STOCK

Treasury stock is defined as shares that have been issued by the corporation, but are subsequently reacquired and held by the issuing corporation. Treasury shares do not reduce the number of issued shares, but are considered to be a reduction of outstanding shares.

The acquisition of treasury stock results in a decrease in assets as well as a decrease in total stockholders' equity, as the treasury shares are reported as a contra account to the stockholders' equity. There are two acceptable methods of accounting for treasury stock transactions: the cost method and the par value method. The former will be discussed at this time.

When accounting by the cost method, the acquisition and subsequent sale of treasury shares are veiwed as one continuous transaction. An account title should be descriptive of the type of stock it represents and is debited for the total cost incurred to purchase the shares. Subsequent sales of treasury stock may be based on specific identification, FIFO, last in, first out (LIFO), or a weighted average. Any incremental amounts from the sale of treasury shares will be reflected in the contributed capital account.

In reporting treasury stock on the balance sheet when either method is used, the total amount of stockholders' equity will be the same. The only difference is in the classification of the accounts and their balances. The method chosen is left up to the practitioner, yet it must be consistently applied.

Many times stock is donated by shareholders to the corporation. The donated shares are classified as treasury stock until they are retired. A donation does not result in an increase or decrease in total assets or total capital. The accounting process is consistent with accounting for treasury stock transactions.

AN OVERVIEW OF RETAINED EARNINGS AND DIVIDENDS

Retained earnings represent income and/or losses accumulated by the organization over time. If accumulated losses exceed the income, a deficit retained earnings balance will exist. However, in most cases, the balance will be positive. The retained earnings account is decreased (debited) for items such as net losses, prior period adjustments, and cash, stock, or property dividends. The account is increased (credited) for prior period adjustments and net income.

Dividends normally reduce retained earnings and represent a pro-rata allocation of corporate profits to the shareholders. Types of dividends include cash, stock, property, and liquidating dividends. It should be noted that liquidating dividends represent a return of corporate capital, and therefore the contributed capital account is debited as opposed to retained earnings.

Although dividends normally reduce retained earnings, they are not actually paid out of this account because retained earnings do not represent substantive assets. When paying dividends, usually the retained earnings account is reduced along with the appropriate asset account. However, when stock dividends are paid, the retained earnings account is decreased while the appropriate stock accounts are increased.

In accounting for dividends, four dates are important and an explanation of each is warranted.

Date of declaration: The date on which the board of directors formally announces a dividend. If the type of dividend is cash, liquidating, or property, the distribution is irrevocable and must be recorded on this date.

Date of record: This date is specified by the board of directors, and represents the cutoff date for stockholders to receive dividends. Stockholders of record as of this date will receive the dividend regardless of subsequent sales and purchases of stock.

Ex-dividend date: This date occurs one day after the date of record and shares sold from this date forward do not transfer the dividend rights. Consequently, this fact is usually reflected in the market price of the stock.

Payment date: The date on which checks are made available to the shareholders, or when property or stock is actually distributed. The accounting treatment involves a debit to dividends payable and a credit to the appropriate asset or equity account.

FOREIGN OPERATIONS

In December 1981, the FASB issued SFAS No. 52, entitled "Foreign Currency Translation." This statement was issued in direct response to the criticism the FASB received on its previous foreign currency pronouncement SFAS No. 8, "Accounting for the Translation of Foreign Currency Transactions and Foreign Currency Financial Statements." SFAS No. 52 provides for translation of foreign currency financial statements at the current exchange rate in most instances. Thus, it represents a significant departure from previous requirements. A further departure from SFAS No. 8 occurs owing to the requirement to aggregate translation adjustments in stockholders' equity.

The FASB issued SFAS No. 8 in October 1975. From its inception, the document was extremely controversial. The need for guidance in translating foreign currency statements was quite evident since existing standards were extremely diverse. The majority of the controversy centered around the following issues: (1) Should a statement permit reserve on allowance accounts? (2) Should a statement be based on historical cost? After lengthy deliberation, the FASB decided the temporal method of translation should be used. This method is consistent with historical cost and does not reflect actual current values. The FASB also disallowed adjustment accounts because of their perceived inconsistency with the all-inclusive concept of income determination.

However, the conclusions reached by the FASB in SFAS No. 8 did not settle the controversy concerning the treatment of foreign currency financial statements. The FASB asked for comments on its first 12 SFASs in May 1978, and No. 8 was the most criticized document. Respondents argued that elimination of reserve accounts would, at times, encourage management to make unwise and unnecessary moves to hedge against bookkeeping exposure when no actual economic exposure existed. Additionally, it was argued that historical cost simply does not reflect economic reality in an environment of high inflation and fluctuating exchange rates. These and other criticisms of SFAS No. 8 caused the FASB to restudy the matter and led to the issuance of SFAS No. 52.

Overview of SFAS No. 52

Owing to the perceived deficiencies of SFAS No. 8, the FASB reconsidered that pronouncement and eventually issued SFAS No. 52 on foreign currency translations. These modified requirements revise the standards of financial accounting and reporting for foreign currency transactions in financial statements of a reporting enterprise. In addition, SFAS No. 52 revises the standards for translating foreign currency financial statements that are incorporated in the financial statements of a reporting enterprise by consolidation, combination, or the equity method of accounting.

Objectives of Translation

Because multinational enterprises and their subsidiaries operate in diversified economic and currency environments, it is necessary to consolidate the financial statements of each separate entity. The resultant consolidated financial statements are presented as though they were the financial statements of a single enterprise, i.e., the multinational enterprise. To facilitate this presentation, it is necessary to translate into a reporting currency (i.e., the U.S. dollar) those assets, liabilities, revenues, expenses, gains, and losses that are measured or denominated in a foreign currency. Recognizing these assertions, the FASB concluded that the objectives of translation are to provide information that is generally compatible with the expected economic effects of a rate change on an enterprise's cash flows and equity and reflect, in consolidated statements, the financial results and relationships of the individual consolidated entities as measured in their functional currencies in conformity with U.S. GAAP.

Measurements

SFAS No. 52 requires that assets, liabilities, and operations of a foreign entity first be measured using the functional currency of that entity. An entity's functional currency is defined as the currency of the primary economic environment in which the entity operates and generates net cash flows. For example, the functional currency of a foreign entity operating in Germany would generally be German marks. This general rule, however, does have exceptions. For example, if a foreign entity operating in Germany were a direct and integral component or extension of a U.S. parent company's operations, the functional currency would be the U.S. dollar. In addition, if each entity has more than one distinct and separable operation (e.g., a branch or division), each operation may be considered an entity. It is therefore possible for each entity to have a different functional currency if their operations are conducted in different economic environments. Determining a single functional currency for an entity will be difficult in some instances. In those cases, the judgment of management should determine the functional currency of a foreign entity.

Once the functional currency for a foreign entity has been determined, that determination should be consistently applied for each foreign entity unless changes in the economic facts and circumstances clearly indicate that the functional currency has changed.

Remeasurement into functional currency is required for entities that do not maintain records in their functional currency prior to translation. The remeasurement process should produce asset and liability measures that would have resulted if financial records were maintained in the functional currency. However, to accomplish this, historical exchange rates should be utilized to remeasure certain accounts while the current exchange rate should be used on all others.

Translation of Foreign Currency Statements

Once measured in the functional currency, all assets and liabilities must be translated utilizing the current exchange rate as of the balance sheet date, while revenues, expenses, gains, and losses are translated at the current exchange rate in effect at the dates on which those elements are recognized during the period. In order to derive meaningful results without a burdensome record keeping system, it is acceptable to translate revenue and expense items at the average rates in effect during the period.

It should be noted that if the functional currency is the U.S. dollar, remeasurement into the dollar is all that is required; i.e., the need for translation is eliminated. Thus, in instances where the functional currency of an entity is the U.S. dollar and the records are maintained in a foreign currency, the translation principles of SFAS No. 8 virtually are retained. Many foreign entities operate in countries that experience high rates of inflation. Recognizing this fact, the FASB concluded that for financial statements of foreign entities operating in countries experiencing cumulative inflation rates of approximately 100 percent or more over a three year period, the functional currency will be defined as the reporting currency of the consolidated enterprise, i.e., the U.S. dollar. As stated previously, this results in maintaining the translation principle established in SFAS No. 8.

For entities whose functional currency is not the reporting currency, translation of financial statements into a reporting currency (usually the U.S. dollar) at the current exchange rate will result in translation adjustments if there has been a change in the exchange rate since the financial statements were last translated. SFAS No. 52 provides that these adjustments be excluded from net income until a sale or complete or substantially complete liquidation of the net investment in the entity occurs. (SFAS No. 8, by contrast, required that these adjustments be included in income.) As a result, translation adjustments will be reported separately and accumulated as a separate component of consolidated stockholders' equity until liquidation occurs. While excluded from the determination of net income, translation adjustments may result in timing differences pursuant to APBO Nos. 11, "Accounting for Income Taxes," 23, "Accounting for Income Taxes—Special Areas," and 24, "Accounting for Income Taxes," and thus be reflected in stockholders' equity net of tax.

Translation adjustments may result from either translating a foreign entity's financial statements using a current exchange rate that differs from the exchange rates used during the period or translating a foreign entity's financial statements using a current exchange rate that differs from the exchange rate used to translate the foreign entity's financial statements at the end of the previous period.

Foreign Operations Disclosures

SFAS No. 52 requires enterprises to disclose the aggregate amounts of translation gains or losses that are reflected in income (this includes gains or losses on forward contracts that have been recognized). Additionally, since the translation adjustments are included in equity, the changes in the translation adjustment should be disclosed along with other stockholders' equity changes. SFAS No. 52 requires, at a minimum, enterprises to disclose

1. The beginning and ending amount of cumulative translation adjustments
2. The aggregate adjustment for the period resulting from translation adjustments and gains and losses from certain hedges and intercompany balances that are deferred
3. The amount of income taxes for the period allocated to translation adjustments
4. The amounts transferred from cumulative translation adjustments and included in determining net income for the period as a result of the sale or complete or substantially complete liquidation of an investment in a foreign entity.

In certain instances, the FASB calls for additional disclosures as well. The accounting and auditing literature requires disclosure of material subsequent events that will impact operations in subsequent reporting periods. Consistent with this policy, SFAS No. 52 requires that if the exchange rate changes subsequent to the balance sheet date, and its effects on the open foreign currency transactions are material, this effect should be disclosed. However, the financial statements would not be restated in these instances.

ILLUSTRATIVE DISCLOSURES

Exhibit 12.1 provides an example of disclosures applicable to stockholders' equity. As can be seen, Champion International Corporation has three classes of stock outstanding. The preferred stock classes both indicate that they can be converted into common stock. Note 10 amplifies upon the conversion rights of the preferred stockholders. For example, each share of the 1.20 preferred stock can be converted into one share of common.

Additionally, the disclosures include liquidation preferences ($149,950 for the $4.60) as well as the dividend rate. Further, they indicate that the preferred stock is cumulative as to dividends. Note 10 also discloses common shares actually issued through conversion of preferred during the reporting period (2,789,362 common shares in 1979) and shares of common reserved for future conversion (1,416,842 at December 31, 1981).

Relative to common stock, the disclosures include the par value ($0.50 per share), shares authorized (100,000,000 shares), and shares issued at the reporting date (55,681,757 shares at December 31, 1981). Additionally, note 10 reconciles the beginning number of shares outstanding to these outstanding at year-end by explaining the causes of share issu-

Exhibit 12.1
Illustrative Stockholders' Equity Disclosures: Champion International Corporation

Liabilities and Shareholders' Equity December 31	1981	1980
Current Liabilities:		
Notes payable (Note 6)	$ 39,523	$ 18,110
Current installments of long-term debt	22,563	35,649
Accounts payable and accrued liabilities (Note 7)	388,379	417,423
Income taxes (Note 14)	17,180	6,921
Total current liabilities	467,645	478,103
Long-Term Debt (Note 8)	924,884	811,015
Other Liabilities	38,127	37,324
Deferred Income Taxes (Note 14)	219,425	217,662
Minority Interest in Subsidiaries	39,701	42,124
Commitments and Contingent Liabilities (Notes 9 and 19)	—	—
Capital Shares (Notes 10 and 11):		
Preference stock, $1 par value:		
$1.20 Cumulative convertible series (liquidation preference aggregates $27,056)	7,040	8,892
$4.60 Cumulative convertible series (liquidation preference aggregates $149,950)	145,152	145,200
Common stock, $.50 par value, authorized 100,000,000 shares; in 1981, issued 55,681,757 shares; in 1980, issued 55,324,154 shares	383,341	380,832
Retained Earnings (Note 8)	1,240,735	1,234,684
	1,776,268	1,769,608
Less:		
Treasury shares, at cost (Note 10)	16,105	16,318
Cumulative translation adjustment (Note 12)	6,719	—
	1,753,444	1,753,290
	$3,443,226	$3,339,518

Note 10. Capital Shares:

Preferred Shares

Each $1.20 and $4.60 preference share is cumulative and is convertible into one share and 1.667 shares of common stock, respectively, unless called for redemption, in which case the right to convert may end several days prior to the redemption date.

(continued)

Exhibit 12.1 (continued)

Each $1.20 preference share may be redeemed for $22.50 plus accrued dividends. At December 31, 1981 and 1980, respectively, 1,416,842 and 1,879,933 of such shares were authorized, and 1,212,640 and 1,545,095 were issued.

Changes in $1.20 preference shares (net of treasury) during the three years ended December 31, 1981 are as follows:

(in shares and thousands of dollars)	Shares	Amount
Balance at December 31, 1978	5,157,038	$ 28,712
Conversion to common shares	(2,789,362)	(15,653)
Conversion of long-term debt	5,879	152
Balance at December 31, 1979	2,373,555	13,211
Conversion to common shares	(850,752)	(4,828)
Conversion of long-term debt	12,122	310
Balance at December 31, 1980	1,534,925	8,693
Conversion to common shares	(335,831)	(1,938)
Conversion of long-term debt	3,376	86
Balance at December 31, 1981	1,202,470	$ 6,841

Each $4.60 preference share may be redeemed currently at $54.14 and thereafter at prices that decline to $50.00 at October 1, 1990, plus accrued dividends in each case. At December 31, 1981 and 1980, 3,000,000 shares were authorized and 2,999,000 and 3,000,000 shares were issued, respectively. The shares were issued in 1980 and the 1981 reduction in the issued amount is attributable to conversion.

At December 31, 1981 and 1980, 8,531,431 preference shares, for which no series has been designated, were authorized and unissued.

Common Shares

Changes in common shares (net of treasury) during the three years ended December 31, 1981 are as follows:

(in shares and thousands of dollars)	Shares	Amount
Balance at December 31, 1978	50,418,752	$333,003
Conversion of preference shares	2,789,362	15,653
Exercise of stock options	57,089	1,025
Conversion of long-term debt	30,058	769
Contingent compensation plan	4,715	81
Balance at December 31, 1979	53,299,976	350,531
Conversion of preference shares	850,752	4,828
Exercise of stock options	2,781	66
Conversion of long-term debt	29,962	779
Contingent compensation plan	5,541	100
Acquisition of timberlands	336,250	8,409
Balance at December 31, 1980	54,525,262	364,713
Conversion of preference shares	337,498	1,986
Exercise of stock options	3,469	83
Conversion of long-term debt	20,105	524
Contingent compensation plan	7,084	129
Balance at December 31, 1981	54,893,418	$367,435

Exhibit 12.1 (continued)

At December 31, 1981, common shares of the company are reserved for:

Conversion of preference shares	6,275,631
Conversion of long-term debt	97,027
Stock options granted or available for grant	2,055,355
Contingent compensation plan	1,707,982
Conversion of preferred shares of subsidiary	46,506
	10,182,501

Note 11. Stock Options:

The company has granted officers and key employees options, generally accompanied by stock appreciation rights, to purchase common shares at the market price of the shares on the date of grant. The options become exercisable in installments and expire ten years from the date of grant.

Transactions in 1981 under the plans are summarized below:

	Shares
January 1, 1981 – Shares under option	1,120,528
Options granted	254,900
Options exercised at prices ranging from $17.00 to $27.50 per share or stock appreciation rights exercised	(66,790)
Options surrendered or cancelled	(32,933)
December 31, 1981 – Shares under option	1,275,705
Options exercisable at December 31, 1981	689,561
Shares available for grant:	
January 1, 1981	1,007,115
December 31, 1981	779,650

At December 31, 1981, the common shares under option were at prices ranging from $12.25 to $27.50 per share with an aggregate option price of $30,314,000.

ances (i.e., conversion of preferred stock, exercise of stock options, conversion of long-term debt, contingent compensation plan).

The shares of preferred stock held in the treasury are disclosed as a reduction of total stockholders' equity ($16,318 at December 31, 1980). Further, the disclosure includes the shares held in the treasury and the basis of accounting for these shares (i.e., at cost).

The stock options outstanding are discussed in note 11. The disclosure includes the term of the options, those granted, the exercise price, and the shares issuable upon conversion of the options.

Finally, as required, note 12 provides an analysis of the cumulative translation adjustment at December 31, 1981, beginning with the aggregate adjustment resulting from the application of the new accounting standards.

13
Earnings per Share Disclosures

THE NATURE OF EARNINGS PER SHARE

EPS data are used by external parties in evaluating the past operating performance of the reporting enterprise. While EPS is only one of many useful financial ratios, it has received widespread prominence in reporting earnings figures. As such, the APB required that EPS be prominently displayed on the face of the income statement when financial statements that purport to present results of operations in conformity with GAAP are issued by the reporting entity. Thus, EPS has been designated by the accounting profession as the most important financial ratio by requiring that it be reported in the audited financial statements.

An exception to this reporting requirement is allowed to nonpublic enterprises. SFAS No. 21, "Suspension of the Reporting of Earnings per Share and Segment Information by Nonpublic Enterprises," suspends the requirements for nonpublic enterprises to report either EPS or segment information. A nonpublic enterprise is defined by SFAS No. 21 as an enterprise other than one (1) whose debt or equity securities trade in a public market on a foreign or domestic stock exchange or in the over-the-counter market (including securities quoted only locally or regionally) or (2) that is required to file financial statements with the SEC. While nonpublic enterprises are not required to report EPS data, if they voluntarily choose to do so, the computation and disclosure principles of APBO No. 15, "Earnings per Share," must be applied.

As the following illustrations show, a reporting enterprise may be required to present two EPS figures (dual presentation) on the face of the income statement. Also, the reporting enterprise is required to show EPS for several different income numbers (e.g., income before extraordi-

Exhibit 13.1
EPS Disclosures on the Income Statement

	Required on the Income Statement	Required, but May Be in the Notes	Optional, but Encouraged
Income from continuing operations	X		
Discontinued operation			
Income (loss) from operations		X	
Gain (loss) on disposal		X	
Income before extraordinary items	X		
Extraordinary items			X
Cumulative effect of a change			
in accounting principle	X		
Net income	X		

nary items and net income). Exhibit 13.1 presents a model income statement and the EPS requirements for each income component.

COMPUTING BASE EARNINGS PER SHARE

If an enterprise has a simple capital structure, it will report only one EPS figure for each of the income components illustrated in Exhibit 13.1. In computing EPS for a simple capital structure (designated "base EPS"), the computations should be based on the weighted average number of common shares outstanding during the period and the income available to common stockholders.

Paragraph 47 of APBO No. 15 requires that the computation of EPS be based upon the weighted average number of common shares outstanding during each period presented. This is necessary to properly reflect the effect of increases and decreases in the outstanding common shares in proportion to the time that they were actually outstanding.

Stock dividends, stock splits, and reverse stock splits change the number of shares outstanding. However, the change is proportional for each stockholder. Therefore, each stockholder (theoretically) maintains the same percentage ownership after the stock dividend, stock split, or reverse stock split as before the transaction. Accordingly, the effect of such transactions should be reflected retroactively for all periods presented. Further, changes in common shares outstanding from stock dividends, stock splits, or reverse stock splits that occur after the close of the reporting period but prior to the issuance of the financial statements also should be reflected retroactively for all periods presented. In such instances, disclosure of the fact that the change occurred subsequent to the end of the reporting period should be provided in the notes.

Since the denominator reflects only shares of common stock outstanding, the numerator should also be adjusted to reflect the earnings available to common stockholders (EAC). Since senior securities have a claim on income before the common stockholders, the claims of senior securities should be deducted in determining the EAC.

The interest accrued on senior debt securities should be reflected as a component of income. Therefore, no further adjustment should be necessary. However, the claims of senior stockholders (e.g., preferred stock) have not been deducted in computing income for the period. These claims on income (i.e., dividends) thus must be deducted from income in computing the EAC. Likewise, they should be added to any loss for the period in determining the EAC. This adjustment should be made for each income component for which EPS will be disclosed, i.e., income from continuing operations, income before extraordinary items, and net income (see Exhibit 13.1).

Once the EAC and the weighted average shares of common stock outstanding for the period are computed, the base EPS can be computed as follows:

$$\text{Base EPS} = \frac{\text{EAC}}{\text{Weighted Average Common Shares Outstanding}}.$$

Base EPS is critical in the process of computing and disclosing EPS, serving as a basis for determining the capital structure of the firm and as the underlying framework for computing primary and fully diluted EPS.

CAPITAL STRUCTURE—SIMPLE VERSUS COMPLEX

In determining the computations necessary for disclosing EPS data, the reporting enterprise must assess whether its capital structure is simple or complex. If simple, the enterprise will report only one EPS number for each disclosure indicated in Exhibit 13.1. This EPS number will be designated "earnings per common share."

The capital structure is deemed to be simple if it consists of only common stock or if there are no potentially dilutive securities that could in the aggregate dilute earnings per common share. Among the securities that may have a dilutive impact on EPS are convertible preferred stock, convertible debt, options, warrants, participating securities, different classes of common stock, and agreements to issue such securities or shares of common stock in the future (contingently issuable shares). These securities would be considered potentially dilutive if their inclusion in the computation of EPS would reduce the EPS or increase a loss per share. If the inclusion of such securities would increase EPS or decrease loss per share, they are considered, for purposes of applying the provisions of APBO No. 15, to be anti-dilutive securities.

Although the definition of a simple capital structure calls for no potentially dilutive securities, APBO No. 15 does provide a materiality threshold to be used for determining whether the capital structure is simple or complex. Footnote 2 to APBO No. 15 states:

Any reduction of less than 3 percent in the aggregate need not be considered as dilution in the computation and presentation of earnings per share data as discussed throughout [APBO No. 15]. In applying this test only issues which reduce earnings per share should be considered. In establishing this guideline the [AFB] does not imply that a similar measure should be applied in any circumstances other than the computation and presentation of earnings per share data under [APBO No. 15].

Therefore, as a practical matter, to determine if the capital structure is simple, each potentially dilutive security must be identified (anti-dilutive securities would be excluded) and then the aggregate dilutive effect must be determined. If the aggregate dilutive effect on base EPS is less than 3 percent, the capital structure is simple. If the aggregate dilutive effect on base EPS is 3 percent or more, the capital structure is complex.

If the enterprise has a complex capital structure, it is required to provide dual presentation of EPS data: primary EPS and fully diluted EPS. Further, EPS data must be presented for all periods covered by an income statement or earnings summary. If the capital structure is complex for any of the periods presented, dual presentation of primary and fully diluted EPS must be provided for all periods presented.

Primary EPS is the amount of earnings attributable to each share of common stock outstanding and common stock assumed to be outstanding to reflect the dilutive effect of common stock equivalents. It should be noted that the terms "primary" and "fully diluted" are used here (as well as in APBO No. 15) for ease of reference to one set of EPS figures; it is not, however, suggested as a caption to be used on income statements. Suggested captions will be presented later in this chapter.

Fully diluted EPS is the amount of earnings attributable to each share of common stock outstanding and common stock assumed outstanding to reflect the dilutive effect of common stock equivalents and other potentially dilutive securities that are not common stock equivalents. Therefore, the purpose of fully diluted EPS presentation is to show the maximum potential dilution of current earnings per share on a prospective basis.

CAPTIONS

While precise captions of EPS data are not prescribed by APBO No. 15, except that the term "earnings per common share" should be used if the enterprise has a simple capital structure, various alternatives are suggested. Exhibit 13.2 provides five potential captions and the situations in which they may be used.

If dual presentation is required in one period, it then is required for all periods presented in comparative form. Therefore, in a comparative income statement, the captions used should be the captions that are appropriate for the most dilutive presentation.

ADDITIONAL DISCLOSURES

Paragraphs 20 and 21 of APBO No. 15 suggest that a schedule or note relating to EPS data should explain the bases upon which both primary

Exhibit 13.2
Captions for EPS Data

Suggested EPS Captions

1. Earnings per common share
2. Earnings per common share—assuming no dilution
3. Earnings per common share—assuming full dilution
4. Earnings per common and common equivalent share (If both dilutive and anti-dilutive common stock equivalents are present, the caption may be earnings per common and dilutive common equivalent share.)
5. Earnings per common share—assuming issuance of all dilutive contingent shares

Table Indicating Use of EPS Captions

Common Stock Equivalents Present	Other Potentially Dilutive Securities Present	Caption for Single Presentation	Dual Presentation Primary Caption	Dual Presentation Fully Diluted Caption
No[a]	No[a]	1		
No[a]	Dilutive		2	3
No[a]	Anti-dilutive	1[b]		
Dilutive	No		4	3[c]
Dilutive	Dilutive		4	3
Dilutive	Anti-dilutive		4	5[b,c]
Anti-dilutive	No[a]	1[b]		
Anti-dilutive	Dilutive		2[b]	5[b]
Anti-dilutive	Anti-dilutive	1[b]		

[a]Or dilution is less than 3 percent if such securities are present.
[b]In a note, disclose the existence of the anti-dilutive securities.
[c]Primary and fully diluted amounts will be the same.

200 FINANCIAL STATEMENT DISCLOSURES

Exhibit 13.3
EPS Disclosures: Scovill Inc.

Scovill Inc. and Consolidated Subsidiaries	Fiscal Year Ended		
	December 27, 1981	December 28, 1980*	December 30, 1979*
Revenues			
Net sales	$817,862,000	$793,040,000	$788,072,000
Other income	7,832,000	6,171,000	5,444,000
	825,694,000	799,211,000	793,516,000
Costs and Expenses			
Cost of sales	572,392,000	561,275,000	554,250,000
Selling, administrative, research and general expenses	159,925,000	153,822,000	145,761,000
Interest on borrowed money (Notes D and E)	26,666,000	27,435,000	24,908,000
Other deductions	6,841,000	2,699,000	2,698,000
	765,824,000	745,231,000	727,617,000
Earnings from Continuing Operations before Income Taxes and			
Minority Interest	59,870,000	53,980,000	65,899,000
Federal, Foreign and State Income Taxes (Note G)	27,585,000	24,388,000	29,491,000
Earnings from Continuing Operations Before Minority Interest	32,285,000	29,592,000	36,408,000
Minority Interest in Net Earnings of Subsidiaries	2,304,000	2,205,000	1,152,000
Earnings from Continuing Operations	29,981,000	27,387,000	35,256,000
Loss from Discontinued Operations (Note B)	(34,515,000)	(3,376,000)	(3,256,000)
Net Earnings (Loss)	$ (4,534,000)	$ 24,011,000	$ 32,000,000
Net Earnings (Loss) per Share of Common Stock			
(Note J)			
Primary:			
Earnings from continuing operations	$3.18	$2.92	$3.81
Loss from discontinued operations	(3.68)	(.36)	(.35)
Net earnings (Loss)	$(.50)	$2.56	$3.46
Fully diluted:**			
Earnings from continuing operations	$3.13	$2.87	$3.69
Loss from discontinued operations	—	(.36)	(.34)
Net earnings (Loss)	$ —	$2.51	$3.35

*Reclassified for comparative purposes.
**Dash indicates anti-dilutive and, accordingly, is not shown.
See notes to consolidated financial statements.

EPS and fully diluted EPS were calculated. This schedule or note should identify which potentially dilutive securities are Common Stock Equivalents (CSEs) and were included in the computation of primary EPS.

In addition, supplementary computations in tabular form may be desirable to provide users with a clear understanding of the manner in which EPS amounts were derived. If provided, this information should include data on each potentially dilutive security included in the EPS computations. These supplementary data must be clearly distinguished from the income statement as a separate schedule.

DISCLOSURE OF EPS

Exhibit 13.3 illustrates disclosure of EPS data by Scovill Inc. As can be seen, both primary and fully diluted EPS data are presented for each income component beginning with earnings from continuing operations

Exhibit 13.3 (continued)

J. Earnings Per Common Share   Primary earnings per share are computed based on the average number of common shares outstanding during each year. Fully diluted earnings per share are computed assuming the conversion of all outstanding Preferred Stock and further assuming that the outstanding stock options having a dilutive effect had been exercised and the proceeds applied to purchase common shares for the treasury.

Earnings per share of Common Stock have been calculated as follows:

	Fiscal Year Ended		
	Dec. 27, 1981	Dec. 28, 1980*	Dec. 30, 1979*
Primary:			
Earnings from continuing operations	$29,981,000	$27,387,000	$35,256,000
Preferred Stock dividend requirements	182,000	234,000	355,000
Earnings from continuing operations applicable to Common Stock	29,799,000	27,153,000	34,901,000
Loss from discontinued operations	(34,515,000)	(3,376,000)	(3,256,000)
Net earnings (loss) applicable to Common Stock	$ (4,716,000)	$23,777,000	$31,645,000
Earnings per share:			
Continuing operations	$ 3.18	$ 2.92	$ 3.81
Discontinued operations	(3.68)	(.36)	(.35)
Net earnings (loss)	$ (.50)	$ 2.56	$ 3.46
Weighted average shares outstanding	9,380,295	9,289,205	9,158,453
Fully diluted:**			
Earnings from continuing operations	$29,981,000	$27,387,000	$35,256,000
Loss from discontinued operations	(34,515,000)	(3,376,000)	(3,256,000)
Net earnings (loss)	$ (4,534,000)	$24,011,000	$32,000,000
Earnings per share:			
Continuing operations	$ 3.13	$ 2.87	$ 3.69
Discontinued operations	—	(.36)	(.34)
Net earnings (loss)	$ —	$ 2.51	$ 3.35
Weighted average shares outstanding	9,581,540	9,558,294	9,561,370

*Reclassified for comparative purposes.
**Dash indicates anti-dilutive and, accordingly, is not shown.

(primary 3.18 for 1981). Additionally, it should be noted that dual presentation is used for all periods presented.

Further, note J to their financial statements describes the basis used for computing EPS figures. This discussion is supplemented with the detailed schedule (as suggested by APBO No. 15) showing the computation of the EPS numbers.

14

A Practitioner's Guide To Segment Disclosures as Required by Generally Accepted Accounting Principles

In SFAS No. 14, "Financial Reporting for Segments of a Business Enterprise," the FASB introduced a new concept in financial reporting as required by GAAP. This new concept was one of reporting on a less-than-total-enterprise basis. SFAS No. 14, as amended by SFAS Nos. 18, 24, and 30, and also suspended for nonpublic companies by No. 21, requires that public companies disaggregate and disclose total enterprise financial information in terms of business industry segments, foreign operations, export sales, and major customers.

NATURE OF SEGMENT DISCLOSURES

The primary purpose underlying segment disclosure requirements, as specified in SFAS No. 14, is to permit a better assessment of an enterprise's past and prospective economic performance. Therefore, interperiod comparability should be a major concern in preparing segment disclosures.

Interenterprise comparability should not be a primary concern in preparing segment disclosures. The FASB has not attempted to prescribe disaggregation and reporting procedures that would produce information valuable for comparisons between enterprises. Although, in general, total enterprise accounting methods and policies are applicable to individual segments, several important decisions regarding segment information policies have been left to the discretion of individual enterprise management. These decisions include those of choosing the bases of disaggregating the enterprise along with the methods of accounting for intersegment transactions and segment cost allocations.

METHODS OF PRESENTING SEGMENT INFORMATION

The FASB has also provided options in the required methods of presenting segment information. Segment information may be included in the financial statements of an enterprise in any one of the three following ways:

1. Within the body of the financial statements, with appropriate footnote explanations
2. Entirely in the footnotes of the financial statements
3. In a separate schedule that is an integral part of the financial statements. If the schedule is not clearly a part of the financial statements, a reference should be made to the schedule within the financial statements.

WHEN SEGMENT DISCLOSURES ARE REQUIRED

Generally, segment disclosures are required when a complete set of year-end financial statements is presented for a public company. However, SFAS No. 24, "Reporting Segment Information in Financial Statements That Are Presented in Another Enterprise's Financial Report," provides for exemptions from this general requirement.

A parent company, subsidiary, corporate joint venture, or 50 percent or less owned investee that would normally be required to report segment information is exempted from making these disclosures if its complete set of financial statements is included in the financial report of another enterprise and if the statements are

1. Consolidated or combined in a complete set of financial statements and both sets of financial statements are presented in the same financial report.
2. Presented for a foreign investee that is not a subsidiary of the primary reporting enterprise, unless that foreign entity's separately issued financial statements are required to disclose segment information.
3. Those of investee companies accounted for by the cost or equity method, if that segment information is not significant in relation to the consolidated or combined financial statements. Significance should be determined separately in terms of business industry segments, foreign operations, export sales, and major customers, as described in the following discussion.
4. Presented in the financial report of a nonpublic entity.

Unless these specific exemptions are met, complete sets of year-end financial statements for public investee companies, included in the financial report of another enterprise, must include segment information in accordance with SFAS No. 14, as amended.

Interim Financial Statements

As noted above, segment disclosures are required only in year-end financial statements. SFAS No. 18, "Financial Reporting for Segments of a Business Enterprise—Interim Financial Statements," amended SFAS No. 14 and eliminated segment reporting requirements for interim financial statements. However, if segment information is presented in interim financial statements, it should be consistent with the requirements of SFAS No. 14, as amended.

Nonpublic Companies

SFAS No. 21, "Suspension of the Reporting of Earnings per Share and Segment Information by Nonpublic Enterprises," suspended the segment disclosure requirements for nonpublic enterprises. A nonpublic enterprise is defined by SFAS No. 21 as "an enterprise other than one (a) whose debt or equity securities trade in a public market on a foreign or domestic stock exchange or in the over-the-counter market . . . or (b) that is required to file financial statements with the Securities and Exchange Commission."

SEGMENT DISCLOSURE REQUIREMENTS—IN GENERAL

As mentioned previously, SFAS No. 14 prescribes segment disclosures in four areas: business industry segments, foreign operations, export sales, and major customers. General disclosure requirements for business industry segments and foreign operations focus on revenues, profitability, and identifiable assets, while export sales and major customers disclosures are related only to revenues.

Each of these four disclosure areas will be analyzed individually in the following. Two questions in relation to each disclosure area will be addressed: (1) What are the required disclosures? (2) How are those disclosures derived?

REQUIRED DISCLOSURES—BUSINESS INDUSTRY SEGMENTS

Exhibit 14.1 highlights the required disclosures for business industry segments. These disclosures are required individually for business industry segments determined to be reportable and in the aggregate for nonreportable business industry segments. The flowchart, as shown in Exhibit 14.2, summarizes the process of determining reportable segments.

DERIVING BUSINESS INDUSTRY SEGMENT DISCLOSURES—DETERMINING REPORTABLE SEGMENTS

As shown in the flowchart in Exhibit 14.2, the initial step in determining reportable segments is to identify the revenue producing products and services of an enterprise. The revenues produced from these products or services should be primarily from sales to unaffiliated customers.

Exhibit 14.1
Business Industry Segment Disclosures

Revenue Disclosures
1. Sales to unaffiliated customers
2. Sales or transfers to other industry segments
3. Basis of accounting for intersegment sales and transfers
4. Reconciliation of total segment revenues to consolidated revenues

Profitability Disclosures
1. Operating profit or loss
2. Nature and amount of unusual *or* infrequently occurring items included in operating profit or loss
3. Reconciliation of total segment operating profits and losses to consolidated pre-tax income from continuing operations
4. Optional disclosure—additional profitability measures and description of differences from operating profit or loss

Identifiable Assets Disclosures
1. Aggregate carrying amount
2. Aggregate amount of depreciation, depletion, and amortization expense
3. Capital expenditures
4. Reconciliation of total segment identifiable assets to total consolidated assets with assets maintained for general corporate purposes separately identified in the reconciliation

Interperiod Comparability Disclosures
1. Nature and effect on operating profit or loss in the period of change for changes in the basis of accounting for intersegment sales and transfers
2. Nature and effect on operating profit or loss in the period of change for changes in the method of allocating operating expenses among segments
3. Effect on operating profit or loss in the period of change for changes in accounting principles
4. Restatement and disclosure of nature and effect of restatement if financial statements of prior periods have been retroactively restated
5. Restatement and disclosure of nature and effect of restatement if the method of grouping industry segments has been changed
6. Explanation of significant industry segments not considered reportable and reportable segments not considered significant, as determined by the interperiod comparability test described in the text

Other Required Disclosures
1. Types of products and services from which individual segment revenues are derived
2. Accounting policies relevant to segment information that are not adequately explained elsewhere in the financial statements
3. Equity in net income from and investment in net assets of unconsolidated subsidiaries or other equity method investees whose operations are vertically integrated with operations of an individual business industry segment
4. Types of industries in which all unconsolidated subsidiaries or other equity method investees operate

Exhibit 14.2
Determining Reportable Industry Segments

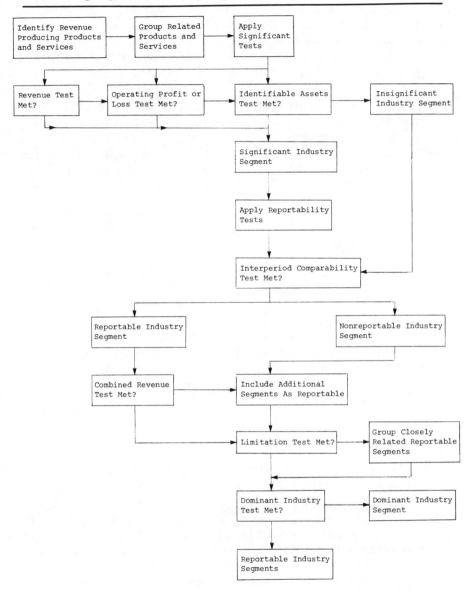

Grouping Products and Services

Once identified, related products and services should be grouped to form industry segments. SFAS No. 14 states that no single authoritative industrial classification system exists for determining groupings of related products and services. Therefore, this grouping process must depend largely on the judgment of individual enterprise management. Factors to be considered, as suggested in SFAS No. 14, include the nature of the product or service, the nature of the production process, and the customer markets and marketing methods.

SFAS No. 14 does, however, give a few specific guidelines for disaggregating the total enterprise into industry segments:

1. Foreign operations should be disaggregated by industries only if practical. If considered impractical to disaggregate, foreign operations may be considered a single industry segment.
2. Vertically integrated operations of an enterprise should not be disaggregated by industries.
3. Unconsolidated subsidiaries or other equity method investees are not required to be disaggregated by industry segments; however, vertically integrated investees should be identified with related industry segments.

Analyzing Segments for Significance

As shown in the flowchart in Exhibit 14.2, significant business industry segments have been defined in terms of three tests: (1) the revenue test, (2) the operating profit or loss test, and (3) the identifiable assets test. These tests must be applied separately in each fiscal year for which segment information is presented. Industry segments are required to meet only one of the three tests to be considered significant and subject to additional reportability tests.

Before discussing the mechanics of each of the three significance tests, definitions of the terms "revenue," "operating profit or loss," and "identifiable assets" must first be established.

Revenue

Segment revenue should include both sales to unaffiliated customers and intersegment sales and transfers. Intersegment sales and transfers should be from products and services similar to those sold to unaffiliated customers and should not include billings for joint costs between segments or charges for use of shared facilities. Intersegment sales and transfers should be included on the basis used by the enterprise to price such transactions.

Interest revenue should also be included in segment revenue if the interest earning asset is included in the segment's identifiable assets, as defined below. Interest earned on advances or loans to other industry segments should be included in segment revenue for financial service segments only.

Operating Profit or Loss

Segment operating profit or loss is defined as segment revenue less segment operating expenses. Segment revenue has been previously defined; only segment operating expenses will be defined here.

Generally, segment operating expenses include expenses related to segment revenue from both unaffiliated customers and other segments. Intersegment purchases should be included in expense on the same basis as used in pricing intersegment sales.

Operating expenses that are not directly traceable to a segment, yet are incurred for a segment's benefit, should be allocated on some reasonable basis related to the benefits received. Amortization of intangible assets, included in segment identifiable assets, should also be included in computing segment operating profit or loss.

SFAS No. 14 specifically excludes the following from segment operating profit or loss:

1. Revenue earned at the corporate level that was not the direct result of operations of any industry segment
2. General corporate expenses
3. Interest expense, except for financial service segments
4. Domestic and foreign income taxes
5. Equity in income or loss from unconsolidated subsidiaries or other equity method investees
6. Gains or losses from discontinued operations
7. Extraordinary items
8. Minority interests
9. Cumulative effect of a change in accounting principle.

Identifiable Assets

Segment identifiable assets should include all tangible and intangible assets used by or associated with the segment. Intangible assets that represent part of an enterprise's investment in a segment should be included in that segment's identifiable assets. Assets used jointly with other segments should be allocated on a reasonable basis between the user segments. However, assets used only to transfer goods or services between segments should not be considered joint assets and should be identified only with the segment producing the goods or services.

Advances or loans to other segments should be considered segment assets only if the segment is a financial services one. Contra asset accounts associated with identifiable segment assets should also be included as a part of total segment identifiable assets. General corporate assets should be excluded from individual segment identifiable assets.

Significance Tests

With these definitions in mind, the mechanics of the three tests used to determine significant segments can be discussed. The discussion will follow the order of the flowchart presentation in Exhibit 14.2. However, if any one of the three tests is met, the segment should be considered significant and subject to the reportability tests.

Revenue Test

In order to meet the revenue test for significance, an individual industry segment's revenues must equal 10 percent or more of combined segment revenues. Combined segment revenues should include revenue from unaffiliated customers and intersegment sales and transfers for all industry segments.

Operating Profit or Loss Test

Individual segment operating profit or loss amounts should be measured against the greater of total operating profits for all segments with an operating profit or the absolute value of the total operating losses of all segments with an operating loss. Any industry segment with an operating profit or loss greater than or equal to 10 percent of the measurement value will be considered significant.

Identifiable Assets Test

Any segment with identifiable assets equal to or greater than 10 percent of combined identifiable assets for all segments will be considered significant.

Reportability Tests

Significant segments, as determined by any of the three significance tests, will then be subject to three additional reportability tests. These tests will determine which of the significant segments will be considered reportable ones and which, if any, of the insignificant segments should also be considered reportable. Reportable segments are those for which individual segment information is required to be reported.

Interperiod Comparability Test

Significant and insignificant segments should be evaluated in terms of actual reportable segments of the past and expected reportable segments of the future. If a segment is significant in the current year, but has not been a reportable segment in the past and is not expected to be one in the future, it would be appropriate to exclude that segment from the current reportable segments even though it has met at least one of the significance tests.

Conversely, if a segment is not currently significant, but was reportable in the past and is expected to be reportable in the future, it would be appropriate to include that segment as a reportable one in the current year, even though it has not met any of the significance tests.

Combined Revenue Test

The combined revenue test ensures that reportable segments do, in fact, compose a substantial part of the enterprise's total operations. Only segment revenues from sales to unaffiliated customers should be considered in applying this test. Revenues from all unaffiliated customers for reportable segments should be combined and then compared with combined sales to unaffiliated customers for all segments. Reportable segment revenues from unaffiliated customers must equal 75 percent or more of total segment sales to unaffiliated customers.

If this test is not met, additional segments must be considered reportable. Insignificant segments with the largest amounts of revenues from unaffiliated customers should now be considered reportable in order to increase unaffiliated sales to the level needed to meet the combined revenue test.

Limitation Test

Finally, the number of reportable segments should not exceed a practical limit. SFAS No. 14 suggests this limit should be ten. If more than ten reportable segments exist, closely related reportable segments should be combined in order to meet the limitation test.

Dominant Industry Test

If one of the reportable segments is unusually significant, the dominant industry test should be applied. In order to meet the dominant industry test, the following two conditions must exist: (1) One segment's revenues, operating profit or loss, and identifiable assets must each equal or exceed 90 percent of the combined totals for all segments; and (2) No other industry segment meets any of the three significance tests.

If these two conditions are met, the enterprise has a dominant industry and is not subject to the business industry disclosure requirements as shown in Exhibit 14.1. Only the identity of the dominant industry must be disclosed in accordance with SFAS No. 14.

DERIVING BUSINESS INDUSTRY SEGMENT DISCLOSURES—REPORTING CONSIDERATIONS

Industry segment disclosures, as shown in Exhibit 14.2, should be presented for each reportable industry segment and in the aggregate for all nonreportable industry segments, as indicated. The definitions of revenue, operating profit or loss, and identifiable assets, as discussed earlier, should provide general guidelines for deriving the revenue, profitability, and identifiable assets disclosures.

Interperiod comparability disclosures require the disclosure of the nature and effect of changes affecting the comparability between segment disclosures for the periods presented. These disclosures should be adequate to present a clear understanding to financial statement users of the changes that affect the interperiod comparability of the segment disclosures presented. Specifically, these disclosures should include a description of the change and the effect of the change, in terms of dollar amounts, on the appropriate segment disclosures for the year in which the change occurred.

Other required disclosures include the types of industries in which all unconsolidated subsidiaries or other equity method investees operate. Financial information about investees whose operations are vertically integrated with those of specific industry segments should also be disclosed. Required financial information disclosures for vertically integrated investees include (1) the amount of equity in net income from the investee recognized during the period and (2) the amount of investment in net assets of the investee.

REQUIRED DISCLOSURES—FOREIGN OPERATIONS

Exhibit 14.3 highlights the required disclosures for foreign operations. These disclosures should be presented if foreign operations are considered significant to total enterprise operations.

DERIVING FOREIGN OPERATIONS DISCLOSURES

The flowchart shown in Exhibit 14.4 summarizes the process of deriving foreign operations, export sales, and major customer disclosures. This two step process includes (1) determining if foreign operations, export sales, and major customers are significant to total enterprise operations, and thereby determining if disclosure of these operations is required, and (2) the process of disaggregating an enterprise into bases for reporting the required disclosures.

Determining If Foreign Operations Disclosures Are Significant

As shown in the flowchart, analyzing a corporation in terms of its domestic and foreign operations is the first step in determining if foreign operations disclosures are required.

SFAS No. 14 defines foreign operations as revenue producing operations that are located outside of the enterprise's home country and that are generating revenue either from sales to unaffiliated customers or from intraenterprise sales or transfers between geographic areas.

Domestic operations are defined as revenue producing operations lo-

Exhibit 14.3
Foreign Operations Disclosures

Revenue Disclosures
1. Sales to unaffiliated customers
2. Sales or transfers between geographic areas
3. Basis of accounting for sales and transfers between geographic areas
4. A reconciliation of total revenue for all geographic areas to consolidated revenue

Profitability Disclosures
1. A common profitability measure for each geographic area including either:
   a. Operating profit or loss or
   b. Net income or
   c. Profitability measure between operating profit or loss and net income
2. A reconciliation of total profitability of all geographic areas to total profitability on a consolidated basis

Identifiable Assets Disclosures
1. Aggregate carrying value of assets identifiable with each geographic area
2. Reconciliation of identifiable assets for all geographic areas with total consolidated assets

Interperiod Comparability Disclosures
1. Nature and effect of a change in the method of accounting for sales and transfers between geographic areas
2. Restatement and disclosure of nature and effect of restatement, if financial statements of prior periods have been retroactively restated
3. Restatement and disclosure of nature and effect of restatement, if the method of grouping foreign operations has been changed

Other Required Disclosures
1. Identification of significant geographic areas
2. Identification of geographic areas in which unconsolidated subsidiaries and other equity method investees operate

---

cated in the enterprise's home country that generate revenue either from sales to unaffiliated customers or from intraenterprise sales or transfers between geographic areas. As in determining industry segments, unconsolidated subsidiaries or other equity method investees should not be considered in determining foreign and domestic operations.

Once foreign operations have been identified, two significance tests should be applied: a revenue test and an identifiable assets test. If either of these two significance tests is met, foreign operations disclosures are required.

Revenue Test

Foreign operations are considered significant if sales to unaffiliated customers generated by foreign operations are 10 percent or more of consolidated revenues.

Exhibit 14.4
Determining Bases for Reporting Foreign Operations, Export Sales, and Major Customers Disclosures

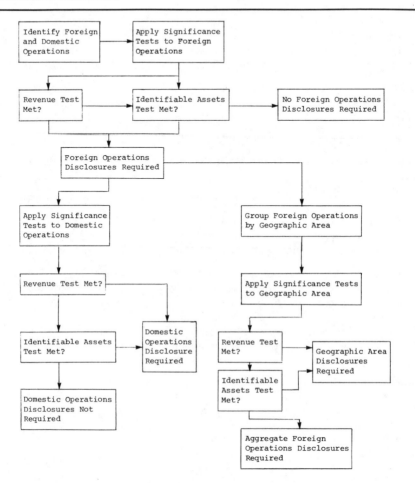

Identifiable Assets Test

Foreign operations are also considered significant if the identifiable assets associated with foreign operations are 10 percent or more of consolidated total assets. If neither the revenue nor the identifiable assets test is met, foreign operations disclosures are not required. However, if one of these two significance tests is met, foreign operations must be further analyzed to determine the bases for reporting the required disclosures.

Determining the Bases for Reporting

Foreign operations should be disaggregated into geographic areas for reporting purposes. The appropriate geographic areas are determined on an individual enterprise basis. Geographic areas may include individual foreign countries or groups of countries. Factors to be considered in determining geographic areas, as suggested in SFAS No. 14, include proximity, economic affinity, similarities in business environments, and the nature, scale, and degree of interrelationships of the operations in various foreign countries.

Once geographic areas have been determined, the two significance tests for revenue and identifiable assets, as described above, should be applied to each.

An enterprise must report the required foreign operations disclosures for each geographic area that meets at least one of the two significance tests and for all other geographic areas in the aggregate. If there are no individually significant geographic areas, foreign operations disclosures should be made in the aggregate only.

Disclosures are also required for domestic operations if either revenue or identifiable assets associated with domestic operations meet the appropriate significance test.

DERIVING FOREIGN OPERATIONS DISCLOSURES— REPORTING CONSIDERATIONS

Foreign operations disclosure requirements are similar in nature to the disclosure requirements for business industry segments. Such disclosures should be made based on "revenue," as defined in the discussion of business industry segments. That definition of revenue is summarized below:

Segment revenue includes both sales to unaffiliated customers and intersegment sales and transfers. Intersegments sales and transfers should be included in revenue at the basis used by the enterprise to price such transactions and should not include billings for joint costs or charges for use of shared facilities. Interest revenue should be included in segment revenue if the interest earning assets are included in the segment's identifiable assets.

Profitability disclosures for foreign operations can be made based on operating profit or loss, net income, or some measure inbetween operating profit or loss and net income. If operating profit or loss disclosures are made, operating profit or loss should be defined, generally, as segment revenues less the expenses related to those segment revenues. The computations of operating profit or loss for foreign operations disclosures should be consistent with the more specific definition used in the preceding discussion of business industry segments.

Identifiable assets disclosures should also be based on the definition of identifiable assets presented in the discussion of business industry segments earlier. Generally, identifiable assets for foreign operations disclosures should include all assets used by or normally identified with operations in a foreign country.

Interperiod comparability disclosures, as discussed for business industry segments, should also be presented for foreign operations. Based on these disclosures, financial statement users should have a clear understanding of the changes affecting the interperiod comparability of the segment information presented.

Identification should also be made of the geographic areas in which unconsolidated subsidiaries or other equity method investees operate. SFAS No. 14 does not require the disaggregation of unconsolidated subsidiary or other equity method investee operations for foreign operations disclosures.

REQUIRED DISCLOSURES—EXPORT SALES

Exhibit 14.5 highlights export sales disclosure requirements.

DERIVING EXPORT SALES DISCLOSURES

Export sales disclosures are required if export sales are 10 percent or more of total consolidated revenues.

Export sales should include only sales generated by domestic operations that were made to unaffiliated customers in foreign countries. Domestic operations include operations located in an enterprise's home country, as defined earlier.

This disclosure test should be made separately from the significance tests for business industry segments and foreign operations. Export sales disclosures are required if this test is met, regardless of whether or not business industry segment or foreign operations disclosures are made.

REQUIRED DISCLOSURES—MAJOR CUSTOMERS

Exhibit 14.6 summarizes the disclosure requirements for major customers.

Exhibit 14.5
Export Sales Disclosures

---

1. Aggregate export sales to unaffiliated customers
2. Export sales to unaffiliated customers for each geographic area
3. Restatement and disclosure of nature and effect of restatement if financial statements of prior periods have been retroactively restated

---

Exhibit 14.6
Major Customers Disclosures

1. Fact that 10 percent or more of enterprise (consolidated) revenues were derived from single customers
2. Amount of revenue derived from each such customer
3. Identity of industry segment or segments making these sales (required only if industry segment disclosures are required for the enterprise)
4. Restatement and disclosure of nature and effect of restatement if financial statements of prior periods have been retroactively restated

DERIVING MAJOR CUSTOMER DISCLOSURES

Major customer disclosures are required if revenue from a single customer is 10 percent or more of consolidated revenues.

Identifying Total Revenues by Single Customer

Total enterprise revenues must first be divided into sales to single customers. Single customers, as defined in SFAS No. 14 and amended by SFAS No. 30, include (1) individual enterprises, (2) enterprises under common control (e.g., two subsidiaries of the same parent company), (3) a federal government, (4) a state government, (5) a local government, and (6) a foreign government. Total revenues from any single customer, as defined above, should then be compared with total enterprise revenue.

Total Revenue Test

If revenue from a single customer is equal to or greater than 10 percent of total enterprise revenue, major customer disclosures are required for that customer. Major customer disclosures are required if this test is met regardless of whether or not the enterprise reports other types of segment disclosures.

ANALYZING FINANCIAL STATEMENT SEGMENT DISCLOSURES

The preceding discussion addressed the questions related to the specific segment disclosure requirements and how those disclosures are derived for each of the four disclosure areas: business industry segments, foreign operations, export sales, and major customers.

The concluding discussion will analyze segment disclosures as recently reported in the annual financial statements of two public companies—U.S. Steel and Du Pont. These segment disclosures will be analyzed in terms of the segment disclosures required by SFAS No. 14, as presented in Exhibits 14.1, 14.3, 14.5, and 14.6.

ANALYSIS OF SEGMENT DISCLOSURES—U.S. STEEL

Exhibit 14.7 shows segment disclosures as reported in the 1981 annual report of U.S. Steel. U.S. Steel presented segment information primarily in the footnotes of the financial statements. Additional segment information was also presented outside of the financial statements and appropriately referenced in the footnotes. Segment information was presented for three annual periods, 1981, 1980, and 1979. Complete financial statements were included in the annual report for 1981 and 1980. Therefore, only 1981 and 1980 segment disclosures were required under GAAP. Selected financial information for 1979 was presented in the 1981 annual report including consolidated statements of income and changes in financial position.

Business Industry Segment Disclosures—U.S. Steel

U.S. Steel presented industry segment disclosures for each of six reportable segments. As shown in the industry segment disclosure of Exhibit 14.7, these industry segments include (1) steel, (2) chemicals, (3) resource development, (4) fabricating and engineering, (5) manufacturing and other, and (6) domestic transportation and utility subsidiaries. Foreign operations have been disaggregated by industry segments. Worldwide disaggregation by industry segments is prescribed by SFAS No. 14 only if practical.

Revenue Disclosures

U.S. Steel presented the required revenue disclosures in columns 2, 3, and 4 of the industry segment disclosure schedule. All consolidated sales were allocated to industry segments, and intersegment sales were appropriately included in total segment revenues. The basis of accounting for intersegment sales was disclosed in the first paragraph of the footnote disclosure, as shown in Exhibit 14.7.

Profitability Disclosures

Operating income or loss was disclosed for each industry segment and reconciled to consolidated operating income, as shown in the fifth column of the industry segment disclosure schedule. Total consolidated operating income is reconciled to pre-tax income from continuing operations in the consolidated income statement. SFAS No. 14 requires that total operating profit or loss from all industry segments be reconciled to consolidated pre-tax income from continuing operations.

Identifiable Assets Disclosures

The last three columns of the industry segment disclosure schedule present the required identifiable assets disclosures. Segment totals were appropriately reconciled to consolidated assets totals, with corporate

Exhibit 14.7
Segment Disclosures: U.S. Steel

STEEL MANUFACTURING

	$ Millions	
	1979	1978
Sales	$9,754	$8,820
Operating Income (Loss)	(102)	26

The increase in sales during 1979 resulted primarily from steel price increases, which only partially covered increased costs. Price increases were voluntarily restricted in compliance with the Federal government's Anti-Inflation Program (see "Wage-Price Guideline Program", page 16).

With strong steel markets in the first half of 1979, operating income trended upward. However, income in the second half was adversely impacted by a decline in demand, continued cost-price pressures, and substantial costs to implement major programs necessary to maintain and improve future operations.

The loss for 1979 came principally from operations at four unprofitable plants. These steel operations have many new facilities which have not yet attained expected performance and productivity levels. Correcting problems at these locations has been costly in terms of increased maintenance and facility outages, disrupted production schedules, and reduced productivity. By year-end, many major maintenance programs were virtually complete. In addition, comprehensive programs utilizing the best available technical expertise are under way to resolve remaining problems.

Many improvements were evident by year-end and more are expected. At Gary Works, the Corporation's largest blast furnace was completely rebuilt and resumed operation in January 1980. Upon completion of start-up, production from this rebuilt furnace is expected to be about 50 percent above its level during 1979. Three smaller furnaces have been shut down. With completion of a blast furnace program in late 1979, South Works has efficient iron production facilities which complement a modern oxygen steelmaking shop and electric furnaces.

At Fairfield Works, efficient, consistent production of quality iron is now being achieved from the new 5,000-ton-per-day blast furnace, which began production in late 1978. It is now exceeding its expected production level. Texas Works began operations in 1970 as a plate mill. It has been expanded and includes modern electric furnaces, continuous casting facilities and a large diameter pipe mill. The new pipe mill is expected to be the leader in the production of pipe products, including the rigid specification, high quality Arctic grades.

The steelmaking facilities and many of the finishing facilities at these four locations are as modern as those anywhere. Some investment will be required, however, to increase production of flat rolled products at Fairfield, to provide new rail production facilities at a location to be determined, and to obtain additional continuous casting and annealing capability. These investments are expected to provide an attractive rate of return.

Strengthening the Organization

Low-cost production on modern, competitive facilities is only one part of the business plan for Steel Manufacturing. The other major part is renewed emphasis on customer service and product quality. To accomplish this, marketing, product allocation and production planning functions in steel were centralized. This change will enable more effective coordination of production and sale of the most profitable products by the most efficient plants. The plan does not contemplate production of every possible product.

Also, to insure the greatest return from the investment dollar, all aspects of facility planning, process engineering and construction management were placed under centralized control.

Enhancing Product Quality

In a continuing effort to further improve product quality, all plants are well into the most comprehensive quality improvement program ever undertaken in the Corporation. The program includes an ongoing monitoring system to indicate whether standards are met. It defines responsibilities and establishes authority and accountability for quality control management.

Improving Steelmaking

To benefit from the best steelmaking practices available, U. S. Steel is supplementing its own expertise with the best proven practices available worldwide.

The Corporation has substantial reserves of high-quality coking coal and ore. U. S. Steel intends to use the most efficient manufacturing practices to convert coal and ore economically into iron for steelmaking. The objective is to lower costs, reduce energy requirements, decrease investment in facilities and be virtually self-sufficient in cokemaking capacity. As a corollary, fewer blast furnaces and less coke will be needed to produce the required iron. Already, usage of coke has declined and blast furnace productivity has improved. Further improvements in productivity are expected upon

(continued)

Exhibit 14.7 (continued)

completion of projects under way to produce higher quality coke consistently.

Facilities are under construction at three steel producing locations to accomplish de-sulphurization of iron, and similar facilities are planned for three additional locations. Benefits will include reduced coke consumption, increased productivity in both ironmaking and steelmaking processes, and production of more prime grade steel.

Improved Profitability: Target for the 1980's

Steel Manufacturing's strategy is to maximize return from investments already in place. Implementation involves identifying and concentrating on product lines with the greatest profit potential; continuing emphasis on product quality; improving customer service; and consolidating production into those facilities where quality, cost effectiveness and improved product mix will provide optimum results. The full favorable effects from these actions will not be realized immediately; but a steady, gradual improvement is expected. With production directed to the most profitable products and the most efficient facilities, U. S. Steel expects to be a leaner, more profitable, market-oriented steel producer in the 1980's.

CHEMICALS

	$ Millions	
	1979	1978
Sales	$1,256	$808
Operating Income	58	21

With growing markets, with new products available and with higher prices, sales of chemicals in 1979 exceeded the billion dollar level for the first time—a year ahead of earlier projections. Cost increases, primarily raw materials and energy, were substantial—as were preproduction and start-up expenses associated with major construction projects. Operating income increased significantly.

Seven major projects, most of which came on stream late in 1979, are expected to reach full production capability in early 1980. With these projects completed, the year 1980 should be largely free of preproduction and start-up costs. Annual sales potential from these new facilities is nearly $350 million per year at current prices.

Highlights

The new chemical facilities will provide a stronger raw materials base, expand existing

Steel Manufacturing

	1979	1978	1977	1976	1975
SALES BY PRODUCT GROUPING		Percent of Total Dollars			
Sheet, Strip and Tin Mill	41%	41%	42%	44%	33%
Plates, Structural and Piling	19	20	18	17	22
Bars and Rods	12	13	13	14	12
Pipe and Tubing	15	15	14	11	19
Other Steel Products	7	7	8	10	9
All Other Products and Services	6	4	5	4	5
Total	100%	100%	100%	100%	100%
OPERATING STATISTICS		Millions of Net Tons			
Shipments of Steel	21.0	20.9	19.6	19.4	17.6
Production:					
Raw Steel	29.7	31.3	28.8	28.3	26.4
% Capability Utilization	83.5%	82.4%	75.5%	74.6%	74.1%
Iron	23.4	24.8	23.1	23.2	21.5
Coal Mined	16.1	11.5	14.0	16.0	17.1
Coke	14.5	13.6	15.4	15.5	16.0
Iron Ore—Natural and Agglomerated					
Mesabi and Western Ore Operations	22.8	20.5	12.2	20.8	22.0
Quebec Cartier Mining Company*	16.7	9.0	17.1	16.5	9.1
Total Iron Ore	39.5	29.5	29.3	37.3	31.1
% Iron Ore Sold to Others	38%	26%	31%	28%	23%

*Resource Development segment

Chemicals—Sales by Product Grouping

	Percent of Total Dollars				
	1979	1978	1977	1976	1975
Industrial & Coal Chemicals..........	39%	39%	45%	46%	42%
Plastic Resins.......................	23	13	5	9	8
Agriculture...........................	38	48	50	45	50
	100%	100%	100%	100%	100%

Exhibit 14.7 (continued)

product lines, supply new products and provide entry into new markets.

Styrene monomer and olefin cracker units were acquired in January 1979. The styrene monomer facility operated throughout 1979. The olefin cracker unit was placed in operation in the fourth quarter after installation of additional environmental control equipment. Production from both of these units will be used to satisfy a portion of existing raw material requirements of other industrial chemical and plastic resin facilities.

New and expanded facilities for producing nitrogen-based fertilizers began operations in 1979, increasing sales potential for these products by 20 percent. New phenol and unsaturated polyester resins facilities will increase the sales potential of these products, many of which ultimately go into construction and automotive products.

New chemical products were added to the existing line with the start-up of facilities in 1979 to produce bisphenol-A, acrylic sheets, polypropylene, ABS resins and latex materials. These products are used in a wide variety of consumer products. The more diversified product line enables USS Chemicals to enter new markets and to broaden its participation in existing markets.

Further Growth: Plan for the 1980's

USS Chemicals and Texaco, Inc., have formed a joint venture to market high-density polyethylene. This product is widely used in containers, housewares and other consumer products; high rates of growth appear likely in the 1980's. Engineering studies are under way for a proposed manufacturing plant for the joint venture that could commence operation in 1983.

In December 1979, USS Chemicals and Tenneco Chemicals, Inc., signed a letter of intent to form a joint venture to manufacture phthalic anhydride and a plasticizer alcohol. The agreement contemplates construction of new world-scale production facilities in the Houston, Texas area. The units could be in production during 1982. These materials will further strengthen the raw materials base for certain product lines.

During 1979, USS Agri-Chemicals and its partner in a joint venture agreed to expand and extend the life of their existing phosphate

rock mine near Ft. Meade, Fla. Phosphate rock is the base material for phosphatic fertilizers. This action will insure Agri-Chemicals' continued self-sufficiency in terms of its phosphate rock requirements through the Eighties.

USS Agri-Chemicals has programs under way to increase sales to consumer markets through additional retail facilities. This approach, coupled with expected strengthening of worldwide phosphatic and nitrogen fertilizer markets, should improve profitability.

RESOURCE DEVELOPMENT

	$ Millions	
	1979	1978
Sales	$576	$396
Operating Income	55	25

The improvement in sales and operating income during 1979 primarily reflected higher volume for iron ore, ocean shipping services and energy products, as well as improved earnings from equity investments in overseas mining companies.

Following organization changes made in late 1979, the management of these business activities is now responsible for all the Corporation's mineral resources, including those necessary to support steel operations.

Capital Investments Beginning to Pay Off

Though world iron ore markets continued depressed, Quebec Cartier Mining Company (QCM), a wholly owned Canadian subsidiary, sold 16.3 million net tons in 1979—80 percent of its annual capacity. Higher customer commitments are already in hand at increased prices for 1980.

The international bulk shipping market experienced a dramatic improvement in 1979. Volume for Navios Corporation, U. S. Steel's ocean transportation subsidiary, was 20 million tons in 1979—up 25 percent with public cargoes accounting for most of the gain. Navios initiated a program in 1976 to replace chartered vessels with owned vessels. This program has moved ahead rapidly and successfully. With the acquisition of two additional vessels in 1979, twelve are now under Navios ownership and management. Owned vessels accounted

Resource Development—
Sales by Product Grouping

	Percent of Total Dollars				
	1979	1978	1977	1976	1975
Minerals..........................	51%	56%	60%	63%	36%
Transportation Services............	28	26	21	26	48
Other..............................	21	18	19	11	16
	100%	100%	100%	100%	100%

(continued)

Exhibit 14.7 (continued)

for 32 percent of the total tonnage transported in 1979. Based on business already in place for 1980 and a continued strong international bulk shipping market, further profit improvements are expected.

U. S. Steel's uranium operations in Texas have undergone three expansion programs since commencement of operations in 1976. With the latest brought on stream in the third quarter of 1979, production capacity has grown to 1.5 million pounds annually, compared with 275,000 pounds annually in 1976.

In 1979, U. S. Steel continued to participate with other companies in oil and gas exploration and drilling. Half the drillings were successful. Revenues from these ventures will play a significant role in Resource Development's future profitability and cash flow.

Highlights

A major extension of dock loading facilities is currently under way at Port Cartier, a commercial port on the St. Lawrence River owned and operated by QCM. Upon completion in late 1980, the port will have loading capability for over 29 million tons of bulk commodities and will also be able to handle efficiently the growing number of grain carriers, oil tankers and general cargo vessels that use the port on a fee basis.

In November, U. S. Steel's Whitwell, Tennessee coal property was leased to Tennessee Consolidated Coal Company (TCC), a wholly owned subsidiary of St. Joe Minerals Corporation. TCC will extend its adjacent current mining operations to the Whitwell reserve. The lease arrangement will provide income for the Corporation over the next 28 years.

Improved Profitability: Target for the 1980's

Resource Development has continued performing geological surveys, mine planning and other pre-engineering to enable quick reaction to anticipated growing markets for coal and other commercial minerals. Profitability will be further enhanced by securing long-term contracts for most future uranium production, by concentrating oil and gas exploration activities in proven producing areas and by increasing participation in the international bulk shipping

FABRICATING & ENGINEERING and OTHER

	$ Millions	
	1979	1978
Sales	**$2,333**	$1,971
Operating Income	**91**	88

Benefits from business planning decisions and capital investments in recent years began to materialize in 1979, as both sales and operating income increased.

As a result of facility expansions over the past four years, as well as the introduction of new products into new market areas, Oilwell Division again achieved record sales and operating income. The order backlog for drilling rig units extends into 1981.

Improved results were also reported by U. S. Steel's real estate operations as its activities continued to grow. A new joint venture shopping center near Pittsburgh, Pa., was opened in 1979. The shopping center includes the largest enclosed mall in Pennsylvania and will be one of the largest shopping complexes in the United States.

Alside, Inc., continued its expansion program during 1979 through the addition of four new retail warehouses. Over the past five years, 26 new retail outlets have been opened for the distribution of siding and related building materials as well as installation service.

At mid-year, U. S. Steel's container manufacturing unit was merged into its steel service center division, United States Steel Supply Division (USD). The merger provides opportunities for improved utilization of the resources of both units. Advantages will occur in product planning, design, development, transportation, customer services and marketing. USD has continued to increase emphasis on the sale of carbon steel sheet products, which represent a significant portion of the domestic steel service center market. USD's carbon sheet shipments in 1979 were over 20 percent higher than in 1978. USD was formerly included in the Steel Manufacturing industry segment.

American Bridge Division (ABD) order bookings, though down from 1978, remained above the depressed levels experienced in 1976 and 1977. Significant projects booked included a

Fabricating & Engineering and Other—	Percent of Total Dollars				
Sales by Product Grouping	**1979**	1978	1977	1976	1975
Manufactured & Fabricated Products...........................	**51%**	51%	52%	50%	57%
Buildings & Bridges..................	**14**	16	14	20	10
Services & Technical Assistance.....	**25**	23	24	21	24
Cement & Other.....................	**10**	10	10	9	9
	100%	100%	100%	100%	100%

Exhibit 14.7 (continued)

series of bridges near Mobile, Ala.; a 4,000-foot bridge across the Mississippi River near St. Louis, Mo.; and two 20-story office buildings for the Renaissance Center in Detroit, Mich. The barge construction business continues strong and ABD's backlog extends through 1980.

In February 1980, U. S. Steel signed a letter of intent to sell its Universal Atlas Cement Division to Heidelberger Zement A.G. of Heidelberg, Germany. The sale price substantially exceeds $100 million. Heidelberger Zement intends to continue to operate the Universal Atlas Cement facilities with substantially the present organization, thereby boding well for the communities in which they are located. No decision has been made by Heidelberger with respect to the facilities whose discontinuance had been previously announced by U. S. Steel.

Improved Profitability: Target for the 1980's

Manufacturing and marketing activities for U. S. Steel's wire rope—a specialty product—have recently been consolidated under a single responsibility. Production capability for larger diameter, high strength special purpose ropes is also being expanded to meet growing demand. Upon completion, U. S. Steel will be the only domestic producer capable of manufacturing large diameter 8-strand wire rope which provides consumers with a more flexible, higher strength product.

During the 1980's, Oilwell Division will continue to expand its domestic manufacturing facilities to meet growing energy-related markets and will actively pursue new international manufacturing ventures. ABD has been reorganized to emphasize fabrication and construction activities as two separate profit responsibilities. This action will enable the division to serve its customers more effectively. USS Engineers and Consultants, Inc., will pursue the worldwide sale of technical assistance, management services and complete industrial plants through increased participation with multinational engineering firms, construction companies, and equipment suppliers. Alside, Inc., whose business is not tied to new housing starts, will continue to penetrate the home improvement market. USS Realty Development will further expand in the domestic real estate market and profitably reemploy other unused

Corporate properties. International Manufacturing operations will stress increased growth through self-supporting expansions of existing businesses.

DOMESTIC TRANSPORTATION & UTILITY SUBSIDIARIES

	$ Millions	
	1979	1978
Sales	$663	$549
Operating Income	152	120

Record sales and operating income were achieved again in 1979, reflecting increased rail and river shipments, authorized tariff rate changes and improved operating efficiency.

Performance of these subsidiaries continues to be outstanding. Since 1975, operating income has increased over 170 percent. During the same period, total sales have risen approximately 75 percent. Sales to non-affiliated customers have also increased, amounting to 34 percent of total sales in 1979.

Highlights

New taconite pellet storage and shiploading facilities of the Duluth, Missabe and Iron Range Railway Company at the port of Two Harbors, Minn., were operated throughout 1979. The complex, honored by the National Society of Professional Engineers as one of the Ten Outstanding Engineering Achievements of 1978, is well equipped to handle efficiently the increasing taconite production from U. S. Steel and others in Minnesota.

Expansion of Bessemer and Lake Erie Railroad's coal handling and storage facilities at Conneaut, Ohio, was completed in 1979. With capability increased by 50 percent, the facilities will be able to handle increases expected in Great Lakes coal movements.

Improved Profitability: Target for the 1980's

The companies will continue an aggressive marketing program to obtain maximum utilization of existing facilities and equipment. This, in conjunction with ongoing emphasis on increased productivity, should lead to further improvement in the 1980's.

Domestic Transportation & Utility Subsidiaries—
Sales by Commodity Handled

	Percent of Total Dollars				
	1979	1978	1977	1976	1975
Iron Ore & Agglomerates	26%	26%	23%	25%	28%
Coal	15	14	16	14	15
Steel & Other Metals	8	10	10	10	11
Switching, Demurrage & All Other	51	50	51	51	46
	100%	100%	100%	100%	100%

(continued)

Exhibit 14.7 (continued)

23. INDUSTRY SEGMENT & GEOGRAPHIC AREA INFORMATION (In millions)

By Industry Segment: (1976 and 1975 Unaudited)

| | Sales | | | Operating | | Wear | |
	Unaffiliated Customers	Between Segments	Total	Income (Loss)(2)	Identifiable Assets	and Exhaustion	Capital Expenditures
Steel Manufacturing:(1)							
1979	$ 9,022.5	$ 731.1	$ 9,753.6	$(102.5)(3)	$ 5,890.2	$375.2	$524.3
1978	8,135.6	684.5	8,820.1	25.5	5,736.7	316.7	395.2
1977	7,021.7	553.8	7,575.5	(59.9)	5,514.8	265.7	599.0
1976	6,313.4	522.1	6,835.5	145.0	5,121.0	228.2	659.0
1975	5,815.6	607.2	6,422.8	272.5	—	—	—
Chemicals:							
1979	$ 1,207.1	$ 48.5	$ 1,255.6	$ 57.9	$ 794.3	$ 44.2	$280.5
1978	763.1	44.7	807.8	21.0	457.3	23.6	100.0
1977	664.5	35.4	699.9	32.7	353.6	17.5	67.5
1976	609.3	38.8	648.1	62.4	270.8	16.1	49.9
1975	621.6	34.1	655.7	124.8	—	—	—
Resource Development:							
1979	$ 433.3	$ 143.0	$ 576.3	$ 55.4	$ 1,066.9	$ 48.8	$ 78.7
1978	271.1	124.9	396.0	25.1	1,085.7	41.3	54.1
1977	242.1	143.4	385.5	26.3	1,057.8	38.0	65.0
1976	198.9	160.2	359.1	68.5	1,063.6	23.8	143.7
1975	247.1	106.2	353.3	69.3	—	—	—
Fabricating & Engineering and Other:(1)							
1979	$ 2,040.7	$ 292.1	$ 2,332.8	$ 90.7	$ 1,105.9	$ 38.3	$ 53.5
1978	1,705.9	264.6	1,970.5	88.1	1,029.2	35.2	33.8
1977	1,545.7	272.3	1,818.0	95.4	870.8	34.8	39.3
1976	1,357.7	307.6	1,665.3	163.9	845.5	24.2	48.6
1975	1,367.1	222.1	1,589.2	192.9	—	—	—
Domestic Transportation & Utility Subsidiaries:							
1979	$ 225.5	$ 437.6	$ 663.1	$ 152.2	$ 743.6	$ 25.8	$ 42.0
1978	173.8	374.7	548.5	119.9	713.1	19.5	84.7
1977	135.9	310.4	446.3	71.3	630.2	16.4	93.9
1976	128.5	317.6	446.1	81.3	562.8	15.0	56.1
1975	119.9	259.5	379.4	55.7	—	—	—
Corporate Assets, Adjustments & Eliminations:(1)							
1979	$ —	$(1,652.3)	$(1,652.3)	$ 7.8	$ 1,429.0	$ (.8)	$ —
1978	—	(1,493.4)	(1,493.4)	6.5	1,514.3	(.7)	—
1977	—	(1,315.3)	(1,315.3)	9.7	1,487.2	(.4)	—
1976	—	(1,346.3)	(1,346.3)	3.4	1,304.2	1.3	—
1975	—	(1,229.1)	(1,229.1)	(11.0)	—	—	—
Total Consolidated:							
1979	$12,929.1	$ —	$12,929.1	$ 261.5(3)	$11,029.9	$531.5	$979.0
1978	11,049.5	—	11,049.5	286.1	10,536.3	435.6	667.8
1977	9,609.9	—	9,609.9	175.5	9,914.4	372.0	864.7
1976	8,607.8	—	8,607.8	524.5	9,167.9	308.6	957.3
1975	8,171.3	—	8,171.3	704.2	8,155.0	297.2	787.4

(1) Years 1978-1975 restated to reflect transfer of steel service center operations from Steel Manufacturing segment to Fabricating & Engineering and Other.

(2) For exclusions see "General."

(3) The current year effects of accounting changes (Note 21) included in Steel Manufacturing Operating Income (Loss) was $20.4 million. The effects on other segments were immaterial.

assets shown separately. The composition of corporate assets, although not required by SFAS No. 14, is also disclosed, as noted in the second paragraph of the footnote disclosure.

Interperiod Comparability Disclosures

U.S. Steel restated industry segment data for 1980 and 1979, as noted in the fourth paragraph of the footnote disclosure. The restatement resulted from a change in the method of grouping the industry segments. No other changes were disclosed that affected the interperiod comparability of the segment information.

Exhibit 14.7 (continued)

23. INDUSTRY SEGMENT & GEOGRAPHIC AREA INFORMATION (In millions) (continued)

By Geographic Areas: (1976 Unaudited)

	Sales			Operating	
	To Unaffiliated Customers	Transfers Between Geographic Areas	Total	Income (Loss)	Identifiable Assets
United States (Domestic):					
1979	$12,335.6	$ 20.3	$12,355.9	$169.2	$ 8,433.7
1978	10,642.6	15.6	10,658.2	239.0	7,943.9
1977	9,205.5	13.1	9,218.6	105.7	7,404.1
1976	8,369.0	7.7	8,376.7	428.8	6,835.9
North America (Excl. U.S.):					
1979	$ 417.6	$ 135.9	$ 553.5	$ 82.7	$ 984.2
1978	259.5	122.6	382.1	40.8	947.5
1977	254.2	145.0	399.2	56.6	909.8
1976	225.8	176.2	402.0	88.9	1,009.7
Other Foreign:					
1979	$ 175.9	$ 6.6	$ 182.5	$ 1.8	$ 138.3
1978	147.4	5.5	152.9	(.2)	130.6
1977	150.2	3.6	153.8	3.5	113.3
1976	13.0	—	13.0	3.4	18.1
Corporate Assets, Adjustments & Eliminations:					
1979	$ —	$(162.8)	$ (162.8)	$ 7.8	$ 1,473.7
1978	—	(143.7)	(143.7)	6.5	1,514.3
1977	—	(161.7)	(161.7)	9.7	1,487.2
1976	—	(183.9)	(183.9)	3.4	1,304.2
Total Consolidated:					
1979	$12,929.1	$ —	$12,929.1	$261.5	$11,029.9
1978	11,049.5	—	11,049.5	286.1	10,536.3
1977	9,609.9	—	9,609.9	175.5	9,914.4
1976	8,607.8	—	8,607.8	524.5	9,167.9

(In millions)

GENERAL—Intersegment sales and transfers, for the most part, are accounted for at commercial prices. Steel Manufacturing transfers of coal chemical by-products to the Chemicals segment reflect the current value of the raw by-product material as a replacement for purchased fuels plus the costs incurred to convert the raw material to the transferred product.

Operating income for 1979 does not include those costs included in Unusual Items, which by nature are ordinarily considered operating expenses. These costs are:

Employee related costs included in provision for shutdown of facilities (Steel Mfg. $339.4, Other $73.9)	$413.3
Other costs included in provision for shutdown of facilities (Steel Mfg. $352.5, Other $63.9)	416.4
Estimated provision for occupational disease claims (Steel Mfg.)	88.1
Total	$917.8

In addition, operating income does not include re-valuation of investments; profit or loss from the sale of investments and property, plant and equipment; equity

(continued)

Other Required Disclosures

The types of revenue generating products and services of each industry segment are described separately in the annual report. An appropriate reference to this description is included in paragraph 4 of the footnote disclosure. The description itself is included in Exhibit 14.7.

Information about the company's unconsolidated subsidiaries and other equity method investees is presented in the sixth column of the industry segment disclosure schedule included in the footnote presentation. This column allocates all U.S. Steel's equity in the net income of "unconsolidated subsidiaries and other non-vertically integrated affiliates" to individual industry segments. This information, along with the

Exhibit 14.7 (continued)

---

23. INDUSTRY SEGMENT & GEOGRAPHIC AREA INFORMATION (continued)

in the income of unconsolidated investees; dividend and interest income on marketable securities and other outside investments; interest and other financing costs; and income taxes and other items considered to be general corporate income or expense. Selling, general and administrative expenses have been allocated to segments.

Corporate Assets consist largely of cash, notes receivable, marketable securities and other investments.

Export sales from domestic operations were not material. U. S. Steel has no single customer from which it derives 10 percent or more of its revenue.

STEEL MANUFACTURING—Includes domestic iron ore, coal and limestone operations integrated with steel plants which produce and sell a wide range of steel mill products. Also included are the Great Lakes transportation operations, principally involving the movement of ore and limestone to steel plants, and sales of steel mill products by export distributors. Some of the steel mill products are sold to other industry segments of U. S. Steel for further processing and fabrication.

CHEMICALS—Includes the production and marketing of various industrial and coal chemicals, petrochemicals, polyolefin & styrenic plastics and agricultural chemicals.

RESOURCE DEVELOPMENT—Includes the operation of both domestic and foreign businesses, either wholly or majority owned. These involve certain iron ore, coal, uranium and other mineral properties; the development of commercial outlets for currently owned mineral resources considered as excess to U. S. Steel's requirements, either by outright sale or development; the activities of the ocean transportation companies; and the search for and development of new mineral and energy reserves.

FABRICATING & ENGINEERING AND OTHER—Includes the fabrication and erection of structural steel for buildings, bridges, storage tanks and other structures; the fabrication of barges, ship sections, transmission towers, large diameter pipe and a variety of

standard fabricated steel products; sales of steel mill products by a network of domestic steel service centers; the manufacture and marketing of gas and oil field drilling and pumping equipment, electrical cable and products for residential housing; the production of cement; and technology licensing, engineering and consulting services. Also includes real estate and miscellaneous operations.

DOMESTIC TRANSPORTATION & UTILITY SUBSIDIARIES—Includes common carrier railroads, domestic barge lines, gas utility companies and a dock company. These subsidiaries, operating autonomously, serve the general public including U. S. Steel and charge for their services on the basis of rates filed with and approved by regulatory agencies as applicable or by contract rates.

24. SEC REPLACEMENT COST REQUIREMENTS (Unaudited)—Inflation continues to increase both production costs and capital spending requirements. Depreciation allowances based on the historical costs of existing facilities are inadequate to support the increasing capital requirements for replacements, modernization, and environmental control facilities at the higher current costs of the new facilities. These added costs which at present can only be recovered through depreciation over many future years, are in effect currently taxed as if they were profits. The result is the taxing away of much of the capital needed to meet the steadily rising costs of inflation. U. S. Steel's annual report on Form 10-K filed with the Securities and Exchange Commission contains quantitative replacement cost information in accordance with SEC Accounting Series Release 190. After three years of disclosure, the conceptual shortcomings of this approach have been acknowledged by the SEC. Accordingly, this requirement is terminated commencing with 1980 reporting when the Supplementary Information on Changing Prices must include the required data on a current cost basis as well as the constant dollar basis required (reported on page 19) for 1979.

---

amount of investment in net assets of equity method investees and unconsolidated subsidiaries, is required by SFAS No. 14 only for vertically integrated investees.

In a separate supplementary schedule, appropriately referenced in another footnote of the financial statements, U.S. Steel included detail information about the types of industries in which each of its "unconsolidated affiliates" operate. This schedule is presented in Exhibit 14.7. Identification of the types of industries in which all unconsolidated and other equity method investees operate is required under SFAS No. 14.

Foreign Operations Disclosures—U.S. Steel

U.S. Steel presented information about its foreign operations primarily in the footnote schedule as shown in Exhibit 14.7. Disclosures were presented for each of three geographic areas, including (1) the United States—domestic operations, (2) other North American countries, and (3) other foreign countries.

Revenue Disclosures

The schedule as shown in Exhibit 14.7 presents the required revenue disclosures, including sales to unaffiliated customers and transfers between geographic areas. All consolidated revenues have been allocated to geographic areas and transfers between areas eliminated in the reconciliation to consolidated revenue. The basis of accounting for transfers between geographic areas was disclosed in the first paragraph of the footnote disclosure.

Profitability Disclosures

Operating profit or loss has been used as the common measurement of profitability for each geographic area. Operating profit or loss from all geographic areas was disclosed for each geographic area and reconciled to consolidated operating profit.

Identifiable Assets Disclosures

The last column of the geographic area information schedule shows the carrying value of identifiable assets of each geographic area and a reconciliation of total geographic area identifiable assets to consolidated assets. Corporate assets have been appropriately identified in the reconciliation to consolidated assets.

Interperiod Comparability Disclosures

No changes were disclosed that affected the interperiod comparblility of the foreign operations information presented.

Other Required Disclosures

Significant geographic areas have been separately identified in the footnote schedule, as previously noted. Countries in which "unconsolidated affiliates" operate have been disclosed, as required by SFAS No. 14, in a separate schedule outside of the financial statements. This schedule, as previously mentioned in the analysis of industry segment disclosures, was appropriately referenced in another footnote of the financial statements, and is presented in Exhibit 14.7.

Export Sales Disclosures—U.S. Steel

As noted in the third paragraph of the footnote disclosure, export sales were not material to total enterprise revenues for the periods presented. Therefore, export sales disclosures were not presented.

Major Customers Disclosures—U.S. Steel

Also as noted in the third paragraph of the footnote disclosure, U.S. Steel had no major customers during the periods presented. Therefore, major customers disclosures were not presented.

ANALYSIS OF SEGMENT DISCLOSURES—E. I. DU PONT DE NEMOURS AND COMPANY

Segment disclosures reported in the 1981 annual report of Du Pont are presented in Exhibit 14.8. Du Pont presented segment information in the footnotes of the financial statements, in the supplementary information to the financial statements, and outside the financial statements in the corporate overview information.

The 1981 annual report included complete financial statements for 1981 and 1980. Selected financial information was also presented for 1979, including consolidated statements of income and changes in financial position. Segment information was presented for 1981, 1980, and 1979. Only 1980 and 1981 disclosures were required based on GAAP reporting requirements.

Business Industry Segment Disclosures—Du Pont

Du Pont reported industry segment information for eight reportable segments in 1981 and five in 1980 and 1979, as shown in the footnote disclosures of Exhibit 14.8. The enterprise was disaggregated on a worldwide basis.

Revenue Disclosures

The industry segment schedules presented in the footnote disclosures clearly reflect sales to unaffiliated customers and intersegment transfers for each period for each reportable segment. Reconciliations to total consolidated revenues were also included in these schedules. The basis of accounting for intersegment transfers was described in the first explanatory paragraph of the footnote disclosure, as shown in Exhibit 14.8. Footnote 1, as shown on page i, provides additional information about the accounting for intersegment transfers.

Profitability Disclosures

Profitability disclosures presented for each reportable segment include operating profit and "after-tax operating income." After-tax operating income was defined in the supplementary information presented with the financial statements as "sales and other income less all directly allocable expenses, net of taxes, but before deduction of certain corporate expenses (net of taxes) and minority interests in earnings of consolidated subsidiaries."

Exhibit 14.8
Segment and Foreign Operations Disclosures: E. I. Du Pont de Nemours and Company

21—Industry Segment Information

Industry segment information includes Conoco results for the year 1982 and for the five months beginning August 1, 1981. See pages 4-5 for an overview of each segment and pages 6-25 for an analysis of segment operations. A presentation of segment results on a pro forma combined basis is included with Management's Discussion and Analysis on pages 37-41. Products are transferred between segments on a basis intended to reflect as nearly as possible the "market value" of the products.

1982	Biomedical Products	Industrial and Consumer Products	Fibers	Polymer Products	Agricultural and Industrial Chemicals	Petroleum Exploration and Production	Petroleum Refining, Marketing and Transportation	Coal	Consolidated
Sales to Unaffiliated Customers[1] ..	$1,032	$2,499	$4,085	$3,051	$3,768	$2,053	$15,177[2]	$1,666	$33,331
Transfers Between Segments	—	32	15	74	696	3,023	854	4	—
Total	$1,032	$2,531	$4,100	$3,125	$4,464	$5,076	$16,031	$1,670	$33,331
Operating Profit	$ 222	$ 237	$ 181	$ 94	$ 142	$2,459	$ 345	$ 238	$ 3,918
Provision for Income Taxes	(92)	(107)	(56)	(16)	(18)	(2,005)	(141)	(59)	(2,494)
Equity in Earnings of Affiliates ...	—	(1)	11	—	46	—	11	—	67
After-Tax Operating Income	$ 130	$ 129	$ 136	$ 78	$ 170	$ 454	$ 215	$ 179	1,491
After-Tax Interest and General Corporate Expenses									(597)
Net Income									$ 894
Identifiable Assets at December 31	$ 589	$1,481	$3,042	$1,969	$2,734	$5,348	$ 3,853	$2,433	$21,148
Investment in Affiliates									362
Corporate Assets									2,833
Total Assets at December 31 ...									$24,343
Depreciation, Depletion and Amortization[3]	$ 44	$ 123	$ 333	$ 196	$ 288	$ 512	$ 71	$ 123	$ 1,747
Capital Expenditures[4]	$ 86	$ 155	$ 395	$ 332	$ 356	$1,180	$ 350	$ 312	$ 3,295

[1] Sales of crude oil and refined products of $6,639 and $9,434, respectively, exceeded 10% of consolidated sales.
[2] Includes $5,227 of crude oil sales at the approximate cost of the crude oil to the segment.
[3] Includes $46 of depreciation on research and development facilities reported as research and development expense in the Consolidated Income Statement. Also includes $76 of impairment of unproved properties reported as exploration expenses.
[4] Excludes $25 of investment in affiliates.

(continued)

The presentation of this profitability measure is not required by SFAS No. 14. Proper disclosure has been made of the differences in operating profit or loss and after-tax operating income.

Both operating profit and after-tax operating income have been reconciled to consolidated "income before cumulative effect of change in accounting for investment tax credit." After-tax interest and minority interests were properly excluded from segment profitability measures.

Identifiable Assets Disclosures

Identifiable assets disclosures were presented for each industry segment and reconciled to consolidated totals in the industry segment schedules. Footnotes 3 and 4 of Exhibit 14.8 provide additional explanations necessary to reconcile consolidated totals as presented in the industry segment schedules to those in the consolidated financial statements.

Exhibit 14.8 (continued)

1981	Biomedical Products	Industrial and Consumer Products	Fibers	Polymer Products	Agricultural and Industrial Chemicals	Petroleum Exploration and Production	Petroleum Refining, Marketing and Transportation	Coal	Consolidated
Sales to Unaffiliated Customers ...	$1,003	$2,723	$4,858	$3,219	$3,435	$ 704	$6,067[1]	$ 801	$22,810
Transfers Between Segments	—	46	41	72	604	1,174	515	2	—
Total	$1,003	$2,769	$4,899	$3,291	$4,039	$1,878	$6,582	$ 803	$22,810
Operating Profit	$ 230	$ 323	$ 628	$ 190	$ 331	$ 816	$ 174	$ 162	$ 2,854
Provision for Income Taxes	(89)	(113)	(229)	(48)	(108)	(697)	(78)	(41)	(1,403)
Equity in Earnings of Affiliates ...	—	—	(8)	(7)	26	—	2	3	16
After-Tax Operating Income[2] ...	$ 141	$ 210	$ 391	$ 135	$ 249	$ 119	$ 98	$ 124	1,467
After-Tax Interest and General Corporate Expenses									(386)
Net Income[2]									$ 1,081
Identifiable Assets at December 31	$ 614	$1,549	$3,280	$2,123	$2,764	$5,084	$3,825	$2,280	$21,237
Investment in Affiliates									362
Corporate Assets									2,773
Total Assets at December 31 ...									$24,372
Depreciation, Depletion and Amortization[3]	$ 37	$ 104	$ 369	$ 198	$ 220	$ 192	$ 27	$ 49	$ 1,212
Capital Expenditures[4]	$ 78	$ 163	$ 578	$ 252	$ 379	$ 605	$ 161	$ 134	$ 2,389

1980									
Sales to Unaffiliated Customers ...	$ 919	$2,620	$4,494	$2,990	$2,721	$ —	$ —	$ —	$13,744
Transfers Between Segments	—	20	23	56	400	—	—	—	—
Total	$ 919	$2,640	$4,517	$3,046	$3,121	$ —	$ —	$ —	$13,744
Operating Profit	$ 149	$ 256	$ 358	$ 281	$ 359	$ —	$ —	$ —	$ 1,403
Provision for Income Taxes	(61)	(96)	(123)	(94)	(118)	—	—	—	(492)
Equity in Earnings of Affiliates ...	—	2	8	(2)	11	—	—	—	19
After-Tax Operating Income[2]	$ 88	$ 162	$ 243	$ 185	$ 252	$ —	$ —	$ —	930
After-Tax Interest and General Corporate Expenses									(186)
Net Income[2]									$ 744
Identifiable Assets at December 31	$ 534	$1,484	$2,953	$1,891	$2,061	$ —	$ —	$ —	$ 8,884
Investment in Affiliates									276
Corporate Assets									632
Total Assets at December 31 ...									$ 9,792
Depreciation, Depletion and Amortization[3]	$ 27	$ 74	$ 335	$ 157	$ 207	$ —	$ —	$ —	$ 806
Capital Expenditures[4]	$ 76	$ 248	$ 444	$ 299	$ 230	$ —	$ —	$ —	$ 1,297

[1] Includes $1,710 of crude oil sales at the approximate cost of the crude oil to the segment. Sales of refined petroleum of $4,216 exceeded 10% of consolidated sales.
[2] Excludes the $320 cumulative effect of the 1981 change in accounting for ITC. Data for 1980 are pro forma for ITC.
[3] Includes depreciation on research and development facilities reported as research and development expense in the Consolidated Income Statement: 1981—$39; 1980—$30. 1981 also includes impairment of unproved properties of $30 reported as exploration expenses.
[4] Excludes investment in affiliates: 1981—$67; 1980—$72.

Interperiod Comparability Disclosures

Footnote 2 of Exhibit 14.8 describes the treatment, for segment disclosure purposes, of a change in the accounting method for investment tax credits. Pro-forma amounts were presented in the industry segment disclosures for the years prior to the change, 1979 and 1980. The cumulative effect of the change, reported in the consolidated financial statements, was ignored for industry segment disclosure purposes.

A change in the method of product groupings for industry segments

Exhibit 14.8 (continued)

22—Geographic Information [1]

1982	United States	Europe	Other Foreign	Consolidated
Sales to Unaffiliated Customers	$22,274	$7,016	$4,041	$33,331
Transfers Between Geographic Areas	1,181	202	535	—
Total	$23,455	$7,218	$4,576	$33,331
After-Tax Operating Income	$ 1,003	$ 300	$ 188	$ 1,491
Identifiable Assets at December 31	$15,533	$3,838	$2,073	$21,148
1981				
Sales to Unaffiliated Customers	$16,094	$3,990	$2,726	$22,810
Transfers Between Geographic Areas	1,222	361	395	—
Total	$17,316	$4,351	$3,121	$22,810
After-Tax Operating Income [2]	$ 1,209	$ 202	$ 56	$ 1,467
Identifiable Assets at December 31	$15,888	$3,662	$1,939	$21,237
1980				
Sales to Unaffiliated Customers	$ 9,863	$2,147	$1,734	$13,744
Transfers Between Geographic Areas	1,153	119	57	—
Total	$11,016	$2,266	$1,791	$13,744
After-Tax Operating Income [2]	$ 641	$ 155	$ 134	$ 930
Identifiable Assets at December 31	$ 6,789	$1,084	$1,100	$ 8,884

[1] The geographic breakdown of "Sales to Unaffiliated Customers," "Transfers Between Geographic Areas" and "Identifiable Assets" is presented on a basis specified by Statement of Financial Accounting Standards No. 14. Accordingly, these data are segregated by the location of the corporate unit making the sale or transfer. After-tax operating income for each geographic area represents profits on sales and transfers realized by corporate units located in such areas. Products are transferred between geographic areas on a basis intended to reflect as nearly as possible the "market value" of the products. Sales outside the United States of products mined or manufactured in and exported from the United States totaled $2,559 in 1982, $2,646 in 1981 and $2,197 in 1980.

[2] Income data for 1981 exclude the $320 cumulative effect of the change in accounting for ITC. Data for 1980 are pro forma for ITC.

CONSOLIDATED GEOGRAPHIC DATA

(Dollars in millions)

Capital expenditures, total assets and employees of Du Pont and its consolidated subsidiaries were:

	Capital Expenditures		Total Assets December 31		Employees December 31	
	1982	1981	1982	1981	1982	1981
Europe	$ 567	$ 221	$ 4,187	$ 4,254	17,926	19,263
Other Foreign	216	159	2,177	2,259	16,636	16,729
Total International	783	380	6,364	6,513	34,562	35,992
United States	2,537	2,076	17,979	17,859	130,451	141,243
Total	$3,320	$2,456	$24,343	$24,372	165,013	177,235

Capital expenditures, total assets and employees are assigned to geographic areas generally based on physical location. Employee data exclude government-owned plants.

(continued)

also affected the interperiod comparability of the segment disclosures. As described in the first explanatory paragraph of the footnote disclosure shown on page i, the acquisition of Conoco in 1981 required the company to change its product groupings. Segment information for 1980

Exhibit 14.8 (continued)

	1982	1981	1980	1979	1978
Summary of Operations[2]					
Sales	$33,331	$22,810	$13,744	$12,650	$10,646
Earnings Before Income Taxes	$ 2,806	$ 2,155	$ 1,098	$ 1,503	$ 1,331
Provision for Income Taxes	$ 1,912	$ 1,074	$ 354	$ 538	$ 534
Net Income	$ 894	$ 1,081	$ 744	$ 965	$ 797
Percent of Sales	2.7%	4.7%	5.4%	7.6%	7.5%
Percent of Average Stockholders' Equity	8.4%	13.7%	12.8%	18.4%	16.8%
Earnings Per Share of Common Stock[3]	$ 3.75	$ 5.81	$ 4.73	$ 6.23	$ 5.18
Financial Position at Year End[2]					
Working Capital	$ 4,475	$ 4,890	$ 2,458	$ 2,622	$ 2,272
Total Assets	$24,343	$24,372	$ 9,792	$ 9,134	$ 8,226
Long-Term Borrowings and Capital Leases	$ 5,868	$ 6,579	$ 1,113	$ 1,108	$ 1,103
Stockholders' Equity	$10,850	$10,458	$ 5,944	$ 5,540	$ 4,963
General[2]					
For the Year:					
Capital expenditures	$ 3,320	$ 2,456	$ 1,369	$ 940	$ 795
Depreciation, depletion and amortization	$ 1,625	$ 1,143	$ 776	$ 762	$ 754
Research and development expense	$ 879	$ 718	$ 591	$ 509	$ 461
Average number of shares outstanding (thousands)	235,707	184,260	154,990	153,181	151,828
Dividends paid per common share	$ 2.40	$ 2.75	$ 2.75	$ 2.75	$ 2.41⅔
Dividends as percent of earnings on common stock	64%	47%	58%	44%	47%
At Year End:					
Employees (excluding government-owned plants)	165,013	177,235	136,259	136,942	133,391
Common stockholders of record	252,939	243,082	215,782	210,949	204,163
Book value per common share	$ 44.87	$ 43.60	$ 36.77	$ 34.60	$ 30.95
Historical Summary of Operations[4]					
Income Before Cumulative Effect of Change in Accounting for Investment Tax Credit	$ 894	$ 1,081	$ 706	$ 939	$ 786
Cumulative Effect for Years Prior to 1981 of Change in Accounting for Investment Tax Credit	$ —	$ 320	$ —	$ —	$ —
Earnings Per Share of Common Stock[3]:					
Before Cumulative Effect of Change in Accounting for Investment Tax Credit	$ 3.75	$ 5.81	$ 4.49	$ 6.07	$ 5.11
Cumulative Effect for Years Prior to 1981 of Change in Accounting for Investment Tax Credit	$ —	$ 1.74	$ —	$ —	$ —
Net Income	$ 3.75	$ 7.55	$ 4.49	$ 6.07	$ 5.11

[1] Results of Conoco are included from August 1, 1981; prior years' data are not restated.
[2] Excludes the $320 ($1.74 per share) cumulative effect of the 1981 change in accounting for ITC. Data for prior years are pro forma for ITC.
[3] Based on the average number of common shares outstanding.
[4] Data for 1978-1980 are as reported in the primary financial statements for those years and have not been restated to reflect the change in accounting for ITC.

and 1979 was restated to reflect these new groupings. The explanatory paragraph also refers to the disclosure of the effect of the change in the method of grouping industry segments. This disclosure is presented in Exhibit 14.8.

In disclosing the effect of the change in the method of grouping industry segments, Du Pont has presented revenue and profitability disclosures for the current and four preceding operating periods. In addition, pro-forma revenue and profitability disclosures are presented for each of the eight new industry segments, which reflect the Conoco acquisition as if it had occurred at the beginning of the current year. Comparative revenue and profitability disclosures are presented for 1980.

Other Disclosures

Descriptions of the types of revenue generating products of each industry segment have been included outside the financial statements and appropriately referenced in the footnotes. The first explanatory paragraph of Exhibit 14.8 refers to pages 6 and 7 and 8-37 of the annual report for such a description. The brief descriptions presented on pages 6 and 7 of the annual report are included in Exhibit 14.8.

Equity in earnings of affiliates is allocated separately to the appropriate industry segments in arriving at after-tax operating income, thus identifying all affiliates with industry segments. No distinction is made for vertical or nonvertical operating affiliates. There is also no allocation of the total investment in affiliates to specific industry segments.

Foreign Operations Disclosures—Du Pont

Foreign operations segment information has been presented in a separate footnote immediately following the industry segment disclosures, of Exhibit 14.8. Foreign operations disclosures are presented individually for European countries and in the aggregate for all other foreign countries. Domestic operations disclosures are also presented.

Revenue Disclosures

Revenue disclosures for sales to unaffiliated customers and transfers between geographic areas are presented in the geographic area schedule, of Exhibit 14.8. The basis of accounting for intersegment sales is disclosed in the explanatory paragraph on page ii. Total geographic area revenues were also reconciled to consolidated revenues in the geographic area schedule.

Profitability Disclosures

"After-tax operating income," as previously described, is the common measurement of profitability presented for each geographic area. Geographic area totals were reconciled to consolidated after-tax operating income.

Identifiable Assets Disclosures

Identifiable assets disclosures are presented for each geographic area and reconciled to consolidated assets in the geographic area schedule. Footnote 2 of Exhibit 14.8 incorporates the reconciliation of total segment identifiable assets to consolidated assets on the balance sheet as presented for industry segments into the foreign operations disclosure information.

Interperiod Comparability Disclosures

The change in accounting method for the investment tax credit affected the comparability between periods of the foreign operations disclosures presented. Treatment of that change for foreign operations disclosures, as shown in footnote 1 was consistent with that of industry segment disclosures, as previously discussed. No other changes were disclosed that affected the interperiod comparability of the foreign operations disclosures.

Other Required Disclosures

Significant geographic areas are identified in the foreign operations disclosures, as previously discussed. Geographic areas in which "affiliates" operate are not specifically identified.

Export Sales Disclosures—Du Pont

Export sales disclosures are presented in the explanatory paragraph of Exhibit 14.8. Export sales from the United States are disclosed in the aggregate for 1981, 1980, and 1979. Export sales disclosures by geographic areas are not presented.

Major Customers Disclosures—Du Pont

No major customers disclosures were presented in the 1981 annual report of Du Pont.

15
Supplementary Disclosures

NATURE OF SUPPLEMENTARY DISCLOSURES

FASB views financial reporting in a broader context than the traditional financial statement. In this regard, there are two forms for additional disclosures: required and other. These required supplementary disclosures must be presented by certain entities. The FASB has identified the entities it believes should make them. The two types of required supplementary disclosures relate to the effects of inflation on the entity and the status of oil and gas operations. The purpose of this chapter is to present these required supplementary disclosures.

THE NATURE OF INFLATION DISCLOSURES

Financial statements traditionally have been prepared on a historical cost basis measuring financial statement elements at the fair market value of consideration surrendered or of consideration received, whichever is more clearly determinable. These amounts have not been restated from their initial measurement amount (except in certain cases to reflect LCM or NRV) to reflect either changes in the general purchasing power of the dollar or changes in current cost of specific financial statement elements. The FASB now is requiring disclosure of both historical cost/constant dollar (general) amounts and current cost (specific) amounts in financial statements for fiscal years ended on or after December 25, 1979. These disclosure requirements are presented in SFAS No. 33 issued in September 1979, entitled "Financial Reporting and Changing Prices."

ENTERPRISES REQUIRED TO DISCLOSE SUPPLEMENTARY INFLATION—ADJUSTED INFORMATION

The SFAS No. 33 requirement to disclose current cost information in external financial reports applies only to public enterprises that prepare

their primary financial statements in U.S. dollars and in accordance with
U.S. GAAP and that have, at the beginning of the fiscal year for which
financial statements are prepared, either (1) inventories and property,
plant, and equipment (before deducting accumulated depreciation, depletion, and amortization) amounting in the aggregate to more than
$125 million or (2) total assets amounting to more than $1 billion (after
deducting accumulated depreciation). Except where otherwise stated,
inventory and property, plant, and equipment should include land and
other natural resources and capitalized leasehold interests but not goodwill or other intangible assets. Both of the amounts listed in the criteria
above should be measured in accordance with GAAP used in developing the primary financial statements of the enterprise.

The FASB defines the reporting entity as the consolidated enterprise.
Therefore, constant dollar and current cost disclosures need not be presented separately for a parent company, an investee company, or any
other enterprise(s) in any financial report that includes the results for
that enterprise in the consolidated financial statements. Further, these
disclosures need not be made during the year of a business combination
accounted for as pooling of interests by an enterprise created by the
pooling of two or more enterprises, none of which individually satisfies
the aforementioned size tests.

The current cost disclosures do not apply to interim reports, segment
disclosure, public enterprises not meeting the size tests, and nonpublic
enterprises. The FASB does encourage enterprises to make the constant
dollar and current cost disclosures even if they are not required to implement the provisions of SFAS No. 33. The board emphasizes that while
there are minimum disclosures required by certain enterprises, there is
room for experimentation both in the information disclosed and in the
reporting format.

CURRENT COST DISCLOSURE REQUIREMENTS

Enterprises subject to making the current cost disclosures under SFAS
No. 33 are required to disclose, at a minimum,

1. Information on income from continuing operations for the current fiscal year
   on a current cost basis

2. The current cost amounts of inventory and property, plant, and equipment at
   the end of the current fiscal year

3. Increases or decreases for the current fiscal year in the current cost amounts
   of inventory and property, plant, and equipment, net of inflation. The increases or decreases in current cost amounts should not be included in income from continuing operations.

4. Purchasing power gain or loss.

In certain circumstances, there may be no material difference between the amount of income from continuing operations determined on a historical cost/constant dollar basis and a current cost basis. In these cases, the current cost disclosures enumerated above need not be made for the current fiscal year if constant dollar disclosures are made, but the reporting enterprise should state, in a note to the supplementary disclosures, the reason for omitting the information.

The required current cost disclosures may be presented in either a statement or a reconciliation format. Regardless of the format selected, disclosures should include material amounts of or adjustments to cost of goods sold, depreciation, depletion, and amortization expense.

In these disclosures, inventories should be measured at current cost or lower recoverable amount at the measurement date. Current cost of inventories owned by an enterprise is the current cost to purchase the goods or the current cost of resources required to produce the goods, whichever is appropriate to the reporting enterprise. In determining cost to produce inventories, an allowance for current overhead costs according to allocation bases used under GAAP should be included. The recoverable amount of inventories means the current worth of the net amount of cash expected to be recoverable from use or sale of the assets. Recoverable amounts should be measured in one of the following ways:

Net realizable value: The amount of cash or its equivalent expected to be derived from the sale of an asset, net of costs required to be incurred as a result of the sale. Net realizable values should be considered as a measurement alternative only when the asset being valued is about to be sold.

Value in use: The net present value of future cash flows (including ultimate proceeds of disposal) expected to be derived from the use of an asset by the enterprise. Value in such use should be considered as a measurement alternative only when immediate sale of the asset being valued is not intended. Value in use should be estimated by discounting expected cash flows at an appropriate discount rate that allows for risk of activities concerned.

Recoverable amounts of inventories need not be ascertained by considering individual items unless those items are used independently of other assets.

Property, plant, and equipment (excluding income producing real estate properties and unprocessed natural resources) should be measured at current cost or lower recoverable amount (determined the same as with inventories) of the assets' remaining service potential at the measurement date. If an enterprise presents the current cost disclosure of SFAS No. 33 in annual reports for a fiscal year ended before December 25, 1980, these special assets and expenses may be measured at their historical cost/constant dollar amounts or by reference to an appropriate index of specific price changes.

The current cost of property, plant, and equipment owned by an enterprise is the current cost of acquiring the same service potential (indicated by operating costs and physical output capacity) as embodied by the asset currently owned. Sources of information used in determining current cost of property, plant, and equipment should reflect a method of acquisition currently considered appropriate for the reporting enterprise. There are three ways to measure the current cost of a used asset:

1. Measure the current cost of a new asset that has the same service potential as the used asset had when it was new and deduct a depreciation allowance.
2. Measure the current cost of a used asset of the same age and in the same condition as the currently owned asset.
3. Measure the current cost of a new asset with a different service potential and adjust that cost for the value of differences in service potential due to increases in life, output, capacity, nature of service, and operating costs.

In determining the current cost, enterprises are expected to utilize the types of information appropriate to their particular circumstances. Examples of information that may be used include the following:

1. Indexation
   a. Externally generated price indices for the class of goods or services being measured
   b. Internally generated price indices for the class of goods or services being measured
2. Direct pricing
   a. Current invoice prices
   b. Vendors' price lists or other quotations or estimates
   c. Standard manufacturing costs that reflect current costs.

It should be noted that cost of goods sold measured on a LIFO basis may provide an acceptable approximation of current cost of goods sold, provided that the effect of any decreases in inventory layers is excluded. Further, there is a presumption that the same methods and estimates used for historical cost determination of depreciation expense are utilized in the calculation of current cost depreciation. However, different methods and estimates may be used in current cost calculations if the methods and estimates used in the historical cost financial statements have been selected partly to allow for expected price changes.

Enterprises that present the minimum disclosures required by SFAS No. 33 relating to current cost income from continuing operations should measure cost of goods sold at current cost or lower recoverable amount at the date of sale or at the date on which resources are used or commited to a specific contract. Depreciation and amortization expense should be measured on the basis of average current cost or lower recoverable amount of the assets' service potential during the period of use. Other revenues, expenses, gains, and losses may be measured at the amounts included in the primary financial statements.

The income tax provision in computations of current cost income from continuing operations should be the same as the provision used in the primary financial statements. No adjustments to the tax provision should be made for any timing differences that may be assumed to arise between amounts determined at current cost and historical cost measurements. Further, the income tax provision should not be allocated between income from continuing operations and increases or decreases in the current cost of inventory and property, plant, and equipment.

The increases or decreases in the current cost of inventory and property, plant, and equipment represent the differences between asset measures at the beginning of the year or at the dates of acquisition (whichever is applicable) and asset measures at the end of the year or at the dates of use, sale, or commitment to a specific contract (whichever is applicable). These increases should be disclosed both before and after eliminating the effects of general inflation. When comprehensive current cost/constant dollar financial statements are prepared, enterprises may measure these increases or decreases in average-for-the-year or end-of-the-year constant dollars.

The required disclosure of the purchasing power gain or loss during the period on net monetary items should be equal to the net gain or loss formed by restating in constant dollars the beginning and ending balances of, and transactions affecting, monetary assets and liabilities. A monetary asset is money or claim to receive a sum of money, the amount of which is fixed or determinable without reference to future prices of specific goods or services. A monetary liability is an obligation to pay a sum of money, the amount of which is fixed or determinable without reference to further prices of specific goods or services. All other assets and liabilities are nonmonetary.

FIVE YEAR SUMMARY OF SELECTED FINANCIAL DATA

In addition to the current cost disclosures, SFAS No. 33 requires applicable enterprises to disclose the following information for each of the five most recent fiscal years:

1. Net sales and other operating revenues
2. Historical cost/constant dollar information
   a. Income from continuing operations
   b. Income per share from continuing operations
   c. Net assets at fiscal year-end

3. Current cost information (except for individual years in which the information was excluded from current year disclosures because there was no material difference between income from continuing operations on a historical cost/constant dollar basis and on a current cost basis)

   a. Income from continuing operations

   b. Income per common share from continuing operations

   c. Net assets at fiscal year-end

   d. Increases or decreases in the current cost amounts of inventory and property, plant, and equipment, net of inflation

4. Other information

   a. Purchasing power gain or loss on net monetary items

   b. Cash dividends declared per common share

   c. Market price per share at fiscal year-end.

   d. Cumulative translation adjustment.

A note to the five year summary should disclose the average-for-the-year or the end-of-the-year CPI, whichever is used for the measurement of income from continuing operations. The information in the five year summary is to be stated in average-for-the-year constant dollars as measured by the CPI for the current fiscal year. Companies that present this information in current year dollars must roll forward prior year information each reporting period to reflect the current CPI.

If an enterprise presents the minimum information required by SFAS No. 33, net assets (i.e., stockholders' equity) should be measured, for purposes of the five year summary, on a current cost basis at the amount reported in the primary financial statements adjusted for the difference between the historical cost amounts and the current cost or lower recoverable amounts of inventories and property, plant, and equipment and restated in terms of constant dollars to the current or base year.

In an effort to simplify transition to the reporting requirements of SFAS No. 33, the FASB requires that only sales, cash dividends per share, market price per share, and the CPI utilized be presented for fiscal years before the enterprise was required to comply with SFAS No. 33. A complete five-year summary of other disclosures is not required until five years after initial application of SFAS No. 33. The FASB does, however, encourage disclosure of the other information in the five-year summary on a retroactive basis during this transition period.

MANAGEMENT DISCUSSION OF THE SUPPLEMENTARY DISCLOSURES REQUIRED UNDER SFAS NO. 33

The most difficult aspect of the SFAS No. 33 disclosure requirements imposed on the management of a reporting enterprise will be attempting to explain and discuss the significance of these supplemental disclosures. This discussion is required in paragraph 37 of SFAS No. 33, which states:

Enterprises shall provide, in their financial reports, explanations of the information disclosed in accordance with this Statement and discussions of its significance in the circumstances of the enterprise.

The purpose of this section is to present some guidance to enterprises attempting to develop this management discussion.

Neither SFAS No. 33 nor any other document provides any standard format for developing the management discussion. These explanations could appear in a variety of places within the financial report, such as footnotes to the supplemental data, the president's letter, a financial review section, etc. In any event, the president's letter probably will contain some general commentary on the meaning of these supplemental disclosures.

An example of the type of explanation that might be included in financial reports follows:

We use the LIFO method of accounting for cost of goods sold, which charges current costs to the results of operations for both financial reporting and income tax purposes. Accordingly, no adjustment to cost of goods sold was necessary for the purpose of determining the supplemental inflation accounting data. Other companies in our industry use the FIFO method of accounting, which generally results in higher income for financial reporting purposes. But these companies will show large adjustments to cost of goods sold in the inflation accounting information, which are not deductible for tax purposes.

Because the inflation adjustments to historical depreciation expense are not deductible for tax purposes, our effective tax rate in the supplemental current cost information has increased to 70 percent, which is well in excess of the statutory rate of 46 percent.

SFAS No. 33 identifies a number of advantages and disadvantages taken into account in deciding what supplementary disclosures are to be required. The following summary of various issues raised in the document may be helpful to management in explaining and discussing the historical cost/constant dollar and current cost disclosures.

1. Estimating future cash flows is an important objective of financial statements users. The supplementary information may provide additional means of estimating such cash flows as follow:
   a. Current cost data may be considered a conservative estimate of net present value of future cash flow.
   b. Current cost margin information together with current cost of inventory may be useful to assess cash flow, especially if selling prices reflect changes in costs.

    c. Assets that are stated at lower recoverable amounts are by definition stated at the present value of management's estimate of future cash flow.

2. Current cost information may be useful in analyzing an enterprise's capability to maintaining its operating capacity without impairing its ability to declare dividends.

3. Alternatively, constant dollar information may be useful in analyzing an enterprise's capacity for maintaining the purchasing power of the shareholders' investment and of sustaining an adequate return on that investment.

4. The use of a uniform unit of measure (constant dollars) should enhance the results of ratio analysis and other usual comparisons of financial data. This uniformity also should enhance the significance of comparisons with other enterprises, both within the same industry and in other industries.

5. Inflation affects different prices in different ways. Therefore, presentation of holding gains or losses, both before and after deducting the effect of general inflation, highlights the specific effects of inflation on an enterprise's activities.

Users of annual financial reports will encounter a plethora of information that the FASB believes will prove useful in assessing the impact of inflation on the reporting enterprise. And management has a vested interest in explaining the significance of the inflation data since, unlike the SEC's replacement cost data, the FASB's disclosures must appear in annual reports to shareholders and will be very visible.

Exhibit 15.1 provides an illustrative disclosure of the inflation adjusted information. Included in the disclosure is information on both a constant dollar and a current cost basis. Additionally, the five year summary information is supplied. Finally, the management discussion of the impact of inflation on the entity's operations is included in the disclosure.

BACKGROUND FOR OIL AND GAS INDUSTRY

Prior to 1977, financial accounting and reporting for oil and gas producing companies had been debated by the accounting profession, regulatory agencies, industry groups, and various companies' managements. The debate focused on the two widely different methods of accounting followed by those companies: the full cost method and the successful efforts method. In an attempt to unify the accounting practices in the oil and gas industry, the FASB in December 1977 issued SFAS No. 19, "Financial Accounting and Reporting by Oil and Gas Producing Companies." This statement required the use of the successful efforts method of accounting for oil and gas producing activities.

In August 1977, prior to the effective date of SFAS No. 19, the SEC issued ASR No. 253, "Adoption of Requirements for Financial Accounting and Reporting Practices for Oil and Gas Producing Activities." In this release, the SEC incorporated into its rules all the substantive provi-

Exhibit 15.1
Illustrative Inflation Disclosures: Atlantic Richfield Company

The financial information contained in this report indicates the magnitude of the dollars received and spent during the past year. The $1.2 billion net income reported is impressive, however, inflation has distorted the real value of the reported profit. Any attempts to measure the impact of inflation on a company with diverse operations is arbitrary. However, a summarized statement of income for the year ended December 31, 1979, prepared on the basis of constant dollars as prescribed by the Financial Accounting Standards Board, is provided. Management feels that this information should be viewed as an indication of the impact of inflation rather than an absolute measurement since there are other equally valid methods which could give materially different results.

The constant dollar amounts were obtained by adjusting historical cost amounts by the Consumer Price Index. The accounting policies used to arrive at historical amounts of costs of goods sold and depreciation, depletion, and amortization expense were also used to determine the constant dollar equivalents. Since the Company uses the last in, first out method of accounting for inventories, historical costs are at recent amounts, and there is only a slight increase in costs of goods sold. Due consideration to the benefit of the purchasing power gain on net monetary assets should be given in evaluating the decrease in net income.

It is important to note that no adjustments to or allocations of the provision for taxes on income in the primary financial statements were made in the computation of the corresponding constant dollar amounts. In doing so, the 45.6 percent effective tax rate as calculated on the historical cost

amounts equates to an adjusted rate of 54.2 percent, a major concern in considering capital formation.

Statement of Income Adjusted for Changing Prices
For the Year Ended December 31, 1979
(Millions of dollars except per share data)

	As Reported Historical Dollars	Constant 1979 Dollars
Revenues	$ 16,818	$ 16,818
Costs and operating expenses	11,777	11,803
Depreciation, depletion and amortization	684	997
Other expenses	1,877	1,877
Interest expense	335	335
Provision for taxes on income	979	979
Net income	$ 1,166	$ 827
Earned per share	$ 9.48	$ 6.73
Gain from decline in purchasing power of net amounts owed		$ 577
Net assets at December 31, 1979	$ 6,120	$ 10,233

Additional supplemental financial data adjusted for effects of changing prices are as follows (in average 1979 dollars):

	Years Ended December 31,				
	1979	1978	1977	1976	1975
Revenues (millions):					
As reported	$ 16,818	$ 12,985	$ 11,540	$ 9,256	$ 7,854
Adjusted	$ 16,818	$ 14,446	$ 13,822	$ 11,801	$ 10,592
Cash dividends declared per common share:					
As reported	$ 2.80	$ 2.40	$ 1.80	$ 1.425	$ 1.25
Adjusted	$ 2.80	$ 2.67	$ 2.16	$ 1.817	$ 1.69
Market price per common share at year-end:					
As reported	$ 80.00	$ 56.875	$ 51.375	$ 57.750	$ 45.188
Adjusted*	$ 80.00	$ 64.439	$ 63.464	$ 76.166	$ 62.467
Average consumer price index (1967 = 100)	217.4	195.4	181.5	170.5	161.2

*Calculated using year-end 1979 dollars.

The foregoing indicates that the Company and the shareholder have partially overcome the adverse impact of inflation indicated by the steady increase in revenues and cash dividends, both on a historical and constant dollar basis. While the inflation adjusted rate of increase for sales and cash dividends is only a little better than half the historical rate, they significantly exceed the average annual inflation rate of about eight percent reflected by the Consumer Price Index over the period presented. Since 1977, the market value per share of common stock has also risen reflecting an increase in the shareholder's investment in constant dollars.

sions of SFAS No. 19 except that the commission's rules permit, as an acceptable alternative for reporting purposes, the use of a prescribed form of the full costing method of accounting. The SEC in ASR No. 257, "Requirements for Financial Accounting and Reporting Practices for Oil and Gas Producing Activities," specified the form of successful efforts accounting identical to the method indicated by SFAS No. 19. At the same time, the SEC in ASR No. 258, "Oil and Gas Producers—Full Cost Accounting Practices," established uniform requirements for financial accounting and reporting practices of oil and gas producers following the full costing method of accounting.

In February 1979, in light of the conflicts between SFAS No. 19 and the SEC's regulations, the FASB issued SFAS No. 25, "Suspension of Certain Accounting Requirements for Oil and Gas Producing Companies." SFAS No. 25 suspended the effective date indefinitely for applying the requirements of SFAS No. 19. Therefore, companies not required to report to the SEC could continue the use of their present methods of accounting. Finally, to harmonize the disclosures required by the SEC and the FASB, SFAS No. 69 "Disclosures about Oil and Gas Producing Activities," was issued.

SUCCESSFUL EFFORTS VERSUS FULL COSTING ACCOUNTING FOR OIL AND GAS PRODUCING ACTIVITIES

The successful efforts and full costing methods of accounting for oil and gas producing activities are used widely by companies of all sizes. Successful efforts accounting is presently prescribed by SFAS No. 19 (as amended and modified by SFAS No. 25) and ASR No. 257. Full costing is prescribed by ASR No. 258.

The basic differences between these two methods of accounting are the treatment of exploratory cost and the size of the cost center. Successful efforts accounting recognizes most costs of exploration as an expense in the period incurred. Full costing accounting treats the majority of exploration costs as a capital expenditure to be amortized over future production. Successful efforts accounting uses a small cost center (such as a property, field, or lease) to amortize capitalized expenditures, while full costing accounting uses a large cost center such as a country.

DEFINITIONS OF KEY TERMS IN OIL AND GAS ACCOUNTING

Development well: A well drilled within the proved area of an oil or gas reservoir to the depths of a stratigraphic horizon known to be productive

Exploratory well: A well drilled to find and produce oil or gas in an unproved area, to find a new reservoir in a field previously found to be productive of oil and gas in another reservoir, or to extend a known reservoir

Field: An area consisting of a single reservoir or multiple reservoirs, all grouped on or related to the same individual geological structural feature

Proved developed oil and gas reserves: Reserves that can be expected to be recovered through existing wells with existing equipment and operating methods

Proved oil and gas reserves: The estimated quantities of crude oil, natural gas, and natural gas liquids that geological and engineering data demonstrate with reasonable certainty to be recoverable in future years from known reservoirs under existing economic and operating conditions

Proved properties: Properties with proved reserves

Proved undeveloped reserves: Reserves that are expected to be recovered from new wells on undrilled acreage or from existing wells where a relatively major expenditure is required for completion

Reservoir: A porous and permeable underground formation containing a natural accumulation of producible oil and/or gas that is confined by impermeable rock or water barriers and is individual and separate from other reservoirs

Unproved properties: Properties with proved reserves.

DISCLOSURES REQUIRED FOR SUCCESSFUL EFFORTS AND FULL COSTING

ASR No. 253, "Adoption of Requirements for Financial Accounting and Reporting Practices for Oil and Gas Producing Activities," requires the disclosure of certain data in the body of the financial statements or the notes thereto or in a separate schedule as an integral part of the financial statements. An oil and gas producing entity shall disclose

1. The method of accounting used (full costing or successful efforts)
2. The aggregate amount of capitalized cost and of related accumulated depreciation, depletion, amortization, and valuation allowance as of the end of each period
3. The cost incurred in producing oil and gas each year segregated into acquisition, exploration, development, and production costs, and whether these costs are capitalized or expensed
4. For each geographic area that reserves are reported, the net revenues from oil and gas production for proved developed reserves and reserves applicable to long-term supply contracts with foreign governments
5. A schedule of estimated quantities of proved reserves (note per SFAS No. 25 that this may be provided as supplementary information)
6. The future net revenues from estimated production of oil and gas reserves using current prices for the same areas as (4) above
7. The present value of future net revenues computed by applying a 10 percent discount rate to the estimated future net revenues.

Reserve Recognition Accounting

The SEC reached the following conclusion regarding oil and gas accounting in ASR No. 253: "Traditional accounting methods fail to provide sufficient information on financial position and operating results of oil and gas producers. . . . Development of an accounting method based on a valuation of proved oil and gas reserves would provide significant useful information and steps should be taken to develop such a method."

Exhibit 15.2
Illustrative Oil and Gas Disclosures: E. I. Du Pont de Nemours and Company

Oil and Gas Producing Activities

The disclosures on pages 64 through 66 are presented in accordance with the provisions of Statement of Financial Accounting Standards No. 69. Unless otherwise noted, these data reflect the oil and gas producing activities of Conoco subsequent to its acquisition by Du Pont on August 1, 1981.

Estimated Proved Reserves of Oil and Gas

The reserve quantities below exclude royalty interests of others. Royalty interests in foreign reserves that are dependent upon rates of production or prices were calculated using projected rates of production and prices that existed at the time the quantities were estimated. Oil reserves comprise crude oil, condensate and natural gas liquids expected to be removed for the company's account from its natural gas deliveries.

	Total Worldwide		United States		Europe		Other Foreign[1]
	Oil	Gas	Oil	Gas	Oil	Gas	Oil
	(Oil in million barrels and gas in billion cubic feet)						
Proved Developed and Undeveloped Reserves							
Acquisition of Conoco on August 1, 1981	1,444	3,537	379	2,621	385	916	680
Revisions of previous estimates	17	(1)	15	8	1	(9)	1
Extensions, discoveries and other additions . .	27	89	14	82	12	7	1
Production	(54)	(136)	(21)	(109)	(9)	(27)	(24)
December 31, 1981	1,434	3,489	387	2,602	389	887	658
Revisions of previous estimates	87	11	57	96	28	(85)	2
Extensions, discoveries and other additions . .	18	187	17	135	—	52	1
Production	(131)	(333)	(50)	(262)	(24)	(71)	(57)
Sales of in-place reserves[2]	(61)	(268)	(61)	(268)	—	—	—
December 31, 1982[2]	1,347	3,086	350	2,303	393	783	604
Proved Developed Reserves							
August 1, 1981	1,052	2,744	364	2,272	35	472	653
December 31, 1981	1,085	2,886	380	2,418	72	468	633
December 31, 1982[2]	1,014	2,616	344	2,199	89	417	581

Capitalized Costs Relating to Oil and Gas Producing Activities

	Total	Proved Properties	Unproved Properties
At December 31, 1981:			
Gross cost	$4,143	$3,369	$774
Accumulated depreciation, depletion, amortization and valuation allowances	177	148	29
Net cost	$3,966	$3,221	$745
At December 31, 1982[2]:			
Gross cost	$4,873	$3,990	$883
Accumulated depreciation, depletion, amortization and valuation allowances	640	534	106
Net cost	$4,233	$3,456	$777

[1] Dubai, Libya and Indonesia.

[2] December 31, 1982 reserve quantities and capitalized costs exclude amounts applicable to properties sold to Petro-Lewis Corporation and others (see page 16); for this purpose, these transactions are reflected as sales of in-place reserves in 1982.

Exhibit 15.2 (continued)

Costs Incurred in Oil and Gas Producing Activities[1]

	Total Worldwide	United States	Europe	Other Foreign[2]
Five months ended December 31, 1981:				
Acquisition of proved properties	$ 18	$ 18	$ —	$ —
Acquisition of unproved properties	101	100	—	1
Exploration	206	138	25	43
Development	304	188	77	39
Year ended December 31, 1982:				
Acquisition of proved properties	6	6	—	—
Acquisition of unproved properties	140	129	—	11
Exploration	458	288	78	92
Development	797	389	338	70

Results of Operations for Oil and Gas Producing Activities[3]

	Total Worldwide	United States	Europe	Other Foreign[2]
Five months ended December 31, 1981:				
Revenues:				
Sales to unaffiliated customers	$ 667	$ 479	$ 98	$ 90
Transfers to other company operations	1,027	367	220	440
Total	1,694	846	318	530
Expenses:				
Exploration	173	130	13	30
Production	497	367	80	50
Depreciation, depletion, amortization and valuation provisions	196	110	41	45
Income taxes	703	138	144	421
Total	1,569	745	278	546
Results of operations	$ 125	$ 101	$ 40	$ (16)
Year ended December 31, 1982:				
Revenues:				
Sales to unaffiliated customers	$1,952	$1,150	$504	$ 298
Transfers to other company operations	2,555	866	318	1,371
Total	4,507	2,016	822	1,669
Expenses:				
Exploration	388	264	56	68
Production	1,100	787	206	107
Depreciation, depletion, amortization and valuation provisions	543	319	122	102
Income taxes	2,014	359	347	1,308
Total	4,045	1,729	731	1,585
Results of operations	$ 462	$ 287	$ 91	$ 84

[1] These data comprise all costs incurred in the activities shown, whether capitalized or charged to expense at the time they were incurred.

[2] Dubai, Libya and Indonesia, except for acquisition of unproved properties and exploration costs which cover all areas outside the United States and Europe.

[3] Revenues are based on market prices determined at the point of delivery from the producing unit. All royalty payments are reflected as reductions in revenues in this tabulation. Results of oil and gas producing activities are included in the Petroleum Exploration and Production segment information in Note 21 on page 60, along with results of tar sands, oil shale and certain other activities; in that tabulation, foreign royalty payments are reflected as costs.

(continued)

Exhibit 15.2 (continued)

Standardized Measure of Discounted Future Net Cash Flows and Changes Therein Relating to Proved Oil and Gas Reserves

The information below has been prepared in accordance with Statement of Financial Accounting Standards No. 69, which requires the standardized measure of discounted future net cash flows to be based on sales prices, costs and statutory income tax rates in effect at the time the projections are made, and a 10 percent per year discount rate.

The projections should not be viewed as realistic estimates of future cash flows nor should the "standardized measure" be interpreted as representing current value to the company. Material revisions to estimates of proved reserves may occur in the future; development and production of the reserves may not occur in the periods assumed; and actual prices realized and actual costs in-curred are expected to vary significantly from those used. The company's investment and operating decisions are not based on the information presented below, but on a wide range of reserve estimates that includes probable as well as proved reserves and on different price and cost assumptions than reflected in this information.

The December 31, 1980 Conoco data shown below predate Du Pont's August 1, 1981 acquisition of Conoco, but are included to provide a basis for explaining changes in the standardized measure for the full-year 1981. The December 31, 1980 data exclude Conoco's 52.9% interest in Hudson's Bay Oil and Gas Company Limited, which was disposed of during the second quarter of 1981.

	Total Worldwide	United States	Europe	Other Foreign[1]
December 31, 1980				
Standardized measure of discounted future net cash flows	$ 5,379	$ 3,148	$ 1,811	$ 420
December 31, 1981				
Future cash flows				
Revenues	$54,843	$17,550	$15,387	$21,906
Production costs	(11,518)	(7,325)	(3,137)	(1,056)
Development costs	(1,933)	(341)	(1,096)	(496)
Income tax expense	(32,688)	(4,533)	(8,307)	(19,848)
Future net cash flows	8,704	5,351	2,847	506
Discount to present value at a 10% annual rate	(3,849)	(2,241)	(1,379)	(229)
Standardized measure of discounted future net cash flows	$ 4,855	$ 3,110	$ 1,468	$ 277
December 31, 1982[2]				
Future cash flows				
Revenues	$48,355	$15,556	$14,050	$18,749
Production costs	(9,830)	(6,542)	(2,443)	(845)
Development costs	(1,845)	(374)	(993)	(478)
Income tax expense	(28,147)	(3,935)	(7,806)	(16,406)
Future net cash flows	8,533	4,705	2,808	1,020
Discount to present value at a 10% annual rate	(3,966)	(2,202)	(1,275)	(489)
Standardized measure of discounted future net cash flows	$ 4,567	$ 2,503	$ 1,533	$ 531

[1] Dubai, Libya and Indonesia.
[2] Excludes future cash flows related to reserve quantities sold to Petro-Lewis Corporation and others (see page 16).

The aggregate standardized measure of discounted future net cash flows decreased $288 during 1982. This change reflects pretax decreases of $3,407 due to sales and transfers of oil and gas produced and $1,323 due to net changes in sales and transfer prices and in production costs. Partially offsetting these factors were a $2,180 accretion of the beginning pretax amount of the standardized measure and a net $2,018 decrease in the discounted amount of income taxes. Other, less significant, variances include those attributable to the exclusion from December 31, 1982 balances of amounts applicable to properties sold to Petro-Lewis Corporation and others (see page 16), additions and revisions to reserve estimates, and changes in development costs.

The aggregate standardized measure decreased $524 during 1981. The principal source of this change was a pretax decrease of $3,457 due to sales and transfers of oil and gas produced. Largely offsetting this factor were a $2,337 accretion of the beginning pretax amount of the standardized measure and a net $1,044 decrease in the discounted amount of income taxes. Other, less significant, variances include those attributable to additions and revisions to reserve estimates and changes in development costs.

Exhibit 15.2 (continued)

Undeveloped Petroleum Acreage
(thousands of acres at December 31)

	Gross 1982	Gross 1981	Net 1982	Net 1981
Worldwide	**103,609**	**118,432**	**35,688**	**40,043**
United States operations	**9,062**	**8,130**	**6,180**	**5,640**
Onshore	8,127	7,174	5,835	5,305
Texas	1,790	1,358	1,207	781
Montana	1,284	1,146	588	627
North Dakota	1,097	918	227	309
California	850	613	721	527
Other	3,106	3,139	3,092	3,061
Offshore and Alaska	935	956	345	335
Gulf of Mexico	711	625	211	144
Atlantic	97	193	55	104
Pacific	57	62	35	38
Alaska	70	76	44	49
International operations	**94,547**	**110,302**	**29,508**	**34,403**
Europe	**4,512**	**4,629**	**2,190**	**2,451**
United Kingdom	2,614	2,614	1,612	1,619
Norway	892	784	144	126
Italy	805	875	378	565
The Netherlands	106	106	32	32
Spain	95	250	24	109
Africa	**64,758**	**76,998**	**15,701**	**19,580**
Chad	32,236	32,236	8,059	8,059
Central African Republic	18,200	18,200	4,550	4,550
Libya	12,600	12,600	2,058	2,058
Egypt	1,722	13,962	1,034	4,913
Middle East	**956**	**956**	**287**	**287**
Dubai	956	956	287	287
Asia Pacific	**22,798**	**26,196**	**9,807**	**10,562**
Indonesia	22,798	26,196	9,807	10,562
Latin America	**1,523**	**1,523**	**1,523**	**1,523**
Brazil	1,523	1,523	1,523	1,523

Sources of Refined Products*
(barrels per calendar day)

	1982	1981
Worldwide	**626,608**	**623,128**
United States	**399,925**	**418,703**
Crude oil and condensate processed	282,871	290,987
Other feedstocks processed	14,869	10,539
Natural gas liquids recovered	20,310	18,678
Purchases	75,381	87,494
Inventory decrease	6,494	11,005
International	**226,683**	**204,425**
Crude oil and condensate processed	103,889	97,318
Other feedstocks processed	51,788	43,674
Purchases	63,661	65,359
Inventory decrease (increase)	7,345	(1,926)

*These sources supply products for outside sales and for internal uses, including refinery fuel, petrochemical feedstocks and other uses.

Refinery Capacities and Operations
Rated Crude Oil and Condensate Distillation Capacity at Year End
(barrels per calendar day)

	1982	1981
Worldwide	**546,000**	**596,500**
United States[1]	**381,000**	**431,500**
Lake Charles, Louisiana[2]	156,500	156,500
Ponca City, Oklahoma	134,000	134,000
Billings, Montana[3]	48,500	52,500
Denver, Colorado[4]	32,500	32,500
Santa Maria, California	9,500	9,500
Paramount, California[5]	—	46,500
United Kingdom	**130,000**	**130,000**
Federal Republic of Germany[6]	**35,000**	**35,000**

Crude Oil and Condensate Processed at Refineries by Sulfur Content
(barrels per calendar day)

	1982	1981
Worldwide	**386,760**	**388,305**
United States	**282,871**	**290,987**
Low sulfur[7]	238,241	242,434
High sulfur	44,630	48,553
United Kingdom (low sulfur)[7]	**84,594**	**77,278**
Federal Republic of Germany[6]	**19,295**	**20,040**
Low sulfur[7]	11,423	11,910
High sulfur	7,872	8,130

Product Yields by Volume
(percent of total yield)

	1982	1981
United States:		
Motor gasoline	49.9	48.9
Middle distillate	29.3	27.0
Residual fuel oil and asphalt	9.0	9.6
Other	11.8	14.5
United Kingdom:		
Motor gasoline	27.5	28.4
Middle distillate	41.2	41.8
Residual fuel oil	2.1	.5
Other	29.2	29.3
Federal Republic of Germany[6]:		
Motor gasoline	40.4	46.6
Middle distillate	22.1	23.0
Residual fuel oil	22.3	22.1
Other	15.2	8.3

[1] A 23,500-barrel-per-day refinery in Wrenshall, Minn., operational for the first part of 1981, was shut down in May of that year.

[2] A 32,500-barrel-per-day interest in the refinery, formerly held by Monsanto, was acquired in August 1981 as part of the merger with Conoco.

[3] Decrease in rated capacity resulted from reduced availability of light Canadian condensate.

[4] The Denver refinery, which was extensively damaged by an explosion and fire in 1978, resumed operations in April 1981.

[5] The Paramount refinery was closed in July 1982 and sold in December 1982.

[6] Represents Conoco's 25 percent interest in a refinery at Karlsruhe.

[7] Low-sulfur crude oil and condensate contain no more than 0.5 percent sulfur by weight.

(continued)

Exhibit 15.2 (continued)

Well Completions	Development		Exploration	
	1982	1981	1982	1981
United States:				
Gross wells	969.0	1,134.0	87.0	99.0
Net wells	263.0	358.8	52.1	50.1
Oil	152.4	192.2	5.5	3.9
Gas	86.0	129.9	3.2	6.6
Dry	24.6	36.7	43.4	39.6
International:				
Gross wells	62.0	87.0	40.0	36.0
Net wells	12.3	17.2	10.4	11.0
Oil	11.0	16.5	2.8	1.8
Gas	1.0	—	.3	1.8
Dry	.3	.7	7.3	7.4

Petroleum and Coal Five-Year Review
(Dollars in millions)

	1982	1981	1980	1979	1978
CAPITAL EXPENDITURES[1]					
Petroleum exploration:					
United States operations:					
Acquisition of leases	$ 128.9	$ 166.2	$ 117.6	$ 135.0	$ 44.1
Wells and equipment	137.9	150.6	65.4	51.8	33.7
International operations:					
Acquisition of leases	40.2	45.9	67.9	13.0	8.7
Wells and equipment	68.6	47.3	36.8	15.8	10.4
Subtotal	375.6	410.0	287.7	215.6	96.9
Petroleum production:					
United States operations	396.4	500.7	380.1	242.6	226.3
International operations	408.5	326.6	305.4	275.5	228.9
Subtotal	804.9	827.3	685.5	518.1	455.2
Petroleum refining and natural gas processing:					
United States refining	198.4	148.0	80.9	70.2	39.9
International refining	18.0	39.1	23.4	29.0	23.9
Natural gas processing[2]	33.6	52.3	19.1	24.1	19.9
Subtotal	250.0	239.4	123.4	123.3	83.7
Petroleum marketing:					
United States operations	24.3	18.8	14.9	12.4	8.5
International operations	25.9	26.8	25.4	16.4	20.6
Subtotal	50.2	45.6	40.3	28.8	29.1
Petroleum transportation:					
United States operations	48.7	85.0	65.0	23.9	17.2
International operations	1.2	24.0	4.4	2.9	6.8
Subtotal	49.9	109.0	69.4	26.8	24.0
Total Petroleum	1,530.6	1,631.3	1,206.3	912.6	688.9
Coal:					
Coal and surface lands[3]	60.3	87.9	26.2	17.3	16.2
Plant and equipment	273.3	188.1	173.1	164.9	136.8
Total Coal	333.6	276.0	199.3	182.2	153.0
Total Petroleum and Coal	$1,864.2	$1,907.3	$1,405.6	$1,094.8	$841.9
United States	$ 1,271.5	$ 1,392.3	$ 931.9	$ 734.7	$ 540.4

Exhibit 15.2 (continued)

Petroleum and Coal Five-Year Review Continued
(Dollars in millions)

	1982	1981	1980	1979	1978
CASH EXPLORATION EXPENSES					
United States petroleum operations	$ 148.4	$ 115.1	$ 69.2	$ 44.0	$ 33.3
International petroleum operations	70.7	73.9	44.7	28.0	22.8
Petroleum	219.1	189.0	113.9	72.0	56.1
Coal	9.2	11.8	11.4	12.5	10.2
Total	**$ 228.3**	**$ 200.8**	**$ 125.3**	**$ 84.5**	**$ 66.3**
UNDEVELOPED PETROLEUM ACREAGE (at December 31)[4]					
Net acreage—Worldwide (thousands of acres)	**35,688**	**40,043**	**51,749**	**43,979**	**50,909**
United States operations	6,180	5,640	4,173	3,517	3,290
International operations	29,508	34,403	47,576	40,462	47,619
PROVED PETROLEUM RESERVES (at December 31)[1]					
Petroleum liquids—Worldwide (million barrels)	**1,539**	**1,637**	**1,723**	**1,793**	**1,719**
United States	350[5]	387	403	398	413
Europe	452	446	452	461	409
Africa, Middle East and Asia Pacific	737	804	868	934	897
Natural gas—Worldwide (billion cubic feet)	**3,197**	**3,617**	**3,743**	**4,102**	**4,146**
United States	2,303[5]	2,602	2,660	2,681	2,704
Europe	894	1,015	1,083	1,181	1,158
Africa and Middle East	—	—	—	240	284
PETROLEUM PRODUCTION[1]					
Petroleum liquids production—Worldwide					
(thousands of barrels daily)	**401**	**375**	**389**	**408**	**398**
United States operations	**136**	**139**	**148**	**159**	**165**
Crude oil and condensate	125	126	134	143	151
Onshore	99	105	114	122	128
Texas	51	55	60	64	67
Wyoming	15	17	18	20	20
California	9	10	10	11	11
Other	24	23	26	27	30
Offshore	26	21	20	21	23
Louisiana	25	20	19	20	22
California	1	1	1	1	1
Natural gas liquids	11	13	14	16	14
International operations	**265**	**236**	**241**	**249**	**233**
United Kingdom	53	41	17	16	3
Norway	21	15	6	1	—
Other International (Dubai, Libya and Indonesia)	191	180	218	232	230

[1] See Definition of Terms on page 72.

[2] Includes transportation and storage facilities for natural gas and gas liquids.

[3] Includes $20.5 for the 1982 acquisition of a 49 percent interest in Gollin Wallsend Coal Company Limited.

[4] Does not reflect tar sands and oil shale properties, which at December 31, 1982 contained an estimated 1.4 billion tons of tar, a portion of which is potentially recoverable, and 1.3 billion barrels of shale oil. These resources are not currently under production or development and would not be commercially recoverable under present costs and market prices.

[5] Excludes reserves sold to Petro-Lewis Corporation and others (see page 16).

(continued)

Exhibit 15.2 (continued)

Petroleum and Coal Five-Year Review Continued

	1982	1981	1980	1979	1978
Natural gas deliveries—Worldwide (million cubic feet daily) ...	**931**	**899**	**1,007**	**1,050**	**1,127**
United States operations	**718**	**737**	**778**	**834**	**869**
Onshore	466	511	539	573	567
Texas	164	172	187	206	204
New Mexico	140	171	183	180	178
Oklahoma	78	86	74	90	94
Other	84	82	95	97	91
Offshore	252	226	239	261	302
International operations (United Kingdom)	**213**	**162**	**229**	**216**	**258**
PETROLEUM REFINING (thousands of barrels daily)					
Refinery inputs processed—Worldwide	**453**	**443**	**446**	**323**	**481**
United States operations	**297**	**302**	**293**	**346**	**354**
By own refineries	297	301	293	346	354
Crude oil and condensate	282	290	284	337	344
Other feedstocks	15	11	9	9	10
By others for Conoco	—	1	—	—	—
International operations (Western Europe)	**156**	**141**	**155**	**179**	**127**
By United Kingdom refinery	121	109	115	127	100
Crude oil and condensate	85	77	86	112	84
Other feedstocks	36	32	29	15	16
By nonconsolidated affiliate for Conoco	35	32	37	39	14
Crude oil and condensate	19	20	29	33	14
Other feedstocks	16	12	8	6	—
By others for Conoco	—	—	3	13	13
PETROLEUM MARKETING					
Sales of refined products—Worldwide					
(thousands of barrels daily)	**532**	**526**	**543**	**617**	**638**
United States operations	**321**	**332**	**338**	**394**	**426**
Motor gasoline	163	158	166	188	204
LPG and natural gasoline	25	26	22	23	23
Commercial jet fuel	22	22	19	19	24
Middle distillate	68	59	73	94	92
Residual fuel oil and asphalt	28	49	42	54	66
Other products	15	18	16	16	17
International operations	**211**	**194**	**205**	**223**	**212**
Western Europe	203	187	193	213	204
Motor gasoline	72	69	72	72	65
Middle distillate	89	87	85	88	98
Residual fuel oil	19	11	15	29	20
Other products	23	20	21	24	21
Far East	8	7	12	10	8
Retail marketing outlets—Worldwide[1][2]	**7,542**	**7,741**	**7,628**	**7,362**	**8,462**
United States operations	5,489	5,708	5,605	5,275	6,425
International operations (Western Europe)	2,053	2,033	2,023	2,087	2,037
PETROLEUM TRANSPORTATION					
Pipeline shipments (thousands of barrels daily):					
Pipeline shipments	629	576	648	685	688
Equity in pipeline shipments of nonconsolidated affiliates	328	319	319	349	349

[1] At December 31.

[2] Outlets owned by Conoco and others that sell the company's refined products.

Exhibit 15.2 (continued)

Petroleum and Coal Five-Year Review Continued

	1982	1981	1980	1979	1978
COAL ACTIVITIES (millions of tons)[1]					
Recoverable coal resources at January 1[2]	12,250	14,324	14,511	14,093	14,166
Purchased resources	231	357	485	289	284
Resources sold in place	(2)	(985)[3]	(127)	(200)	(153)
Production	(45)	(39)	(45)	(47)	(38)
Revisions and other changes	(197)	(1,407)	(500)	376	(166)
Recoverable coal resources at December 31[2]	12,237	12,250	14,324	14,511	14,093
Steam coal	10,937	10,758	12,772	12,702	12,201
Eastern and midwestern United States	5,079	5,004	5,478	5,318	5,127
Western United States[4]	5,825	5,669	7,205	7,160	6,851
Canada	33	85	89	224	223
Metallurgical coal	1,300	1,492	1,552	1,809	1,892
Eastern United States	993	1,128	1,138	1,384	1,484
Canada	307	364	414	425	408
Coal production[5]	45	39	45	47	38
Steam coal	39	35	39	42	35
Metallurgical coal	6	4	6	5	3
Average realized mine price (per ton)[6]	$33.30	$29.52	$27.65	$25.94	$23.80

[1] Coal activities data do not include Consol's 49 percent interest, acquired during 1982, in Gollin Wallsend Coal Company Limited, an Australian company, nor do the tables include resource or production data for other affiliates. Such amounts are immaterial in the aggregate.

[2] Not all of these resources are commercially recoverable under present prices and costs. See Definition of Terms on page 72. The breakdown of recoverable coal resources is as follows:

	1982	1981	1980
Demonstrated Reserves	7,253	7,410	7,661
Other Identified Resources	4,984	4,840	6,663
Total	12,237	12,250	14,324

The 12.2 billion tons at year-end 1982 consist of 11 billion tons owned or leased, and 1.2 billion tons for which the company has preferential leasing rights granted by the Federal government. These rights include 0.5 billion tons that are located on an Indian reservation and are currently being contested by the tribal lessors. It is possible that these Indian reservation leasing rights will either be honored or that the rights will be converted to other leases. The leased resources include 1 billion tons leased from the Federal government subject to certain "due diligence" production requirements commencing in 1985. The resources are located in nearly every major coal-producing region in North America.

[3] Includes approximately 650 million tons related to properties that were exchanged for oil shale properties.

[4] West of the Mississippi River.

[5] In addition to its own production, Consol supervises production for certain of its affiliates and other companies. Supervised production totaled 5.9 million tons during 1982, compared with 3.9 million tons during 1981.

[6] The average realized mine price per ton of coal reflects sales of both steam and metallurgical coal sold at a wide range of prices, including substantial sales made under long-term contracts.

The SEC developed a value based method of accounting: RRA. In ASR No. 269, "Oil and Gas Producers—Supplemental Disclosure on the Basis of Reserve Recognition Accounting," the commission required oil and gas producers to include in their financial statements a supplemental summary of oil and gas producing activities on the basis of RRA. RRA is based on the theory that, in the oil industry, recognition of revenue should take place when proved reserves are found. This is intended to provide a better measure of an oil and gas enterprise's success in finding proved reserves than is currently reflected in historical cost financial statements. The SEC planned that the requirement of RRA supplemental information would provide the basis for the eventual decision by the commission as to whether to require RRA as the method of accounting in the primary financial statements of oil and gas producers. The summary of oil and gas producing activities includes the current year's additions and revisions to proved reserves and all nonproductive cost. SFAS No. 69 effectively extends these requirements to most oil and gas producing entities.

ASR No. 269 also requires a reconciliation of beginning and ending total present value of estimated future net revenues. This reconciliation reports changes in purchases of reserves in place and expenditures for development that were accrued when valuing reserves in prior years, and identifies the amounts currently realized from the production and sale of oil and gas.

ILLUSTRATIVE DISCLOSURES OF OIL AND GAS OPERATIONS

Exhibit 15.2 illustrates the disclosures called for by these documents. As can be seen, these requirements result in lengthy disclosures with regard to quantities of all mineral rights which must be included in this disclosure package.

16
Interim Disclosures

THE NATURE OF INTERIM REPORTING

An interim reporting period is any reporting period of less than one year. Interim financial reporting generally is considered to be an essential part of the financial reporting package provided to investors, creditors, and potential investors. Interim financial information provides external financial statement users with timely information as to the progress of the reporting enterprise. As such, the New York Stock Exchange, the SEC and others require enterprises subject to their authority to provide financial information on an interim basis. The APB issued APBO No. 28, "Interim Financial Reporting," to establish guidelines for the measurement of income in interim reporting periods.

Prior to the issuance of APBO No. 28, two general concepts existed as to the basic nature of an interim period. Proponents of one concept viewed each interim period as a separate and discrete reporting period. Thus, results of operations for each interim period are determined as if the interim period were a discrete period—much the same as is done for the annual reporting period. Proponents of the second concept viewed interim reporting periods as being an integral part of the annual reporting period.

The APB concluded that the usefulness of interim information is based upon its relationship with the annual results of operations. Accordingly, the second concept—that interim periods are an integral part of the annual period—is consistent with the conclusion of the APB. Therefore, the primary objective of APBO No. 28 is to mandate measurement rules for interim reporting that will provide results for the interim period that are consistent with the anticipated annual results.

In general, the results for each interim period should be based on the same GAAP used by the enterprise in preparing its annual report. However, in certain circumstances, different principles and practices are necessary so that the interim results will be more indicative of the annual results. This chapter will explain the technical provisions of APBO No. 28, SFAS Nos. 3, "Reporting Accounting Changes in Interim Financial Statements," and 16, "Prior Period Adjustments," and FASBIN No. 18, "Accounting for Income Taxes in Interim Periods," as they relate to the measurement and disclosure of income in interim reporting periods.

DETERMINING INTERIM PERIOD REVENUES

As was noted, since an interim period is viewed as an integral part of the annual reporting period, the same accounting principles, procedures, and methods that are used for annual reporting purposes generally should be used in determining the results of operations for interim reporting purposes.

In determining interim period revenues, revenue from products sold or services rendered should be recognized as earned during an interim period on the same basis as is used for the annual reporting period. As a consequence, the cutoff procedures that would be used in determining which in year revenue should be recognized also would be applied in determining in which interim period within a year the revenue should be recognized. For example, revenues from long-term construction contracts accounted for under the percentage-of-completion method should be recognized in interim periods on the same basis followed for the full year. Losses projected on contracts should be recognized in full during the interim period in which the existence of such losses becomes evident.

DETERMINING INTERIM PERIOD COSTS AND EXPENSES

APBO No. 28 identifies two categories into which costs and expenses may be classified for interim reporting purposes:

Costs associated with revenue: Those costs that are associated directly with or allocated to the products sold or to the services rendered and that are charged against income in those interim periods in which the related revenue is recognized

All other costs and expenses: Those costs and expenses that are not allocated to the products sold or to the services rendered and that are charged against income in interim fiscal periods as incurred, or are allocated among interim periods based on an estimate of time expired, benefit received, or other activity associated with the periods in a systematic and rational manner.

Costs and Expenses Associated with Revenue

Costs and expenses that are associated directly with revenue, such as cost of goods sold, sales commissions, and warranty costs, should be accorded similar treatment for interim reporting purposes as for annual reporting purposes. Therefore, most costs and expenses associated with revenue can be matched against revenue in the interim period in which the revenue is recognized.

However, practices vary in determining the cost of inventory and the cost of goods sold. For example, the cost of goods manufactured may be determined based on standard or actual costs, while the cost of inventory may be determined on the basis of average cost, FIFO or LIFO. While enterprises in general should use the same inventory pricing methods and make provisions for writedowns to market at interim dates on the same basis as used at annual inventory dates, APBO No. 28 allows for some specific exceptions to the general rule so that the interim results will relate more closely to the annual results.

Other Costs and Expenses

For period costs, charges are made to income for all other costs and expenses in annual reporting periods based upon (1) direct expenditures made in the period (e.g., salaries and wages), (2) accruals for estimated expenditures to be made at a later date (e.g., vacation pay), or (3) amortization of expenditures that affect more than one annual period (e.g., insurance premiums, interest, rents). The objective in all cases is to achieve a fair measure of results of operations for the annual period and to present fairly the financial position at the end of the annual period. In accounting for period costs and expenses in interim periods, the following standards apply:

1. Period costs and expenses should be charged to income in interim periods as incurred, or be allocated among interim periods based on an estimate of time expired, benefit received, or activity associated with the periods. Procedures adopted for assigning specific cost and expense items to an interim period should be consistent with the bases followed by the enterprise in reporting results of operations at annual reporting dates. However, when a specific cost or expense item charged to expense for annual reporting purposes benefits more than one interim period within that annual period, the cost or expense item may be allocated to those interim periods on a systematic and rational basis, consistently applied.

2. Some costs and expenses incurred in an interim period cannot be readily identified with the activities or benefits of other interim periods and should be charged to the interim period in which they were incurred. Disclosure should be made as to the nature and amount of such costs unless items of a

comparable nature are included in both the current interim period and the corresponding interim period of the preceding year.

3. Arbitrary assignment of the amount of such costs to an interim period should not be made.

4. Gains and losses that arise in any interim period similar to those that would not be deferred at year-end should not be deferred to later interim periods within the same fiscal year.

The amounts of certain costs and expenses frequently are subjected to year-end adjustments even though they can be reasonably approximated at interim dates. To the extent possible, such adjustments should be estimated and the estimated costs and expenses assigned to interim periods so that the interim periods bear a reasonable portion of the anticipated annual amount. Examples of such items include inventory shrinkage, allowance for uncollectibe accounts, allowance for quantity discounts, and discretionary year-end bonuses.

PROVISION FOR INCOME TAXES

In computing the results of operations for interim reporting periods, APBO No. 28 requires that the provision for income taxes be computed in accordance with the principles established in APBO Nos. 11, "Accounting for Income Taxes," 23, "Accounting for Income Taxes—Special Areas," and 24, "Accounting for Income Taxes" (see Chapter 7 for a discussion of the requirements of these opinons). At the close of each interim period, the reporting enterprise should estimate the effective tax rate for the annual reporting period. The estimated annual effective tax rate then should be used to compute the provision for income taxes on a year-to-date basis.

The effective tax rate should reflect anticipated investment tax credits, foreign tax rates, percentage depletion, capital gains rates, and other available tax planning alternatives. However, in arriving at this effective tax rate, no effect should be included for the tax related to significant unusual or extraordinary items that will be separately reported or reported net of their related tax effect in reports for the interim period or for the fiscal year.

To aid in applying the provisions of APBO No. 28, the FASB issued FASBIN No. 18, which requires that the estimated annual effective tax rate be revised at the end of each interim period during the fiscal year, as necessary, based upon the enterprise's most current estimate of the annual effective tax rate. The estimated annual effective tax rate should be applied to the year-to-date "ordinary" income at the end of each interim period to compute the year-to-date provision for income taxes. The provision for income taxes for the current interim reporting period is the difference between the year-to-date provision for income taxes and the amounts reported in previous interim periods of the current fiscal year. Since the annual effective tax rate is estimated, the revisions in the rate in subsequent interim periods are changes in accounting estimate and therefore are reflected currently and prospectively.

DISCLOSURE OF INTERIM INFORMATION BY PUBLIC ENTERPRISES

Many public enterprises report summarized financial information to their securityholders at periodic interim dates in considerably less detail than that provided in annual financial statements. While this information provides securityholders with more timely information than would result if complete financial statements were issued at the end of each interim period, the timeliness of presentation may be offset partially by a reduction in detail. As a result, APBO No. 28 requires certain minimum disclosures. When public enterprises report summarized financial information to their securityholders at interim dates (including reports on fourth quarters), the following data should be reported, as a minimum:

1. Sales or gross revenues, provision for income taxes, extraordinary items (including related income tax effects), cumulative effect of a change in accounting principles or practices, and net income

Exhibit 16.1
Minimum Interim Disclosures: Union Pacific Corporation

---

10. Quarterly Results of Operations (Unaudited)

The unaudited quarterly results of operations (in thousands of dollars, except per share amounts) for the two years ended December 31 are as follows:

1979	Mar 31	Jun 30	Sep 30	Dec 31
Revenues	$901,776	$978,308	$976,936	$1,171,669
Income before Federal income taxes	134,304	169,298	122,867	136,279
Net income	84,100	112,154	85,468	100,764
Earnings per common share	$1.77	$2.35	$1.79	$2.11
1978				
Revenues	$686,148	$738,823	$730,259	$ 834,198
Income before Federal income taxes	82,681	93,063	98,859	122,976
Net income	56,100	63,489	64,944	79,577
Earnings per common share	$1.18	$1.34	$1.36	$1.67

Exhibit 16.2
Complete Set of Interim Financial Statements: H. J. Heinz Company

Statements of Consolidated Income

H. J. Heinz Company and Consolidated Subsidiaries

(Thousands of Dollars Except for Per Share Amounts)	Three Months Ended		Three Months Ended		Six Months Ended	
	Aug. 1, 1979	Aug. 2, 1978	Oct. 31, 1979	Nov. 1, 1978	Oct. 31, 1979	Nov. 1, 1978
	FY 1980	FY 1979	FY 1980	FY 1979	FY 1980	FY 1979
Sales	$657,105	$536,301	$709,848	$619,627	$1,366,953	$1,155,928
Cost of products sold	431,044	364,971	468,680	415,663	899,724	780,634
Gross profit	226,061	171,330	241,168	203,964	467,229	375,294
Selling and other expenses	169,376	136,042	179,708	155,735	349,084	291,777
Operating income	56,685	35,288	61,460	48,229	118,145	83,517
Other income (expense), net	1,165	2,417	(812)	1,399	353	3,816
Interest expense	7,628	4,443	9,868	6,090	17,496	10,533
	50,222	33,262	50,780	43,538	101,002	76,800
Foreign currency adjustments	(125)	(4,817)	11,033	1,194	10,908	(3,623)
Income before income taxes	50,097	28,445	61,813	44,732	111,910	73,177
Provision for income taxes:						
On operations	24,704	11,662	25,070	18,706	49,774	30,368
U.K. forgiveness	(19,423)	—	—	—	(19,423)	—
	5,281	11,662	25,070	18,706	30,351	30,368
Net income	$ 44,816	$ 16,783	$ 36,743	$ 26,026	$ 81,559	$ 42,809
Preferred dividends	$ 783	$ 786	$ 780	$ 785	$ 1,563	$ 1,571
Average common shares (in thousands)	22,359	22,305			22,367	22,319
Per common share amounts: Net income:						
Primary	$ 1.97	$ .72	$ 1.61	$ 1.13	$ 3.58	$ 1.85
Fully diluted	$ 1.87	$ .70	$ 1.55	$ 1.09	$ 3.42	$ 1.79
Dividends	$ .50	$ .40	$ .55	$ .45	$ 1.05	$ .85

2. Primary and fully diluted EPS data for each period presented, determined in accordance with the provisions of APBO No. 15, "Earnings per Share"

3. Seasonal revenue, costs, or expenses

4. Significant changes in estimates or provisions for income taxes

5. Disposal of a segment of a business and extraordinary, unusual, or infrequently occurring items

6. Contingent items

7. Changes in accounting principles or estimates

8. Significant changes in financial position.

When summarized financial data are regularly reported on a quarterly basis, the foregoing information with respect to the current quarter and the current year to date or the last twelve months to date should be furnished together with comparable data for the preceding year.

Exhibit 16.2 (continued)

Consolidated Balance Sheets

H. J. Heinz Company and Consolidated Subsidiaries

(Thousands of Dollars)	Aug. 1, 1979 FY 1980	Aug. 2, 1978 FY 1979
Assets		
Current Assets:		
Cash	$ 34,822	$ 16,349
Short-term investments	89,455	67,878
Receivables, net	255,775	204,511
Inventories	564,435	501,036
Prepaid expenses	40,472	40,119
Total current assets	984,959	829,893
Investments in and advances to entities, net	35,669	104,565
Excess of investments in consolidated subsidiaries over net assets at acquisition	125,441	16,240
Miscellaneous other assets	14,006	9,203
	175,116	130,008
Property, plant and equipment	839,285	720,429
Less Accumulated depreciation	332,504	300,035
Net property, plant and equipment	506,781	420,394
	$1,666,856	$1,380,295

(Thousands of Dollars)	Aug. 1, 1979 FY 1980	Aug. 2, 1978 FY 1979
Liabilities and Shareholders' Equity		
Current Liabilities:		
Short-term debt	$ 168,105	$ 56,310
Portion of long-term debt due within one year	15,883	16,103
Accounts payable	234,814	196,936
Accrued liabilities	105,033	75,236
Federal, foreign and state income taxes	65,219	70,814
Total current liabilities	589,054	415,399
Long-term debt	145,152	142,217
Deferred Federal and foreign income taxes	53,879	36,333
Future United Kingdom income taxes	23,978	34,687
Other liabilities	37,039	27,190
Minority interests	6,366	5,550
Shareholders' Equity:		
Capital stock	87,800	88,252
Additional capital	83,749	83,747
Retained earnings	654,650	563,095
	826,199	735,094
Less Treasury stock	14,811	16,175
	811,388	718,919
	$1,666,856	$1,380,295

(*continued*)

Exhibit 16.2 (continued)

(Thousands of Dollars)	Oct. 31, 1979	Nov. 1, 1978
	FY 1980	FY 1979
Assets		
Current Assets:		
Cash	$ 22,273	$ 18,315
Short-term investments	122,974	75,886
Receivables, net	259,326	237,664
Inventories	639,952	599,697
Prepaid expenses	44,174	40,214
Total current assets	1,088,699	971,776
Investments in and advances to entities, net	47,286	129,397
Excess of investments in consolidated subsidiaries over net assets at acquisition	124,395	54,414
Miscellaneous other assets	14,071	7,799
	185,752	191,610
Property, plant and equipment	857,612	753,723
Less Accumulated depreciation	337,554	305,035
Net property, plant and equipment	520,058	448,688
	$1,794,509	$1,612,074

(Thousands of Dollars)	Oct. 31, 1979	Nov. 1, 1978
	FY 1980	FY 1979
Liabilities and Shareholders' Equity		
Current Liabilities:		
Short-term debt	$ 246,915	$ 206,600
Portion of long-term debt due within one year	15,860	14,995
Accounts payable	255,739	255,870
Accrued liabilities	116,288	88,725
Federal, foreign and state income taxes	53,986	57,425
Total current liabilities	688,788	623,615
Long-term debt	143,760	143,508
Deferred Federal and foreign income taxes	56,216	39,680
Future United Kingdom income taxes	26,899	35,237
Other liabilities	38,532	31,487
Minority interests	6,385	5,861
Shareholders' Equity:		
Third cumulative preferred stock	17,688	17,997
Common stock	68,362	68,362
Additional capital	83,244	83,721
Retained earnings	678,514	578,287
	847,808	748,367
Less Treasury stock	13,879	15,681
	833,929	732,686
	$1,794,509	$1,612,074

Exhibit 16.2 (continued)

Statements of Consolidated Changes in Financial Position

H. J. Heinz Company and Consolidated Subsidiaries

	Three Months Ended		Six Months Ended	
	Aug. 1, 1979	Aug. 2, 1978	Oct. 31, 1979	Nov. 1, 1978
(Thousands of Dollars)	FY 1980	FY 1979	FY 1980	FY 1979
Source of Funds:				
Funds from operations	$43,764	$31,854	$ 97,908	$ 72,991
Long-term borrowings	7,657	—	9,739	1,451
Other, net	609	846	751	1,307
Total funds provided	52,030	32,700	108,398	75,749
Use of Funds:				
Capital expenditures, net	36,745	16,786	62,187	48,513
Dividends	11,963	9,705	25,045	20,539
Reduction in long-term debt	—	743	3,474	2,132
Increase (decrease) in investments and advances to entities	(1,463)	44,222	7,856	120,870
Increase (decrease) in operating working capital	(28,661)	(51,835)	33,128	21,087
Other, net	10,015	267	11,094	(709)
Total funds used	28,599	19,888	142,784	212,432
Net change in cash and current debt	$ 23,431	$ 12,812	$ (34,386)	$(136,683)
Change in Cash and Current Debt:				
Increase (decrease) in cash and short-term investments	$ 1,996	$ 183	$ 22,966	$ (169)
(Increase) decrease in current debt	21,435	12,629	(57,352)	(136,514)
	$ 23,431	$ 12,812	$ (34,386)	$(136,683)

(*continued*)

When interim financial data and disclosures are not separately reported for the fourth quarter, securityholders often make inferences about that quarter by subtracting data based on the third quarter interim report from the annual results. In the absence of a separate fourth quarter report or disclosure of the results for that quarter in the annual report, disposals of segments of a business and extraordinary, unusual, or infrequently occurring items recognized in the fourth quarter, as well as the aggregate effect of year-end adjustments that are material to the results of that quarter, should be disclosed in a note to the annual financial statements. Additionally, a management discussion of the significant events impacting the interim results is encouraged, but not required.

When condensed interim balance sheet information or funds flow data are not presented at interim reporting dates, significant changes

Exhibit 16.2 (continued)

Notes to Consolidated Financial Statements

H. J. Heinz Company and Consolidated Subsidiaries

1. The financial statements contained herein present comparative consolidated statements of income for the first and second quarters, together with the first six months, of fiscal 1980 and 1979; comparative consolidated balance sheets as of the end of the first and second quarters of fiscal 1980 and 1979; and comparative statements of consolidated changes in financial position for the first three- and six-month periods of fiscal 1980 and 1979.

2. With respect to the first quarter of fiscal year 1980, which ended on August 1, 1979, these results were released to the general public on September 12, 1979. At that time, the company reported net income and earnings per share of $32.1 million and $1.40, respectively, which included a prorata portion of certain previously deferred United Kingdom taxes that have been permanently forgiven. The total taxes forgiven amounted to $19.4 million. The company estimated the allocation of this forgiveness to its first-quarter results in accordance with its understanding of an exposure draft issued by the Financial Accounting Standards Board ("FASB") and FASB Interpretation No. 18.

However, subsequent to the company's announcement of its first-quarter results, the FASB issued a definitive statement on this subject. Under the provisions of this statement, the full amount of the credit should have been included in the company's first-quarter results rather than allocated over the full year. Accordingly, because of this change, as well as a revision in the estimated impact of taxes on dividends expected to be remitted from consolidated operations during fiscal 1980, the company has restated its first-quarter results to net income of $44.8 million and earnings per share of $1.97. There have been no other changes in the previously released statement of consolidated income for the company's first quarter.

3. In April, 1979, shortly before the close of fiscal year 1979, the Audit Committee of the Board of Directors, at the request of the chief executive officer, initiated an inquiry into alleged improper practices in certain of the company's divisions and subsidiaries. The Audit Committee retained the law firm of Cravath, Swaine & Moore, which, in turn, engaged the independent public accounting firm of Arthur Young & Co., to conduct a full inquiry into the practices for the period beginning with fiscal year 1972 through fiscal 1979.

The inquiry is sufficiently complete for the company to state the financial effect of the practices involved. The inquiry has disclosed improper practices in certain subsidiaries and divisions relating to vendor payments and credits as well as treatment of sales and accruals resulting in transferral of income between fiscal periods. The inquiry of the Audit Committee is expected to be completed in the near future.

On the basis of the information developed, the company has determined that restatement of prior years' audited financial statements is appropriate. In addition, published interim financial results for the previous four quarters of fiscal year 1978 and the first three quarters of fiscal year 1979 also have been restated.

The aggregate effect of the adjustments resulting from the inquiry was an increase in net income of $8.4 million during the period 1971 through 1978 and a decrease of a similar amount in the previously reported net income for the first nine months of fiscal year 1979. Details of the restatement on fiscal years 1971 through 1978, as well as the appropriate quarters of 1978 and 1979, were disclosed in the company's Form 10-K as amended by Form 8 filed with the Securities and Exchange Commission on November 20, 1979 and in a press release issued on November 21, 1979.

Note 3 (Continued): The as-reported and as-restated amounts for the first and second quarters of fiscal 1979 are shown in the table below.

	First Quarter		
(Thousands of Dollars Except for Per Share Amounts)	As Reported	Change	As Restated
Sales	$ 555,558	$ (19,257)	$536,301
Gross profit	$ 178,250	$ (6,920)	$171,330
Operating income	$ 42,709	$ (7,421)	$ 35,288
Income before income taxes	$ 35,866	$ (7,421)	$ 28,445
Net income	$ 21,161	$ (4,378)	$ 16,783
Earnings per common share amounts:			
Primary	$ .91	$ (.19)	$ .72
Fully diluted	$ .89	$ (.19)	$ .70

Exhibit 16.2 (continued)

| | Second Quarter | | | Six Months | |
As Reported	Change	As Restated	As Reported	Change	As Restated
$620,230	$ (603)	$619,627	$1,175,788	$ (19,860)	$1,155,928
$203,708	$ 256	$203,964	$ 381,958	$ (6,664)	$ 375,294
$ 52,016	$ (3,787)	$ 48,229	$ 94,725	$ (11,208)	$ 83,517
$ 48,519	$ (3,787)	$ 44,732	$ 84,385	$ (11,208)	$ 73,177
$ 28,204	$ (2,178)	$ 26,026	$ 49,365	$ (6,556)	$ 42,809
$ 1.23	$ (.10)	$ 1.13	$ 2.14	$ (.29)	$ 1.85
$ 1.18	$ (.09)	$ 1.09	$ 2.07	$ (.28)	$ 1.79

4.   The results for the interim periods are not necessarily indicative of the results to be expected for the full fiscal year because of the seasonal nature of the company's business. In the opinion of management, all adjustments (none of which were other than normal recurring accruals) necessary to a fair statement of the results of these interim periods have been included.

5.   During June, 1978, the company acquired through wholly owned subsidiaries all of the outstanding shares of Foodways National, Inc. for approximately $49.6 million and the business of Weight Watchers International, Inc. for approximately $71.2 million. The results of operations of Foodways and Weight Watchers were first consolidated in the second and third quarters, respectively, of fiscal year 1979. The impact of the inclusion of the operations of Foodways and Weight Watchers on consolidated net income after interest charges and amortization of goodwill was not significant.

6.   The provision for income taxes consists of provisions for Federal, state, U. S. possessions and foreign income taxes. The company operates in an international environment with significant operations in various locations outside the United States. Accordingly, the consolidated income tax rate is a composite rate reflecting the earnings in the various locations and the applicable tax rates. Income tax expense for the interim periods is based upon the estimated annual effective tax rates.

As indicated in Note 2 above, the current year's first quarter includes a reduction in taxes of $19.4 million, which represents previously provided deferred United Kingdom taxes applicable to fiscal years 1973 and 1974, which have been forgiven.

Deferred income taxes, which are not material, have been included in the provision for income taxes for all interim periods.

7.   The investments in and advances to entities as shown on the consolidated balance sheet as of August 2, 1978 include the purchase price of Foodways National, Inc., which was consolidated beginning with the second quarter of fiscal year 1979, and the investments in and advances to entities as shown as of November 1, 1978 include the purchase price of Weight Watchers International, Inc., which was consolidated beginning with the third quarter of fiscal year 1979.

8.   During the first quarter of the current fiscal year, the company acquired through wholly owned subsidiaries the common stock of Jerky Treats, Inc. and related manufac-

(*continued*)

Exhibit 16.2 (continued)

turing facilities and the business of Country Kitchen Foods Ltd. Jerky Treats, Inc. manufactures and markets pet food treats in the United States. Country Kitchen Foods Ltd. produces and markets fresh and canned mushrooms in the United Kingdom. These acquisitions were treated as purchases for accounting purposes and have been included in the current year's first-half consolidated operations. The impact of these acquisitions on such operations was not significant.

During November, 1979, the company acquired through wholly owned subsidiaries all of the outstanding shares of Nadler-Werke GmbH and Camargo Foods, Inc. Nadler, a West German company, makes and markets chilled salads, fish marinades, sauces and condiments. Camargo manufactures and sells under the Weight Watchers label a dried apple-based snack food and holds licenses covering a wide range of other nonfrozen food items, such as ice cream mixes, dessert mixes and soft drinks.

The purchase prices of Nadler and Jerky Treats were $49 million and $11 million, respectively, while the purchase prices of Camargo and Country Kitchens were not disclosed. However, the amounts involved with respect to these latter acquisitions were not significant.

9. With respect to the Audit Committee inquiry discussed above in Note 3, the company has informed the Internal Revenue Service of such inquiry. The Internal Revenue Service has not indicated what action, if any, it will take in connection with this inquiry. However, in the opinion of management, should any penalties be assessed, they will not be material to the company's financial position.

Further, the company has been advised that the United States Securities and Exchange Commission has issued a private order of investigation concerning the practices that are the subject of the Audit Committee inquiry. The company has not been informed what action, if any, the Commission may take with respect to these matters. It is possible that the Commission or other governmental authorities may institute proceedings against the company. It is possible also that private plaintiffs may institute suits against the company with respect to such practices. In the opinion of management, the final outcome of such potential action would not have a material adverse effect on the company's consolidated financial position.

10. Foreign currency adjustments result principally from the translation of foreign balance sheets into U. S. dollars.

11. The accompanying financial statements are unaudited.

since the last reporting period with respect to liquid assets, net working capital, long-term liabilities, and stockholders' equity should be disclosed. Exhibit 16.1 provides an illustration of the disclosure of these minimum requirements. In addition, Exhibit 16.2 shows a complete set of interim financial statements that may be issued by the reporting entity.

Bibliography

CHAPTER 1

Brown, "The Economic Impact of Financial Accounting Standards," *Financial Executive* (September 1979).

Burton, "Emerging Trends in Financial Reporting," *Journal of Accountancy* (July 1981).

Conner, "Financial Reporting: Building a Better World," *Journal of Accountancy* (December 1982).

Hepp and McRae, "Accounting Standards Overload: Relief Is Needed," *Journal of Accountancy* (May 1982).

Sommer, "Differential Disclosures: To Each His Own," *Journal of Accountancy* (August 1974).

Wristen, "Financial Information: Have We Reached the Saturation Point?" *Journal of Accountancy* (September 1983).

CHAPTER 2

Guy, "Statements of Income and Retained Earnings," *Journal of Accountancy* (January 1975).

Henry, "A New Funds Statement Format for Greater Disclosure," *Journal of Accountancy* (April 1975).

CHAPTER 3

Bastable and Merriwether, "FIFO in an Inflationary Environment," *Journal of Accountancy* (March 1975).

Davis, "History of LIFO," *Journal of Accountancy* (May 1983).

Hufford, "Cash Discount Losses," *Journal of Accountancy* (November 1983).

Munter and Moore, "Transfer of Receivables with Recourse," *CPA Journal* (July 1984).

Reed and Munter, "The Retail Inventory Method: An Averaging Process," *National Public Accountant* (November 1983).

Roberts, "Carrying Charges on Receivables," *Journal of Accountancy* (July 1981).
Strobel and Powers, "Accounting for Inventories: Where Do We Stand?" *CPA Journal* (May 1981).

CHAPTER 4

Munter and Ratcliffe, "Accounting for Real Estate Projects," *CPA Journal:* Part I (June 1983); Part II (July 1983).
Ratcliffe and Munter, "Accounting for Interest Costs," *National Public Accountant* (September 1980).

CHAPTER 5

Neuhausen, "Consolidation and the Equity Method—Time for an Overhaul," *Journal of Accountancy* (February 1982).
Petri and Stickney, "Business Combinations: Some Unresolved Issues," *Journal of Accountancy* (April 1982).
Ratcliffe and Munter, "Income Recognition on Long-Term Investments: The Controllability Criterion," *Managerial Planning* (January/February 1984).

CHAPTER 6

Bierman and Dukes, "Accounting for Research and Development Costs," *Journal of Accountancy* (April 1975).
Calhoun, "Accounting for Initial Franchise Fees," *Journal of Accountancy* (February 1975).
Ratcliffe and Munter, "Accounting for R & D Activities," *CPA Journal* (April 1983).

CHAPTER 7

Moores and Munter, "Accounting for Debt Extinguishments," *Financial Executive* (Forthcoming).

CHAPTER 8

Ferrara, "The Case for Symmetry in Lease Reporting," *Management Accounting* (April 1978).
Munter and Mondoux, "Determining Contingent Rentals," *National Public Accountant* (December 1981).
Munter and Ratcliffe, "An Assessment of User Reactions to Lease Accounting Disclosures," *Journal of Accounting, Auditing and Finance* (Winter 1983).
Ratcliffe and Munter, "Accounting for Sale-Leasebacks," *National Public Accountant* (March 1982).

CHAPTER 9

Deaton and Weygandt, "Disclosures Related to Pension Plans," *Journal of Accountancy* (January 1975).
Henry, "Disclosure of Pension Liability: A Case Study," *Journal of Accountancy* (May 1982).
Lieber and Dragutsky, "How Accountants Can Keep Pension Costs Down," *Journal of Accountancy* (February 1975).

Lucas and Miller, "Pension Accounting: Impacting the Financial Statement," *Journal of Accountancy* (June 1983).

Munter and Pierre, "The Nature of Pension Assets and Pension Liabilities," *Proceedings of the American Accounting Association (Southwest)* (1982).

Munter and Ratcliffe, "Accounting for Special Termination Benefits," *Oil and Gas Tax Quarterly* (March 1984).

Ratcliffe and Munter, "Reporting by Defined Benefit Pension Plans," *CPA Journal* (December 1980).

Seaman and Hensold, "Pension Plan Obligations: The 'Real' Impact," *Journal of Accountancy* (July 1982).

CHAPTER 10

Hobson, "Tax Allocation," *Journal of Accountancy* (August 1974).

Munter and Ratcliffe, "Accounting for Income Taxes," *National Public Accountant* (October 1983).

Raby and Richter, "Conformity of Tax and Financial Accounting," *Journal of Accountancy* (March 1975).

CHAPTER 11

Munter and Ratcliffe, "Disclosure of Long-Term Obligations," *CPA Journal* (August 1981).

CHAPTER 12

Gibson, "Financial Ratios in Annual Reports," *CPA Journal* (September 1982).

Haley and Ratcliffe, "Accounting for Incentive Stock Options," *CPA Journal* (October 1982).

CHAPTER 13

Alderman and Farmer, "Antidilutive Effects of Stock Options on EPS," *Journal of Accountancy* (September 1981).

Davidson and Weil, "A Shortcut in Computing Earnings per Share," *Journal of Accountancy* (December 1975).

Munter, "On the Usefulness of APBO No. 15," *Mid-Atlantic Journal of Business* (Winter 1981/82).

CHAPTER 14

Lurie, "Selecting Segments of a Business," *Financial Executive* (April 1980).

Munter and Ratcliffe, "An Examination of the Current Status of Segment Reporting," *Ohio CPA Journal* (Winter 1981).

Ratcliffe and Munter, "A Practitioner's Guide to Segment Reporting," *Louisiana CPA* (Summer/Fall 1980).

CHAPTER 15

Barbatelli and King, "How to Comply with FASB 33," *Financial Executive* (March 1980).

Burton, "Financial Reporting in an Age of Inflation," *Journal of Accountancy* (February 1975).

Munter and Ratcliffe, "Financial Statement Disclosures of Oil and Gas Produc-
ing Activities," *Oil and Gas Tax Quarterly* (June 1983).
Munter and Ratcliffe, "Reporting the Effects of Inflation," *Oil and Gas Tax Quar-
terly* (September 1983).
Patrick, "Cash Flow and Return on Investment—A Supplement to FASBIN 33,"
CPA Journal (March 1981).

CHAPTER 16

Hill, "Dollar-Value LIFO Reserves in Interim Statements," *Journal of Accountancy*
(March 1982).
Johnson and Johnson, "Interim Reporting—Redefining the Problem," *Financial
Executive* (May 1979).

Index

About the Authors

PAUL MUNTER, DBA, CPA, is currently Director of the Center for Professional Development and an Associate Professor of Accounting at Texas Tech University. He has authored or co-authored more than 70 articles on accounting and business matters and has also co-authored four books in these fields.

THOMAS A. RATCLIFFE, Ph.D., CPA, is a Professor of Accounting at Troy State University. Formerly an investment advisor, Dr. Ratcliffe has authored in excess of 70 articles in accounting and business journals and has also co-authored four books.